How to Help Every Child Become a Reader

A Portion of This Book's Proceeds Goes to Charity.

We are donating 3 percent of the proceeds from each Your Domain title to nonprofit research, educational, or direct service projects. Our interests are in the areas of career assessment, self-help, literacy, job search, and other important topics—with particular interest in projects that will improve program results and encourage self-directed solutions. Since much of the content of Your Domain titles is based on government sources, we think this is an appropriate way to say thanks to the many good people who work in government positions creating these materials and doing other important tasks.

Your
Domain
PUBLISHING

How to Help Every Child Become a Reader

© 2001 by Your Domain Publishing,
an imprint of JIST Publishing, Inc.
8902-A Otis Avenue
Indianapolis, IN 46216-1033
Phone: 800-648-JIST   Fax: 800-JIST-FAX   E-Mail: editorial@jist.com

Visit our Web site at http://www.jist.com. Get free information on our many books, videos, and other products; find special deals (like half-price books); and order online.

Quantity discounts are available. Very special discounts are available for large orders. Please call our Sales Department at 1-800-648-JIST for more information.

Printed in the United States of America.

03 02 01 00   9 8 7 6 5 4 3 2 1

ISBN: 1-930780-02-8

THIS IS A SHORT BUT IMPORTANT BOOK

This book consists of three little books that were developed by staff at the U.S. Department of Education. Their small formats made them difficult to distribute to as wide an audience as we think they deserve, so we put them together in this one book. We think these are important materials, and we hope this format will help them impact the lives of more youth than otherwise possible.

In various sections of the book is information that falls into three major categories:

1. **The Facts** — There is incredible research support provided for all the important recommendations made in this book. We think this is a major contribution of these materials, since the advice is not simply opinion. You might use the research findings to support changes in how you deal with your own children or to support recommendations to change your school or other program to get better results.

2. **Practical Tips and Action Plans** — The book includes many practical, results-oriented things you can do to improve reading skills and brief tips for parents, teachers, relatives, administrators, even media representatives and public policy makers.

3. **Resources** — From Internet sites providing free information and materials, to model reading programs, sources of funding, suggested books, and many other resources, this publication lists excellent information for everyone.

Please browse the Table of Contents to find the information that will help you most. This book was not designed to be read front to back, so please feel free to go directly to whatever sections seem most relevant.

Where the Information in This Book Comes From

We've already mentioned that the content of this book was developed by the U.S. Department of Education. It was created as part of the "America Reads" project, a grassroots national campaign to challenge every American to help all children learn to read well. America Reads began in 1997 as a federal initiative recognizing that reading is the key to learning. Research shows that students unable to read well by the end of the third grade are more likely to leave school and have fewer good options for jobs as adults. To encourage reading improvements during these critical early years, the America Reads program stresses cooperation between educators, parents, librarians, business people, senior citizens, college students, and community and religious groups. We think the America Reads project makes sense and hope that our making these materials more widely available will help in some small way. For more information about America Reads, there are several ways to contact staff directly:

America Reads Challenge
U.S. Department of Education, 7th Floor
400 Maryland Avenue, SW
Washington, DC 20202-0107
phone: 202-401-8888
AmericaReads@ed.gov

TABLE OF CONTENTS

Quick Table of Contents

Section I: Start Early, Finish Strong

An excellent introduction to the problems related to inadequate reading skills of our youth — and a review of what can and should be done. Includes substantial research findings and suggests things that parents, teachers, citizens, and communities can do to help. **Begins on page 1.**

Section II: You Can Meet the Challenge — Simple Things You Can Do to Help

A series of lists provide results-oriented suggestions and action plans for different groups including families; childcare providers; schools; librarians; grandparents, seniors, and concerned citizens; community, cultural, and religious organizations; universities; employers; and media. We give you permission to photocopy these lists to give them out at PTA meetings, hang on your refrigerator, or any other useful distribution—they are that good. **Begins on page 89.**

Section III: Ideas at Work

Provides an introduction to the America Reads program and a review of federal and state laws and efforts to improve reading. But most of this section presents many examples of innovative programs designed to improve reading. Excellent ideas for others to imitate, including school and library programs, family-based programs, business-sponsored programs, and many other creative approaches. **Begins on page 111.**

EXECUTIVE SUMMARY

The United States is poised for a breakthrough in student reading achievement. If we can move beyond the "reading war" over instructional methods, we have good reason to be optimistic about progress in reading in the near future. This progress can be predicted based on the synergy of four key factors.

1. The need to read has never been greater. As difficult as life has been for illiterate Americans in the past,[1] the economy of the near future will offer even fewer jobs for workers with poor reading skills. [2] The Information Age and the advance of technology into daily life make the job prospects for poor readers bleaker than ever. We must improve reading achievement now, or risk denying a substantial portion of students the opportunity to contribute to and participate fully in our society.[3]

2. More Americans at all levels of society—federal, state, community, school, and family—are mobilizing to improve reading. The American public understands that when our students fail to read, we are failing them. An unprecedented pro-literacy movement, focused on children under age 9, is driving activities in thousands of communities today and could do so in thousands more tomorrow.

   Federal elected officials have created the boldest national reading initiative in 30 years.[4] Governors and legislatures in the majority of states are taking decisive action regarding illiteracy,[5] and many mayors of cities with stubborn illiteracy rates are tackling the challenge head-on.

   Newspapers, businesses, libraries, sports teams, community service groups, employees, college students, and volunteers of all ages are stepping forward to tutor children, work with parents, provide books, and support schools.[6] In fact, we are witnessing unparalleled activity to get more children on the road to reading.

   This crusade is reshaping our view of the reading challenge. No longer can we simply point fingers at schools for failing to teach students to read. Every parent, teacher, and citizen has a role to play to spark dramatic improvement in reading.

   By expanding our view of who contributes to students' reading success, we are increasing the opportunities for millions of Americans to endow our children with this lifelong skill. If we succeed in engaging this untapped pool of adults, the results will revolutionize education in this country.

3. A blueprint for action is now available. The U.S. Department of Education commissioned the National Research Council to write a scholarly and independent review of all reading research on children. The council's 1998 landmark report, Preventing Reading Difficulties in Young Children,[7] clearly lays out what we can and must do to help every child become a reader. This widely respected report calls for an end to the "reading war" over instructional methods and for the adoption of a variety of common sense and research-based techniques.

   The National Research Council found that children benefit from experiences in early childhood that foster language development, cultivate a motivation to read, and establish a link between print and spoken words. Later, students need to develop a clear understanding of the relationship between letters and sounds, and an ability to obtain meaning from what they read.

   Teaching with a flexible mix of research-based instructional methods, geared toward individual students, is more effective than strict adherence to any one approach. Teachers need to understand the most up-to-date reading research and be able to implement it in their classrooms.

   Teachers also must be able to identify reading difficulties in students early on and marshal appropriate interventions in response. Young learners need continuing encouragement and individualized instruction to succeed.

4. For the first time since reading achievement has been measured, national reading scores have improved in all three grades tested. On the latest National Assessment of Educational Progress (NAEP) Reading Report Card,[8] average reading scores in grades 4, 8, and 12 rose from one-third to one-half of a grade level between 1994 and 1998. While much remains to be done, this modest progress reflects a renewed commitment to improve reading and reveals the potential for greater success if everyone works together, using the best and latest research.

The Task Ahead

Powered by the dynamics of the economy, the reading crusade of our citizens, a blueprint for action, and unprecedented momentum, a significant reading breakthrough is within our grasp. Section I of this book, "Start Early, Finish Strong" lays out what we must do to accelerate the pace, and to leave no child behind.

Start Early

By starting early, we address the fact that the roots of reading take hold well before children go to school. We cannot focus only on fourth-grade reading scores as the problem, because children's reading habits and skills are already well-established by that age. We now know we should start much earlier—even from birth—to develop a child's reading ability. Research shows we can improve reading achievement by starting in early childhood to build cognitive and language skills.[9]

Parents and early caregivers play an essential role in laying the foundations for literacy by talking and reading daily to babies and toddlers. A recent parent survey offers a hopeful sign: More preschoolers are being read to daily by family members than in recent years.[10] Yet more than 4 in 10 preschoolers, 5 in 10 toddlers, and 6 in 10 babies are not read to regularly.[11] All parents of young children need encouragement to read to their children. Grandparents and other adults can become a child's daily reader too.

Six in 10 children spend a substantial part of each day in the care of someone other than a parent.[12] Childcare providers and early childhood teachers can do much more to prepare young children for reading success.

Working in preschools, childcare centers, nursery schools, and home-based care settings, this corps of adults has tremendous potential to enhance young children's language development and thus prepare them to read better. Many of these providers and teachers, however, need better training[13] and higher wages[14] to more effectively promote the cognitive, language, social, and emotional development that are the foundations of reading success.

Finish Strong

When a child enters school ready to read, what happens next? That's when all adults in the child's life must be prepared—to "finish strong." Schools can't do it alone. But improvements in primary school—kindergarten through third grade—present a tremendous opportunity to boost reading achievement. We now know how to finish the job that parents and caregivers start: Parents must stay involved, and nothing is more important than a highly skilled, well-prepared teacher.[15]

Universities, colleges of education, state teacher licensing boards, and legislatures must raise standards for proficiency in reading instruction for teacher candidates.[16] Veteran teachers need high-quality, ongoing professional development in research-based reading instruction.[17] Teachers need time to work together to improve their teaching techniques, and elementary school principals can integrate a schoolwide focus on reading achievement.[18] Parents and community members can form reading compacts with schools to marshal all their resources to help more children succeed.[19]

A key factor for a strong finish is the involvement of the whole community in the pro-literacy crusade. The seeds of this crusade are already sprouting in cities and towns nationwide, and these examples can be shared with and replicated in many communities.

Every elementary school child who needs a tutor should have one, for extra reading practice during or after school.[20] All students, but especially poor children, benefit from summer reading programs to prevent erosion of reading skills and promote the joy of reading.[21] Many more children need books to read and adults to read to them.[22] Every citizen can help and millions more can contribute to make every child a proficient reader.

The momentum is with us for a breakthrough in student reading achievement. To seize this moment in history, we must lay down our weapons in the old reading war and engage new troops in the right kind of reading war—the war on illiteracy. If we all commit to "start early, finish strong," we can achieve a breakthrough and help every child become a good reader.

Endnotes

1 Low literacy is strongly related to unemployment, poverty, and crime. About 43 percent of those with the lowest literacy skills live in poverty, and 70 percent of the prison population falls into the two lowest levels of reading proficiency. 1998 National Institute for Literacy Fact Sheet.

2 Eight of the 10 fastest-growing jobs in the next decade will require either a college education or moderate to long-term postsecondary training. U.S. Department of Labor: Bureau of Labor Statistics, Silvestri, G.T. (1997). "Occupational Employment Projections to 2006." *Monthly Labor Review*, November 1997, Table 3, p. 77.

3 In 1998, nearly 4 in 10 fourth-graders nationwide failed to achieve even partial mastery of the reading skills needed for school success. In our highest-poverty schools, nearly 7 in 10 fourth-graders fail to read at this Basic level. U.S. Department of Education, National Center for Education Statistics. (1999). The 1998 NAEP Reading Report Card for the Nation. NCES 1999–459, by Donahue, P.L., Voelkl, K.E., Campbell, J.R., and Mazzeo, J. Washington, D.C.: Author.

4 The Reading Excellence Act authorized $260 million in 1999 for professional development of teachers, out-of-school tutoring, family literacy and transitional programs for kindergartners. The U.S. Department of Education issues competi-

tive grants to the states, which then hold grant competitions that favor school districts with children most in need.

`www.ed.gov/offices/OESE/REA/index.html`

5 Forty-two states reported significant new literacy activity at the National Reading Summit in September 1998, and more than 20 states enacted reading improvement legislation between 1996 and 1999. Many governors have pledged further action. U.S. Department of Education, Office of Intergovernmental and Interagency Affairs.

`www.ed.gov/inits/readingsummit`

6 More than 2.2 million children have been tutored in reading through the Corporation for National Service. More than 22,000 college students served as reading tutors under the Federal Work-Study program in 1997–98, and thousands more serve as volunteers. The President's Coalition for America Reads and many other organizations are active across the nation. U.S. Department of Education, America Reads.

`www.ed.gov/inits/americareads`

7 National Research Council. (1998). Washington, D.C.: National Academy Press.

8 U.S. Department of Education, National Center for Education Statistics. (1999). The 1998 NAEP Reading Report Card for the Nation. NCES 1999-459, by Donahue, P.L., Voelkl, K.E., Campbell, J.R., and Mazzeo, J., Washington, D.C.: Author.

9 Counting, number concepts, letter names and shapes, associating sounds with letters, interest in reading, and cooperation with other children are all relevant to learning to read. Wells, C. G. (1985). "Preschool Literacy-Related Activities and Success in School." *Literacy, Language, and Learning*. London: Cambridge University Press.

10 About 57 percent of children ages 3 to 5 were read to daily by a family member in 1996, up from 53 percent in 1993. U.S. Department of Education. (1996). National Household Education Survey, 1995. Washington, D.C.: Author.

11 Only 48 percent of parents of toddlers ages 1 to 3, and 39 percent of parents of infants reported reading daily to their children in 1996. Young, K. T., Davis, K., and Schoen, C. (1996). The Commonwealth Fund Survey of Parents with Young Children. New York: The Commonwealth Fund.

12 U.S. Department of Education, National Center for Education Statistics. (1996). "Child Care and Early Education Program Participation of Infants, Toddlers, and Preschoolers." Statistics in Brief. NCES 95-824. Washington, D.C.: Author.

[13] Higher education and specialized training enhance the ability of early childhood teachers to do a better job of advancing children's language skills, a key predictor of later reading success. Whitebook, M., Howes, C., and Phillips, D. (1990). The National Child Care Staffing Study. Oakland, CA: National Center for Early Childhood Workforce.

[14] Inadequate funding is the primary reason for the low quality of care experienced by most children. Gomby, D., Larner, M., Terman, D., Krantzler, N., Stevenson, C., and Behrman, R. (1996). Financing Child Care: Analysis and Recommendations. The Future of Children: Financing Child Care, 6(2), 5–25.

[15] National Research Council. (1998). *Preventing Reading Difficulties in Young Children*. Washington, D.C.: National Academy Press.

[16] ibid.

[17] ibid.

[18] ibid.

[19] Effective compacts between parents and schools increase parental involvement in their children's education, with positive student outcomes, particularly in high-poverty schools. D'Agostino, J., Wong, K., Hedges, L., and Borman, G. (1998). "The Effectiveness of Title I Parent Programs: A Multilevel Analysis of Prospects Data." Paper presented at the annual meeting of the American Educational Research Association, San Diego, Calif., April 1998. Note: A new *Compact for Reading Guide* is available free from the U.S. Department of Education. See Reading Resources, Appendix B at the end of this book.

[20] An analysis of 65 studies of high-quality tutoring programs found positive, modest achievement effects across all the studies. Structured tutoring programs demonstrated higher achievement gains than unstructured programs. Students tutored in reading showed positive results for self-confidence, motivation to read, and views of their control over their reading abilities. Cohen, P.A., Kulik, J.A., and Kulik, C.L.C. (1982). "Educational Outcomes of Tutoring: A Meta-analysis of Findings." *American Educational Research Journal, 19*, 237–248.

[21] Alexander, K. and Entwisle, D. (1996). *Early Schooling and Educational Inequality: Socioeconomic Disparities in Children's Learning*. In J.S. Coleman (ed.) Falmer sociology series, 63–79. London: Falmer Press.

[22] For America's poorest children, the biggest obstacle to literacy may be the scarcity of books and appropriate reading material. Needlman, R., Fried, L., Morley, D., Taylor, S., and Zuckerman, B. (1991). "Clinic-Based Intervention to Promote Literacy." *American Journal of Diseases of Children*, Volume 145, August, 1991, 881–884.

SECTION I

START EARLY,
FINISH STRONG

INTRODUCTION:
THE RIGHT KIND OF READING WAR

The phrase *reading war* has been the popular description for long-running disagreements about the best way to teach children to read. Fierce battles have been waged by academics and theorists since the late 1800s (McCormick, 1999), with classroom teachers often spinning like weathervanes as they tried to align classroom practices with the prevailing winds.

The most recent conflicts, fought in school boards and state legislatures, are just the latest attempts by proponents of phonics and whole language to dominate the teaching of reading.

Through the years, though, the United States has been losing the real reading war—the war against illiteracy. Today, 10 million American schoolchildren are poor readers (Fletcher & Lyon, 1998). As a nation, we have failed to ensure that all children are good readers by the time they leave the primary grades.

Even with changing fashions in curriculum and instruction, and the overall push for education reform, the percentage of children who read well has not improved substantially for more than 25 years (NAEP 1996 Trends Report). Among our poorest children, more than half of all fourth-graders who are eligible for the free lunch program fail to read at the Basic achievement level needed for academic success (NAEP 1998 Reading Report Card). In our highest-poverty public schools, a whopping 68 percent of fourth-graders fail to reach the Basic level of achievement. Only 1 in 10 fourth-graders at these schools can read at the Proficient level, the ideal goal for all students (NAEP 1998 Reading Report Card).

Clearly, pursuit of the same old strategies won't help more children master reading. To win this real reading war, it's time to broaden our views on responsibility for reading, and enlist new and more effective troops—involved parents, highly skilled childcare providers, effective primary schoolteachers, and committed communities. We must start early and finish strong, to help every child become a good reader.

A National Crusade

In his 1996 State of Education address, U.S. Education Secretary Richard W. Riley issued a clarion call for a new national crusade: Every American child must become a good reader by the end of third grade. President Clinton's 1997 State of the Union address launched a national literacy initiative, The America Reads Challenge, to pursue Riley's goal. And in 1998, a landmark study by the National Research Council of the National Academy of Sciences provided a blueprint for action to create a nation of readers. Significantly, the report, *Preventing Reading Difficulties in Young Children,* calls for an end to the old reading war and recommends a new research-based mix of instruction that suits each individual child.

Each of these recent actions has emphasized a common strategy for success: We must start early by preparing young children to read, and we must finish strong by providing excellent instruction and community support in the primary grades.

By starting early, we look to the roots of reading ability. Broadening our approach gives us the advantage of preparing children to read from birth, with the active involvement of loving families. Millions of early care and education personnel—in childcare centers, preschools, and home-based childcare—present a largely untapped resource for building the foundations for reading success. An early start enables every child to arrive at kindergarten ready to learn to read.

But a large survey of kindergarten teachers reported that 35 percent of children arrive at school unprepared to learn (Boyer, 1991). Children who lack reading readiness are more likely to develop reading problems when formal schooling begins (Scarborough, 1998). The preparation these children need comes from experiences rich with language and text, and from talking and reading with parents and caregivers (National Research Council, 1998).

Once in school, a child needs teachers with strong, research-based skills in reading instruction who have the support required to maintain these skills. Members of the community can help by tutoring children, helping parents, providing books, and supporting schools. Such a strong finish offers every student the best opportunity to become a good reader by the end of third grade.

Following the release of the National Research Council's 1998 report, President Clinton signed The Reading Excellence Act, the most significant child literacy law enacted by Congress in more than three decades.

Most states have redoubled their efforts to significantly improve reading achievement. In recent years, more than 20 state legislatures have passed a flurry of new child literacy laws and budgets. (See Appendix D.)

Mayors, business leaders, community groups, and millions of individual Americans are taking the challenge and tackling the root causes of illiteracy. We are witnessing a time of unparalleled activity to get more children on the road to reading.

The Need to Read

It would be hard to overstate the vital importance of learning to read well. Reading is the key that unlocks virtually all other learning.

Why Third Grade?

Children are expected to learn to read in the primary grades, kindergarten through third, when most reading instruction is given. By fourth grade, students are expected to read to learn.

Over time, learning becomes more complex, with heightened demands on students to use reading skills to analyze or to solve problems. Good reading skills are required to study geography, do math, use computers, and conduct experiments. Even motivated, hard-working students are severely hampered in their schoolwork if they cannot read well by the end of third grade.

Source: *U.S. Department of Education, Office of Special Education and Rehabilitative Services*

Written language often delivers the content of science, mathematics, religion, politics, and other essential subjects. The Bible, the Torah, the Koran, and other great sacred texts are central to the world's religions. Our nation's founding documents also are written, as are the ballots through which we participate in civic life. Reading literature, poetry, and history allows us to reach out beyond our own lives to develop a broader and richer understanding of the human experience. With all its wonder and power, even the Internet remains a text-driven medium: to navigate the World Wide Web, you must be able to read.

Locked Out of the World of Words

For 38 percent of fourth-graders, access to the world of words is endangered because they read below the Basic achievement level, lacking even partial mastery of the reading skills needed for grade-level work (NAEP 1998 Reading Report Card). By eighth grade, 26 percent of the nation's students continue to read below the Basic level set for that grade, and by twelfth grade, 23 percent remain below the Basic level. (The latter figure, of course, does not include students who dropped out before grade 12 due to poor literacy skills.)

These struggling readers are disproportionately from families living in poverty, according to the National Research Council. Poverty, and for some children, language differences, contribute to the large gaps between White and Asian students and Black and Hispanic students.

In fourth grade, 64 percent of Blacks and 60 percent of Hispanics read below the Basic level, compared with 27 percent of Whites and 31 percent of Asian/Pacific Islanders (NAEP 1998 Reading Report Card).

But poor readers should not be stereotyped; reading difficulties occur in every school and in all types of families. While roughly half of all children learn to read with relative ease, the others have more trouble (Lyon, 1997).

As many as one in five children will manifest a significant reading disability (Shaywitz et al., 1992). These students may not learn to connect the sounds of speech to written letters without intensive additional assistance—help that many do not receive (Lyon, 1997).

Without intervention, most poor readers remain poor readers, limiting their academic achievement and their potential. A startling 88 percent of children who have difficulty reading at the end of first grade display similar difficulties at the end of fourth grade (Juel, 1988). According to researchers at Yale University, three-quarters of students who are poor readers in third grade will remain poor readers in high school (Shaywitz et al., 1997).

The United States renewed efforts to reform its schools in 1983 when a blue-ribbon commission warned we were "a nation at risk." Efforts were launched again in the mid-1990s to raise academic standards.

Since then, many important changes have been made by local schools, districts, states, and the federal government. But thus far, instead of producing dramatic reading gains for all students, these changes have only begun to move us in the right direction.

The Right Direction, But a Long Way to Go

A 1991 international study found that American fourth- and ninth-grade students performed well in reading skills assessments compared with those in other advanced nations, surpassed only by students in Finland (U.S. Department of Education, 1996).

But long-term trends seen in the NAEP show only minimal improvements in the reading proficiency of American 9-year-olds since 1971 (NAEP 1996 Trends Report). Thirteen-year-olds have just barely improved, and 17-year-olds read at about the same level as their counterparts did 25 years ago.

Definitions of NAEP Achievement Levels

Basic   Partial mastery of the prerequisite knowledge and skills that are fundamental for proficient work at each grade.

Proficient   Solid academic performance and demonstration of competency over challenging subject matter for each grade.

Advanced   Superior performance.

Source: *National Assessment Governing Board*

The gap in achievement between White and Black children narrowed between 1971 and 1984, a time of substantial new emphasis and resources, but has persisted since. The gap between White and Hispanic fourth-graders has actually increased since 1992 (NAEP 1996 Trends Report).

Signs of Hope

For the first time ever, between 1994 and 1998, NAEP reading scores improved in all three grades tested (grades 4, 8, and 12).

These gains, though modest, are equivalent to improving reading ability from one-third to one-half of a grade level. Lower-performing fourth-graders and most middle school students made the most significant progress.

However, while reversing a downward trend, fourth- and twelfth-graders' 1998 reading scores remained virtually the same as in 1992. (Modest gains were seen by eighth-graders).

Approximately 4 out of 10 fourth-graders remain below the Basic achievement level in reading (NAEP 1998 Reading Report Card).

Small pockets of improvement were seen by some Black students in 1998. Reading scores rose slightly for Black fourth- and eighth-graders since 1994.

Scores for eighth-grade Black children were also better than in 1992. (Black students' twelfth-grade scores remained the same.)

Still, only 10 percent of Black fourth-graders performed at or above the Proficient level, compared with 39 percent of Whites and 13 percent of Hispanics.

Hispanic twelfth-graders did see slight gains between 1994 and 1998. But fourth- and eighth-grade Hispanics students saw no significant change. White fourth-graders saw no change in 1998, but White twelfth- and eighth-graders improved slightly since 1994. White eighth-graders' scores were also an improvement over their 1992 results. The scores for Asian/Pacific Islander and Native American students made no significant change across these assessments.

Aiming High, Falling Short

While proficiency in grade-level reading is the goal for every child, only a small portion of students achieve that high degree of mastery. About 31 percent of fourth-graders, 33 percent of eighth-graders, and 40 percent of twelfth-graders attained a Proficient level or higher in reading in 1998. Across the three grades, 7 percent or fewer reached the Advanced level of reading achievement, indicating superior performance. Fewer boys than girls reached the Basic and Proficient marks. Students whose parents had dropped out of or completed only high school also had significantly lower scores (NAEP 1998 Reading Report Card).

Poor reading ability can deter students from enriching activities and courses. Researchers have found that high school students with low reading skills spent less time in organized extracurricular activities such as clubs, teams, and bands, and more time shopping at the mall and talking on the telephone.

Poor readers are also less likely to take more than one year of math, science, and foreign language—the gateway courses to college (Siegel & Loman, 1991).

It is not surprising that more than 95 percent of high school dropouts score at the two lowest levels of reading proficiency on national assessments (U.S. Department of Education, OERI, 1993). These are the saddest casualties of losing the real reading war.

Poor Readers, Poor Prospects

Clearly, the inability to read well exacts a huge toll on individuals. But it costs the nation as well.

According to the National Institute for Literacy, family illiteracy often persists from one generation to the next. Low literacy is strongly related to unemployment, poverty, and crime. On average, welfare recipients ages 17 to 21 read at the sixth-grade level, well below what is needed to earn a living wage. In fact, 43 percent of those with the lowest literacy skills live in poverty.

Not surprisingly, those sent to prison generally have lower literacy skills than the rest of the population: 70 percent of prisoners fall into the lowest two levels of reading proficiency (National Institute for Literacy, 1998).

Increasingly, a strong work ethic and a strong back will not be enough to support a family. The global economy demands that workers can read, write, compute, solve problems, and communicate clearly. Yet 1 in 4 adults cannot perform the basic literacy requirements of a typical job (U.S. Office of Technology Assessment, 1993). Seventy-five percent of today's jobs require at least a ninth-grade reading level (National Institute for Literacy, 1998). College-educated Americans are earning, on average, 76 percent more than Americans who have only a high school diploma (U.S. Department of Labor, 1999b).

In early 1999, Education Secretary Richard W. Riley issued a challenge to America's students: Reach beyond a high school diploma and aim to complete at least some college coursework. This challenge acknowledges a hard reality: of the 10 fastest-growing jobs in the next decade, 8 will require either a college education or moderate to long-term postsecondary training (U.S. Department of Labor, 1997).

But literacy is about more than economics. Our ability to share information through the written word is vital in a democratic society. In order to live up to our democratic ideals and to share the richness that comes from thoughtful reflection, we must all be able to communicate and to make wise decisions.

It is clear that the United States cannot afford to lose the real reading war: We can no longer allow so many children to leave the third grade without the reading skills needed for school success.

To help all our children succeed and to compete as a nation, we must start early and finish strong; we must ensure that every American child becomes a reader.

The Secrets of Reading Success

A bumper sticker states, "If you can read this, thank a teacher." But the latest research indicates the situation is more complex.

Who plays the critical roles in preparing a successful reader?

First, as an essential starting point, families can maximize the benefits of parent-child communication from birth.

Second, caregivers and preschool teachers can be given training and resources to stimulate emergent literacy.

Third, children deserve well-trained teachers who understand reading development, who can pinpoint problems, and who can address them effectively (National Research Council, 1998).

But the consequential task of ensuring that children learn to read should not be left to families, providers, and teachers alone. Entire communities can rally around their children for literacy success. This means more partnerships between schools and communities. It means greater engagement of private enterprises, colleges, universities, and cultural groups. It means more volunteers and more opportunities for legions of mentors and tutors.

Americans from all walks of life must step forward to win the war against illiteracy.

Unlike children who are struggling to decode words, we as a nation have already unlocked the secrets to better reading. If we start early and finish strong, we can help every child become a good reader.

The momentum is with us for a breakthrough in student reading achievement. The only question that remains is whether we are committed to literacy for every American child.

CHAPTER 1

Raising Readers: The Tremendous Potential of Families

Recent research into human brain development is proving that parents truly are their children's first teachers. What parents do, or don't do, has a lasting impact on their child's reading skill and literacy. For example, there is considerable evidence of a relationship between reading regularly to a child and that child's later reading achievement (National Research Council, 1998).

Parents as Teachers

Parents as Teachers (PAT) is an international family education program for parents of children from birth through age 5. Parents learn to become their children's best teachers. Evaluations have shown that PAT children at age 3 have significantly enhanced language, problem-solving, and social development skills. PAT parents read more often to their children and stay involved in their children's education.

The program has four main components: 1) home visits by trained parent educators; 2) group meetings for parents to share successes, concerns, and strategies; 3) developmental screenings to determine early if a child needs assistance; and 4) families' connections with community resources, including lending libraries, diagnostic services, and help for children with special needs.

Contact:
Parents as Teachers National Center
10176 Corporate Square Drive Suite
230 St. Louis, MO 63132
(314) 432-4330
Fax: (314) 432-8963
www.patnc.org

But many parents are not yet making the most of simple, vital opportunities to stimulate full and healthy child development in the early years, and by extension, good reading readiness. As U.S. Education Secretary Richard W. Riley has said, "If every child were read to daily from infancy, it would revolutionize education in this country!"

BRAIN DEVELOPMENT AND READING

Children develop much of their capacity for learning in the first three years of life, when their brains grow to 90 percent of their eventual adult weight (Karoly et al., 1998). A child's intelligence, so long as it falls within a normal range, does not determine the ease with which the child will learn to read. Rather, as children grow and experience the world, new neural connections are made. This orderly and individualized process, varying from child to child, makes reading possible.

As parents talk, sing, and read to children, the children's brain cells are literally turned on (Shore, 1997). Existing links among brain cells are strengthened and new cells and links are formed. That is why infants' and toddlers' health and nutrition, along with good functioning of the senses, are so important. The opportunity for creating the foundation for reading begins in the earliest years. Moreover, many pediatricians now believe that a child who has never held a book or listened to a story is not a fully healthy child (Klass, 1998).

Given the course of brain development, it is not surprising that young children who are exposed to certain experiences usually prove to be good readers later. Just as a child develops language skills long before being able to speak, the child also develops literacy skills long before being able to read (National Research Council, 1998).

HOW PARENTS HELP

By cooing, singing lullabies, or reading aloud to a baby, toddler, or preschooler, parents stimulate their children's developing minds and help build a base for literacy skills. Counting, number concepts, letter names and shapes, associating sounds with letters, interest in reading, and cooperation with other children are all relevant to learning to read (Wells, 1985). Researchers studying high school seniors found early educational experiences—such as learning nursery rhymes, watching Sesame Street, playing word and number games, and being read to—are all good predictors of later reading ability (Hanson et al., 1987).

Positive parental attitudes toward literacy can also help children become more successful readers (Baker et al., 1995). Enthusiasm about books and reading can be shared between a parent and child and deepen the child's interest in learning to read (Snow & Tabors, 1996). Children who learn from parents that reading is fun may be more likely to sustain efforts to learn to read when the going gets tough (National Research Council, 1998). Some experts believe that parental emphasis on reading as entertainment, rather than as a skill, develops a more positive attitude toward reading in children (Baker et al., 1997).

Wise parents understand that play is the work of children. Parents can use the arts to help develop early language skills, from the first lullaby to dramatization of a favorite story (Council of Chief State School Officers, 1998). Dramatic play can develop vocabulary, concepts and creativity, all part of pre-literacy skill building. Music and other language-rich creative arts can stimulate a young child's language and literacy development through one-on-one interaction with a caring adult.

Reach Out and Read

Developed at Boston City Hospital by Dr. Barry Zuckerman, Reach Out and Read is a national pediatric literacy program that trains pediatricians and volunteers to read aloud to children as part of their well-baby check-ups. The doctors also "prescribe" reading as essential to raising a healthy child from infancy through age 5.

At each check-up, the child is sent home with age-appropriate books, and parents are encouraged to develop the habit of reading with their children. This trailblazing program, with over 350 sites in 45 states, relies on funding from businesses and private foundations, in addition to book donations from publishing companies.

Contact:
Reach Out and Read
Boston Medical Center
Boston, MA
(617) 414-5701
www.reachoutandread.org

DOCTORS PRESCRIBE READING

Reading aloud to young children is so critical that the American Academy of Pediatrics recommends that doctors prescribe reading activities along with other advice given to parents at regular check-ups.

Dr. Perri Klass, Medical Director of Reach Out and Read, a national pediatric literacy program involving hundreds of hospitals, clinics, and independent practices, strongly agrees. "With confidence," says Dr. Klass, "I tell parents to read to their children, secure in the knowledge that there's good evidence that it will help their language development, help them be ready to read when the time comes, and help parents and children spend loving moments together."

Yet studies show that many parents have not yet heard of this "prescription for reading." A national survey found that less than half (48 percent) of parents said they read or shared a picture book daily with their children ages 1 to 3. Even fewer, 39 percent of parents, read or looked at a picture book with their infants at least once a day. Most alarmingly, 1 in 6 parents of an infant (16 percent) said they do not read to their child at all (Young et al., 1996). Only 4 to 5 percent of adults are unable to read a children's book, although more may be uncomfortable doing so (National Institute for Literacy, 1998).

The 1996 National Household Education Survey, however, found some positive trends involving preschoolers. Fifty-seven percent of children ages 3 to 5 were read to every day by a family member in 1996, up slightly from 53 percent in 1993. When oral storytelling is also considered, the percentage of children exposed to narrative rose to 72 percent (up from 66 percent in 1993). Nonetheless, the growth in the percentage of children being read to has occurred mostly in families least at risk—those at or above the poverty level, those headed by two parents, and those in which the mother has some college education.

DIFFERENCES AMONG FAMILIES

Five for Families!

Researchers have identified five areas where the home and family can influence reading development in children:

1. Value Placed on Literacy: Parents show their own interest in reading by reading in front of their children and encouraging them to read, too.

2. Press for Achievement: Parents let children know that they are expected to achieve and help them develop reading skills.

3. Availability and Use of Reading Material: Homes with reading and writing materials for children—such as books, newspapers, writing paper, pencils, and crayons—create more opportunities to develop literacy.

4. Reading with Children: Parents who read to preschoolers and listen as older children read aloud help children become readers.

5. Opportunities for Verbal Interaction: The quantity and content of conversation between parents and children influence language and vocabulary development, both building blocks for later reading success.

Source: *Hess & Holloway, 1984. Family and School as Educational Institutions*

The single most significant predictor of children's literacy is their mother's literacy level (Educational Testing Service, 1995). The more education a mother has, the more likely she is to read to her child. Studies show that 77 percent of children whose mothers have a college education were read to every day, while only 49 percent of children whose mothers had a high school education were read to daily (National Household Education Survey, 1996).

Similarly, children in poor families are less likely to be read to daily. The 1996 National Household Education Survey found that 46 percent of children in families in poverty were read to every day, compared with 61 percent of children in families living above the poverty line.

Some researchers have found that the home literacy environment can be an even stronger predictor of literacy and academic achievement than family income. That home environment includes the literacy level of the parents, the parents' educational achievement, and the availability of reading materials, among other factors (Dickinson, 1991).

While the overall economic status of the family has a great impact on whether families read to children, the employment status of the mother does not. The 1996 National Household Education Survey found little difference between mothers who work more than 35 hours a week and those who work less than that or are not employed. In families with mothers who worked full time, 54 percent of children were read to daily. When the mother worked part time, or was not employed, 59 percent of the children were read to daily.

In contrast, big differences are seen between dual-parent and single-parent households, according to a recent study by the University of Michigan's Institute for Social Research. Researchers found that parents in "traditional" families with a working father and an at-home mother spent an average of 22 hours a week directly engaged with their children under age 13. That was slightly more than the 19 hours spent by parents in dual-income families and more than double the 9 hours spent by single mothers (Hofferth, 1998). The National Household Education Survey found that 61 percent of preschoolers in two-parent households, vs. 46 percent in households with one parent or no parents, were read to daily.

Differences were also seen in the National Household Education Survey among racial and ethnic groups. Sixty-four percent of White families reported reading every day to children ages 3 to 5, compared with 44 percent of Black families and 39 percent of Hispanic families.

THE VALUE OF WORDS

Research demonstrates that the size of a young child's vocabulary is a strong predictor of reading—preschoolers with large vocabularies tend to become proficient readers (National Research Council, 1998). Children's vocabulary can be greatly enhanced by talking and reading with parents. In fact, the vocabulary of the average children's book is greater than that found on prime-time television (Hayes & Ahrens, 1988).

Children from lower-income families are at greater risk of having smaller vocabularies than other children. One study of the actual vocabulary of first-graders found that those from high-income families had double the vocabulary of those from lower-income families (Graves & Slater, 1987).

None of these statistics should be used to blame parents. Rather, we should use evidence of what works to rally and support all families to take full advantage of their tremendous opportunity to prepare their children for reading success.

Given what we know about brain development, it is clear that parents should not leave to schools alone the important tasks of language and literacy development. We must do more to enable and encourage parents to talk with their children and invest 30 minutes daily for reading. When parents are unable, grandparents, neighbors, babysitters, siblings, and other adults should step in to serve as the child's designated reader for the day. It is an experience that children will remember for a lifetime, and one that will form the foundation for all later learning.

The Consequences of Conversation with Children

More than 40 families were observed over several years to study how, and how often, parents talk with children. Researchers found a tremendous variety in the amount of words spoken to children in the first three years of life and in the quality of feedback they received. These verbal interactions with adults are major predictors of how prepared children will be to succeed in school.

While family income was highly related to levels of children's language exposure, the relationship was not absolute. Some middle-income families behaved more like high-income families, preparing their children for higher achievement through vocabulary development and other language skills. Other middle-income families behaved more like low-income families, with a paucity of language exposure for children.

An average child growing up in a low-income family receiving welfare hears one-half to one-third as many spoken words as children in more affluent households. At these rates the low-income child would know about 3,000 words by age 6, while the child of the high-income family would have a vocabulary of 20,000 words. To provide the low-income child with weekly language experience equal to that of a child from a middle-income family, it would require 41 hours per week of out-of-home word exposure as rich as those heard by the most affluent children.

Number of words heard at home per hour by 1- and 2-year-olds learning to talk:

low-income child	620
middle-income child	1,250
high-income child	2,150

Number of words heard by age 3:

low-income child	10 million
middle-income child	20 million
high-income child	30 million

Source: Hart & Risley, 1995. *Meaningful Differences in the Everyday Experiences of Young Children*

ACCESS TO BOOKS

Some experts believe that for America's poorest children, the biggest obstacle to literacy is the scarcity of books and appropriate reading material (Needlman et al., 1991).

In many homes, particularly those with adult non-readers, there simply aren't any books, magazines, or newspapers appropriate for young children.

Yet, studies show that parents who are given books and "prescriptions for reading" by their children's pediatricians are four times more likely to read and share books with their young children (Needlman et al., 1991). Mothers receiving welfare are eight times more likely to read to their children when provided with books and encouragement (Needlman et al., 1991).

The NAEP 1998 Reading Report Card found that students with higher reading scores were more likely to report four types of reading materials in their homes—encyclopedias, magazines, newspapers, and at least 25 books.

BORROWING BOOKS

Feed Me a Story!

What difference can reading aloud to a child for 30 minutes per day make?

If daily reading begins in infancy, by the time the child is 5 years old, he or she has been fed roughly 900 hours of brain food!

Reduce that experience to just 30 minutes a week and the child's hungry mind loses 770 hours of nursery rhymes, fairy tales, and stories.

A kindergarten student who has not been read to could enter school with less than 60 hours of literacy nutrition. No teacher, no matter how talented, can make up for those lost hours of mental nourishment.

Hours of reading books by age 5

30 minutes daily	900 Hours
30 minutes weekly	130 Hours
Less than 30 minutes weekly	60 Hours

Source: *U.S. Department of Education, America Reads Challenge*

Of course, books are available at public libraries, but this resource is under-utilized—only 37 percent of 3- to 5-year-olds visit a library at least once a month (National Education Goals Panel, 1997). Transportation and access can be obstacles for some families. Parents who are unfamiliar with libraries may be unaware that books can be borrowed for free and that librarians can help them select books that are age-appropriate. Librarians also can direct parents with low literacy skills toward picture books and books on tape, also appealing to children who are struggling with reading. Many libraries offer reading support and story hours for families.

Once again, the parent's education level is significant, though even among the highly educated, library participation is not high. The National Education Goals Panel found that about half of the children of college graduates make monthly trips to the library, compared with less than one-sixth of children whose parents never completed high school.

Access to quality reading materials should continue throughout a child's school years. But a 1996 survey found that average book spending for school libraries had frozen in place. Worse, 36 percent of school librarians reported having less money for books than the year before (Miller & Shontz, 1997). In 1998, cash-strapped schools in Seattle found their lack of contemporary titles to be such a deterrent to student reading that a citywide campaign was launched to replenish school libraries. The state of California spent more than $150 million in 1999 to restock school library shelves with new titles (*Los Angeles Times*, 1999).

CHOOSING BOOKS OVER TELEVISION

A powerful barrier to raising readers sits in the living rooms or bedrooms of most American homes. Children of all ages watch as much television in one day as they read for fun in an entire week, according to a 1998 report of the University of Michigan's Institute for Social Research. Overall, children under age 13 spend 90 minutes a day in front of the TV—down from two hours in 1981, but still one-quarter of their free time.

Even the littlest viewers are hooked. Children ages 3 to 5 spend an average of 13 hours and 28 minutes a week watching TV, almost as much as the 13 hours and 36 minutes that 9- to 12-year-olds watch TV weekly (Hofferth, 1998).

The youngest children spend the most time reading at home, but it is only a paltry one hour and 25 minutes a week. The reading habit actually declines among children between ages 6 and 12, who spend roughly 10 minutes less per week with books at home. Girls spend about 11 minutes per day reading, while boys spend 10 minutes. Reading rates did not differ on weekdays or weekends (Hofferth, 1998).

Children of older parents are more likely to read than are children of younger parents. Children of single parents spend less time reading than do children in two-parent households. Children with two working parents watch less television than "traditional" families with a male breadwinner and a mother at home. Children of better-educated parents watch less TV and read more often for pleasure. Kids with more siblings watch more TV than those in small families (Hofferth, 1998).

The imbalance between reading and television has a significant effect on academic results, the Michigan researchers found. Every hour of weekly reading translated into a half-point increase on test scores, while each hour of TV watching corresponded with a tenth of a point drop in scores (Hofferth, 1998).

Imagination Library

The Dollywood Foundation's Imagination Library promotes early learning by encouraging and enabling families to read together. Long committed to dropout prevention, the foundation has responded to research showing that investment in early childhood can build a strong foundation for school success. Administered by singer and actress Dolly Parton, this innovative program provides free books to families in her home region in Tennessee.

Each baby born in Sevier County receives a special locomotive bookcase and a copy of *The Little Engine that Could*. The child then receives a new book each month until he or she begins kindergarten at age 5, for a total library of 60 books.

The program has distributed more than 100,000 books to 5,000 prekindergarten children.

The Imagination Express, a specially designed train, is driven by The Imagineer, who reads aloud and promotes reading at childcare centers and community events throughout the Sevier County region.

Contact:
Madeline Rogero,
Executive Director
The Dollywood Foundation
Pigeon Forge, TN
(423) 428-9606
www.dollywood.com/foundation/library.html

A HOPEFUL TREND

A Wealth of Children's Books in Spanish

The San Marcos campus of California State University hosts the Center for the Study of Books in Spanish for Children and Adolescents. The center aims to help more children develop an early love of reading and to become lifelong readers. The center offers workshops and publications, and boasts an 80,000 volume lending library of children's books in Spanish, believed to be the world's largest collection of its kind. The library also includes books in English on Latino culture.

The center offers a free searchable database of 5,000 recommended books in Spanish from publishers around the world. To assist

Spanish-speaking parents and others, information on each book is provided in Spanish as well as in English, including subject headings, grade-level, bibliography, and brief descriptions.

Contact:
Dr. Isabel Schon
California State University
San Marcos, CA 92096-0001
(760) 750-4070
Fax: (760) 750-4073
ischon@mailhost1.csusm.edu
www.csusm.edu/campus_centers/csb/

There are reasons to be hopeful. The NAEP 1998 Reading Report Card found fewer students were watching excessive amounts of television compared with 1994, and more fourth- and twelfth-graders were watching a minimal amount—one hour or less per day—compared with 1992. In all three grades, students who reported watching three or fewer hours of television each day had higher average reading scores, and those who watched six hours or more had the lowest average scores. The same report also found that fourth-graders who were given time daily to read books of their own choosing had the highest average scores.

Parents cannot assume that schoolwork makes up for too much TV. With in-class assignments and homework, many students report reading 10 pages or fewer each day—43 percent of fourth-graders, 57 percent of eighth-graders and 56 percent of twelfth-graders (NAEP 1998 Reading Report Card). On a positive note, more eighth- and twelfth-graders report reading 11 or more pages per day than in recent years.

When children are plugged into television instead of reading books, they are not developing the key literacy skills that will prepare them for school and help them learn. While there are some educational programs, most notably on public television, they are underutilized. Parents must be motivated to choose those programs more often.

THE VALUE OF PARENTS

Parents serve both as teachers and role models in reading (National Research Council, 1998). Adults pass on to children their own expectations about education and achievement, both positive and negative (Fingeret, 1990). Parents who value reading are more likely to turn off the television, visit the library, and give books as gifts. But adults who rarely read books or newspapers themselves may be less likely to read to their own children (Fletcher & Lyon, 1998). Some parents with limited English proficiency may be reluctant to read aloud in their native language, out of concern that this would impede their children's English acquisition.

Few parents reach out for help from experts, either due to embarrassment, lack of access, or lack of time. Only 12 percent of parents of 3- to 5-year-olds attended a parenting class in 1996, and only 11 percent had taken part in a parental support group (National Education Goals Panel, 1997). It is a great national challenge to reach parents with literacy information and support, to better enable them to raise a family of readers.

Resources for parents and families may be found in Reading Resources, Appendix B of this book.

Parents: Taking Charge of Television Choices

PBS (the Public Broadcasting Service) created the Ready to Learn program to provide preschool children with skills for lifelong learning. Participating stations coach parents and caregivers on how to use television as a learning tool to improve children's reading and social skills.

A recent study by the University of Alabama's Institute for Communication Research found that coaching seminars had a lasting impact on parents' and children's behavior (Bryant, 1999).

Six months after parents attended a workshop, children were reported to watch 40 percent less television than before, and when they did watch, they chose more educational programs. Parents reported that the shows their children watched, to varying degrees, helped them prepare for school and acquire information. They also encouraged more reading.

Participating parents were more likely to set limits on the amount of time children watched TV. Parents and children watched television together much more often than before the workshop. The coached parents also were much more likely to discuss programs with their children, and the children were much more likely to ask questions about what they were viewing.

The coaching also had a significant impact on reading behavior. Parents read to their children more often, and for longer periods, than before the coaching. They chose more educational reading materials and took children more often to the library and bookstore. They also were much more likely to engage children in hands-on activities related to the books they had read.

Contact:
Jean Chase
Ready to Learn
(703) 739-5000
www.pbs.org/kids/rtl

Action Steps for Parents

There are a number of steps that parents can take to help prepare their young children to become readers and to support the reading habit once they are in school. These include:

- Feed your child a diet of rich language experiences throughout the day. Talk with your infants and young children frequently in short, simple sentences. Tell stories, sing songs, recite nursery rhymes or poems, and describe the world around them to expose them to words. Name things. Make connections. Encourage your child's efforts to talk with you.

- Try to read aloud to your children for 30 minutes daily beginning when they are infants. Ask caring adults to be your children's daily reader when you are unavailable.

- Have your child's eyesight and hearing tested early and annually. If you suspect your child may have a disability, seek help. Evaluations and assessments are available at no cost to parents. Call the early childhood specialist in your school system or call the National Information Center for Children and Youth with Disabilities at (800) 695-0285 (Voice/TTY).

- Seek out childcare providers who spend time talking with and reading to your child, who make trips to the library, and who designate a special reading area for children.

- Ask your child's teacher for an assessment of your child's reading level, an explanation of the approach the teacher is taking to develop reading and literacy skills, and ways in which you can bolster your child's literacy skills at home.

- Limit the amount and kind of television your children watch. Seek out educational television or videos from the library that you can watch and discuss with your children.

(continued)

- Set up a special place for reading and writing in your home. A well-lit reading corner filled with lots of good books can become a child's favorite place. Keep writing materials such as non-toxic crayons, washable markers, paints and brushes, and different kinds of paper in a place where children can reach them.

- Visit the public library often to spark your child's interest in books. Help your children obtain their own library cards and pick out their own books. Talk to a librarian, teacher, school reading specialist, or bookstore owner for guidance about what books are appropriate for children at different ages and reading levels.

- You are your child's greatest role model. Demonstrate your own love of reading by spending quiet time in which your child observes you reading to yourself. Show your child how reading and writing help you get things done every day—cooking, shopping, driving, or taking the bus.

- If your own reading skills are limited, consider joining a family literacy program. Ask a librarian for picture books that you can share with your child by talking about the pictures. Tell family stories or favorite folktales to your children.

- Consider giving books or magazines to children as presents or as a recognition of special achievements. Special occasions, such as birthdays or holidays, can be the perfect opportunity to give a child a new book.

- Connect your children with their grandparents and great-grandparents. Encourage them to read books together, talk about growing up, tell stories, and sing songs from their generation.

- Ask about free readings and other programs at bookstores in your community.

CHAPTER 2

Ready to Read: Building Skills Through Early Care and Education

It is a fact of American family life that young children spend a substantial part of their days in the care of someone other than a parent. More than 13 million infants, toddlers, and preschoolers receive regular care from adults other than their parents—roughly 6 out of 10 children under age 6 who are not enrolled in kindergarten (U.S. Department of Education, OERI, 1996). According to the University of Michigan's Institute for Social Research, the average number of hours spent per week by children ages 3 to 5 in school settings nearly doubled from 11.5 hours in 1981 to 20 hours in 1997 (Hofferth, 1998).

The National Center for the Early Childhood Work Force estimates that 3 million people provided childcare in 1998. The U.S. Department of Labor has projected the need for nearly 300,000 new childcare workers between 1996 and 2006, making the occupation among the 10 fastest-growing in the nation.

These statistics give us important information for winning the war against illiteracy. For some children, the support of parents and elementary school teachers is not enough. While most parents are eager to learn more about early childhood development and education, work and family pressures strain their time and resources. Elementary school teachers do not even meet children until well after key periods have passed for cognitive and language development.

ARCHITECTS OF READING SUCCESS

If we are serious about starting early to create a nation of readers, then we must do more to enlist the burgeoning corps of adults who work in early care and education—in preschools, childcare centers, nursery schools, and home-based care settings. We must also address the reality that many of these early care and education providers need assistance with basic skills and training to fulfill their potential. As a nation, we must acknowledge that these Americans are not just children's caretakers. They are architects of foundations that are critical for reading and academic success.

Many studies have established that high-quality early care and education lay the foundation for school success by enhancing cognitive and language development, as well as social and emotional competence (National Institute for Child Health and Development, 1997). More specifically, the 1998 National Research Council report found that early childhood programs can contribute to the prevention of reading difficulties. These programs contribute by providing young children with enriched, research-based literacy environments, and by identifying and removing possible obstacles to reading success.

Unfortunately, fulfilling the promise of early education is easier to imagine than to realize. By the time they enter kindergarten, most children have experienced some kind of early education or childcare. But access to this care, as well as the quality of care, varies greatly. Children from low-income families, who are most apt to benefit from early intervention, are the least likely to attend preschool. In fact, the preschool participation gap between rich and poor has actually widened over the past two decades (National Education Goals Panel, 1997).

When we fail to make the most of this important period in young children's lives, we set the stage for later difficulties. Kindergarten teachers have estimated that 35 percent of America's children start school unprepared to learn (Boyer, 1991). In 1998, teachers in another national survey reported that about half of all children have problems making the transition to kindergarten (National Center for Early Childhood Development and Learning, 1998). Many of these children will have difficulty learning to read.

Bright Beginnings, Charlotte, NC

Bright Beginnings is a public pre-kindergarten program in North Carolina's Charlotte-Mecklenburg Public Schools. Focused on literacy, the program provides 4-year-olds with a literacy-rich, resource-rich, full-day school experience. Each school day is constructed around four 15-minute literacy circles, where teachers engage children in reading and literacy activities.

The school district has developed its own pre-kindergarten curriculum, content standards, and performance expectations that set high goals for every child. Pre-kindergarten standards have been developed in the areas of social and personal development, language and literacy, mathematical thinking, scientific thinking, social studies, the creative arts, physical development, and technology.

Supported mainly through federal Title I funds, the program currently serves more than 1,900 children.

Plans call for reaching all 4,000 children in the school district who need high-quality preschool experiences to get ready for school.

The district collaborates with Head Start, special education, and other public and private partners. All teachers are early childhood specialists with at least a four-year degree and are certified to teach by the state.

Bright Beginnings serves only eligible children who are selected according to federal funding guidelines. An initial program evaluation shows promising outcomes.

Contact:
Tony Bucci, Ellen Edmonds, Barbara Pellin
Charlotte-Mecklenburg
School District
701 East 2nd Street
Charlotte, NC 28202
(704) 379-7111
www.cms.k12.nc.us/k12/curricul/prek/index.htm

MORE CHILDREN IN CHILDCARE

The opportunities for early care and education to help—or hinder—America's victory in the war against illiteracy have multiplied with the expansion of childcare services. Much of this demand has been fueled by the tremendous expansion of women's roles in the workforce. The percentage of mothers of infants and toddlers working outside the home has nearly tripled from 21 percent in 1965 to 59 percent in 1994 (Shore, 1997).

But even among households in which the mother is not employed, one-third use regular childcare for their youngest children (U.S. Department of Education, OERI, 1996). Preschoolers spend an average of 35 hours a week in childcare if their mothers work outside the home, and 20 hours per week if their mothers are not employed (Shore, 1997).

Childcare starts early: 45 percent of infants under age 1 are regularly cared for by someone other than a parent, most by a relative in a private home. As babies grow, their chance of being cared for by non-parental adults also grows, from 50 percent of 1-year-olds to 84 percent of 5-year-olds. Similarly, the percentage cared for outside of private homes grows from 11 percent of

1-year olds to 75 percent of 5-year-olds (U.S. Department of Education, OERI, 1996). Thus, an enormous potential exists for early childhood providers to influence later reading success.

CHOICES IN CHILDCARE

Individual and cultural preferences influence family choices about the use of early childhood programs. More than 6 out of 10 Black children (66 percent) and White children (62 percent) receive supplemental care and education, compared with 46 percent of Hispanic children. There are also wide income differences in families' childcare patterns: only half of all households with incomes of $30,000 or less use childcare, compared with three-quarters of households with incomes of $50,000 or more (U.S. Department of Education, 1996).

Besides influencing whether families use childcare at all, income also influences the type of care that families select. This has significance for the war against illiteracy: the care families choose makes a difference.

Building Literacy Through the Arts in Early Childhood

The Arts Education Partnership, representing more than 100 national organizations, researched the role of the arts in early childhood. The study identifies the best kinds of experiences for babies, toddlers, preschoolers, and young elementary school students to build cognitive, motor, language, and social-emotional development.

Under the philosophy that play is the business of young children, the partnership study found that the arts engage children in learning, stimulate memory, and facilitate understanding. Role-playing games, poems, songs, rhyming, dramatic storytelling, and other creative arts play can develop language skills and a love of learning.

The study's report, *Young Children in the Arts,* includes developmental benchmarks and appropriate arts activities for children from birth to age 8. Parents and adult caregivers are encouraged to use character voices and dramatic gestures when reading or telling stories and to make sock puppets to increase the enjoyment of the tale. Show-and-tell stories can be created with photographs, and young children can pantomime their favorite book characters before a mirror. Older children can write poems and improvise stories with simple costumes.

Resources, research, and programs are available through the database of the Wolf Trap Institute for Early Learning Through the Arts at www.wolftrap.org.

Contact:
    Arts Education Partnership
    Council of Chief State School Officers
    One Massachusetts Avenue, NW
    Suite 700
    Washington, DC 20001-1431
    (202) 326-8693
    Fax: (202) 408-8076
    aep@ccsso.org
    http://aep-arts.org

THE LIMITATIONS OF INCOME

In addition to having greater access to regulated care, higher-income families are much more likely to use center-based care—nursery schools, childcare centers, and preschools—than are lower-income families (National Education Goals Panel, 1995; West et al., 1995). In low-income neighborhoods, the supply of any kind of regulated childcare, whether in centers or family childcare homes, is usually inadequate (Siegel & Loman, 1991).

A Jump Start

Jumpstart recruits college students to help children who are struggling in preschool. The mentors are paired for almost two years with 3- and 4-year-olds in Head Start or other programs for children living in poverty. The Jumpstart mentors work one-on-one with children to teach and reinforce basic academic and social skills.

Jumpstart forms partnerships with early childhood caregivers and involves families in their preschooler's development. The summer program provides an intensive preschool experience for young children during the two months before kindergarten.

Jumpstart serves children in Boston; New Haven, Connecticut; New York City; Washington, D.C.; Los Angeles; and San Francisco. The program aims to engage 1,000 college students as mentors by the year 2000 and to reach more than 12,000 children. Mentors may receive stipends or wages through AmeriCorps or the Federal Work-Study program.

Contact:
    Jumpstart
    93 Summer Street, 2nd Floor
    Boston, MA 02110

(continued)

(617) 542-JUMP
Fax: (617) 542-2557
www.jstart.org

This lack of options increases the number of poor children in unlicensed family childcare or relative care (Fuller & Liang, 1995; Love & Kisker, 1996). Research shows that, in general, unlicensed care arrangements are of lower quality than licensed centers or homes (Cost, Quality and Child Outcomes Study Team, 1995; Kontos et al., 1994). Among those who offer services in a private home, 50 percent of non-regulated providers have been found to offer inadequate care, compared with about 13 percent of regulated providers (Families and Work Institute, 1994).

ADVANTAGES OF CENTER-BASED CARE

Although many families prefer family childcare arrangements for their home-like atmosphere and small numbers of children, center-based care is the preference of most families for their older, preschool children (Leibowitz et al., 1988). Because centers are designed to serve larger groups of children, they often offer greater resources for preschoolers' literacy development, such as books, tapes, and computers.

Additionally, a recent multi-site study found that center care is associated with better cognitive and language outcomes and a higher level of school readiness, compared with outcomes in other settings of comparable quality (National Institute of Child Health and Human Development, 1997b). But not all center-based care is equal. Children who attended centers that met professional guidelines for child-staff ratios, group sizes, and teacher education had better language comprehension and school readiness than did children enrolled in centers without these standards.

But the doors to high-quality early care and education are often closed to low-income families, either because of cost or location. These barriers result in many poor children entering school without the early educational choices available to their affluent classmates, placing them at greater risk of reading difficulties.

LOW FUNDING, LOW QUALITY

Childcare providers have struggled to satisfy the demand for services. Unfortunately, this struggle has resulted in the chronic, twin calamities of low wages and high employee turnover. The under-funding of early care and education—

including fees, subsidies, and donations—is acknowledged to be the chief cause of low quality (Gomby et al., 1996; National Education Association, 1998).

Both parents and childcare teachers bear the burden of the current inadequate funding system. Clearly, parent fees put high-quality early care and education out of reach for many working families. Yet, this system also perpetuates low salaries, which fail to attract and retain highly skilled teachers. The impact is negative for all involved—childcare providers, families, and children—and ultimately, for our nation as well. Low-quality early care and education put children's development at risk, including the development of abilities associated with reading success.

The Gardner Children's Center, San Jose, CA

For this bustling childcare center, serving children from 6 weeks old through seventh grade, literacy is the foundation of all learning. Each child is read to daily. Lesson plans are based on "Ten Best Books," which each teacher chooses to ensure that all children learn the joy of reading. Every classroom has a designated reading area, and both pre-kindergarten and school-age children regularly visit the Biblioteca (the Spanish language library) for story hour and book selection. Teachers aim to make visiting the library a lifelong habit.

The Gardner Children's Center also reaches out to families to promote literacy. At orientation, all parents are given a book in their home language and coached on the importance of reading to and with their children. These messages are reinforced at parent conferences twice a year. A family literacy night is celebrated through a partnership with the local public television station.

Also, parents learn to share literacy activities at home with their children in English and Spanish. Children's books are distributed at the annual health fair. At holiday time, every child enrolled in the program, and each sibling, receives at least one book as a gift. The total environment communicates the value and joy of reading.

Contact:
   Frederick Ferrer, Director
   Gardner Children's Center Inc.
   611 Willis Avenue
   San Jose, CA 95125
   (408) 998-1343
   www.gardnerchildren.com

In 1989, a national study reported that the quality in most childcare centers was "barely adequate" (National Center for the Early Childhood Workforce, 1989). In 1999, the National Institute of Child Health and Human Development (NICHD) found that fewer than 10 percent of American youngsters ages 3 and under are likely to receive "excellent" care (Booth, 1999). About 20 percent of childcare centers are estimated to provide unsafe and unhealthy care (Shore, 1997). The 1995 Cost, Quality, and Child Outcomes Study found that childcare at most centers is poor to mediocre, and almost half of infant and toddler care may be detrimental. The NICHD study found that 61 percent of childcare arrangements—including centers, family childcare homes, in-home sitters, and relative care—to be poor to fair quality (Booth, 1999).

Six for Success!

Both child development theory and research on successful practices point to six key features of high-quality early care and education programs:

1. High staff-child ratios
2. Small group sizes
3. Adequate staff education and training
4. Low staff turnover
5. Curriculum emphasizing child-initiated, active learning
6. Parent involvement

Source: *National Education Association, 1998*

THE STATES TAKE ACTION

Many states are taking action aimed at improving childcare quality, in part because a growing amount of public money is being spent on childcare. Although states traditionally spend the lion's share of funds for children on elementary and secondary education, states increased expenditures on childcare by 55 percent between 1996 and 1998 (National Governors' Association, 1998).

This investment is important not only to meet the demands of the marketplace but also, if the quality of care is high, to put more children on the path to school success. Thus, quality improvement efforts must attend to children's development—cognitive, language, social, and emotional—as well as reduce risks of physical harm.

Forty-four states reported to the National Governors' Association that they were working on childcare quality issues in 1998. One positive trend finds 16 states paying higher reimbursements to childcare providers who meet higher quality standards. Fortunately, reforms to boost health and safety often parallel reforms that can improve opportunities for cognitive and language development.

For example, improving child-staff ratios and requiring smaller class sizes enables teachers to have individual conversations, read with small groups, and implement classroom practices that research shows are necessary to promote literacy and later school success (Cost, Quality and Child Outcomes Study Team, 1995). Research also has found that favorable adult-child ratios increase children's imitation of adults and increase children's verbal interactions (National Education Association, 1998). Despite this evidence, only 18 states maintain requirements for a 10-to-1 ratio throughout the preschool years, and some states allow ratios twice as high (General Accounting Office, 1998).

QUALITY OF EARLY CHILDHOOD TEACHERS

Whether they work in childcare, preschool, or public school, research consistently shows that the quality of teachers is the key to quality education. This is especially true in the early years.

A national study found that when childcare providers had more years of education and more college-level early education training, they provided more sensitive, developmentally appropriate care to children (Cost, Quality and Child Outcomes Study Team, 1995). Higher education and specialized training also allow early childhood teachers to do a better job of advancing children's language skills, a key predictor of later reading success (Whitebook et al., 1990).

But not all childcare teachers get the professional preparation they need. In a study for the U.S. Department of Education, 93 percent of childcare teachers reported having some child-related training, but only 36 percent had formal, college-level teacher preparation, and only 24 percent held a credential from a professional organization. Among home-based providers, only 64 percent reported any child-related training and just 6 percent were accredited by a professional organization (Kisker et al., 1991).

Early childhood teachers find little incentive under current state requirements to prepare themselves better to support literacy development. The National Association for the Education of Young Children (NAEYC) recommends that all early care and education teachers have formal training at the bachelor's level, but most states require that childcare workers hold only a high school diploma. Only nine states require any college credit in early childhood for childcare center teachers. Only two—Hawaii and Rhode Island—require a bachelor's degree in any field with specialized training in early care and education (Azer & Eldred, 1998).

Just as improvements in child-staff ratios and class size benefit all areas of children's development, more professional training opportunities and higher standards for early childhood teachers would enhance children's growth, including their preparation to be successful readers.

EFFORTS TO IMPROVE

Small but promising steps have been taken to enhance the professional preparation of early childhood teachers. One study showed that even a modest increase in high-quality training can benefit children.

A Family Place

The Family Place Library recruits childcare providers to bring children to the library for learning fun. This library also provides Storytime Kits for childcare providers to use in their homes. The kits include books, videos, puzzles, puppets, and activities. Educational toys, including adaptive toys for children with disabilities, can also be borrowed.

This program offers learning opportunities based on family strengths, cultures, and interests.

The Family Place Library, a joint venture between New York's Middle Country Public Library and Libraries for the Future, is funded by the Hasbro Children's Foundation. Family Place Library is a national project operating programs in six communities.

Contact:
Sandy Feinberg
Middle Country Public Library
(516) 585-9393, ext. 200
feinberg@mcpl.lib.ny.us
www.mcpl.lib.ny.us

Libraries for the Future
(212) 352-2330
www.lff.org

These researchers found that even 18 to 36 hours of training for family childcare providers resulted in improved caregiving environments and stronger relationships between adults and children. A taste of professional development also whetted the participants' appetites—after completing the training, 95 percent of the providers said they wanted more instruction (Galinsky et al., 1995).

However promising, this level of preparation does not approach what is needed to provide our youngest children with the foundations for healthy development. More comprehensive approaches to training can strengthen the early childhood work force. The Council for Early Childhood Professional Recognition offers a Child Development Associate (CDA) credential, which is used as one of the standards in the licensing of childcare teachers and center directors in 46 states and the District of Columbia. The credential calls for a high school diploma, 120 hours of training in specified categories, and 480 hours of experience, along with a formal assessment procedure.

With leadership from Wheelock College's Center for Career Development in Early Care and Education, many states are developing more coherent early childhood training systems, with increased collaboration between higher education institutions and community partners.

Other state efforts include the T.E.A.C.H. project (Teacher Education and Compensation Helps). In North Carolina and a small number of other states, this innovative project provides college scholarships for early childhood teachers, administrators, and family childcare providers. Completion of the program leads to higher compensation.

A New Option for Certification in Child Development

The U.S. Department of Labor's Bureau of Apprenticeship and Training (BAT) is taking a collaborative approach to credentialling childcare providers. Through BAT's partnership with the state of West Virginia's apprenticeship program, candidates who take four semesters of college courses and get 4,000 hours of on-the-job training receive certification from the U.S. Department of Labor as a Child Development Specialist.

Hundreds of providers have graduated from the program, and many hundreds more are actively pursuing completion of the requirements. Florida, Minnesota, and Maine have followed suit, with Maine requiring six semesters of college courses.

The program draws on core teams of educators, health professionals, parents, and employers. The system creates a career ladder for childcare providers who earn their salaries while in the program and receive incremental wage increases as their skills, abilities, and knowledge increase.

(continued)

Employers report almost no turnover among participating providers, and the providers report high satisfaction with their careers. Plans are underway to launch similar projects in 10 more states in 1999.

Contact:
> Dana Daugherty
> U.S. Department of Labor
> Bureau of Apprenticeship & Training
> Childcare Development Specialist Registered Apprentice Program
> 200 Constitution Avenue, NW
> Washington, DC 20210
> (202) 219-5921
> www.doleta.gov/bat

These promising trends are consistent with recommendations by experts in the field. The Not By Chance report (Kagan & Cohen, 1997) summarizes four years of discussions by early childhood and policy experts. They recommend that every person employed in early care and education programs hold an individual license to practice, based on demanding standards of education and training.

Licensing Priorities

Hairdressers in more than 40 states are required to have between 1,000 and 2,100 hours of training at an accredited school to get a license (BeautyTech, 1999). Yet 39 states and the District of Columbia do not require childcare providers to have any early childhood training prior to taking children into their homes (Azer & Caprano, 1997).

In the literacy area alone, the 1998 National Research Council's report sets forth a long list of in-depth knowledge and skills that all early childhood educators must have if children are to enter school ready to become successful readers.

The Orton Dyslexia Society calls for all preschool and kindergarten teachers to be able to, at minimum: stimulate oral expressive language, language comprehension, and print awareness; foster phonological awareness and recognition of the links between sounds and letters; and identify language problems of children at risk for reading difficulty. One-shot workshops and minimal training requirements will not be enough to produce the skilled professionals needed to support children's language and literacy development.

Books Aloud: A Childcare Experiment

A recent study called Books Aloud, in and around Philadelphia, found that children's early literacy skills can be enhanced by simultaneously flooding childcare centers with books and training caregivers to read aloud (Neuman, in press).

This $2 million study, funded by the William Penn Foundation, targeted more than 330 childcare centers serving more than 17,000 low-income children. Centers were flooded with nearly 90,000 books—an average of five new, high-quality books per child.

At the start of the study, more centers had TVs than library nooks; the majority had neither. The centers had negligible funding for supplies, so the books they did have were in shabby condition.

Research has found that talk between adults and children in some child-care settings can be dominated by imperatives—adults telling children what to do (Cost, Quality and Child Outcomes Study Team, 1995). The Books Aloud teachers received 10 hours of training from preschool specialists on how to enrich the language and literacy opportunities they offered to children. Caregivers were shown that, in addition to being fun, reading aloud also teaches children about vocabulary, narrative structure, and the relationship between spoken and printed words.

Childcare teachers were encouraged to designate a reading area in their center and storytime in their schedule. They were coached on how to prepare for storytime and extend the concepts of the book through discussions, questions, and hands-on activities, such as puppets.

The frequency of literacy interactions between adults and children, such as talking about stories and developing skills through singing, counting, and rhyming, doubled over seven months. Teachers regarded reading aloud as an opportunity for interactive learning. This increased the children's motivation, interest, and reading time. Books Aloud children frequently asked to be read to, pretended to read, and played with books during their free time more often than similar children who were not in the program. Books Aloud children outperformed their peers in specific abilities that lead to successful reading, such as knowledge of letters and understanding of print, writing, and narrative. Gains were still evident six months after the program had ended.

Contact:
Susan B. Neuman
437 Ritter Hall
Temple University

(continued)

Philadelphia, PA 19122
(215) 204-4982
sneuman@vm.temple.edu

THE NEED FOR COORDINATION

An equally challenging obstacle to the consistent preparation of high-quality early childhood teachers is the isolation and lack of coordination in the early care and education field. Providers range from Head Start teachers to private nursery school teachers to a neighbor caring for a handful of toddlers. Settings range from family homes and churches to private centers and public preschools. Funding ranges from private to local to state to federal.

Watching Kids, Watching Cars

The median hourly wage for parking lot attendants ($6.56) remains higher than the median hourly wage for childcare workers ($6.48).

Source: *U.S. Department of Labor, Bureau of Labor Statistics, 1997*

This fragmented array of early childhood services has resulted in an inequality of resources and lack of communication about good teaching practices, undermining our commitment to provide high-quality education to all children. Greater coordination is needed at the local level to link this mosaic, share resources, increase access, improve overall care, and foster children's language and literacy development.

It is not unusual for children entering a single kindergarten class to display a five-year range of literacy skills. Some children may have the reading ability of an 8-year-old, while others may have the language skills of a 3-year-old (Riley, 1996). Although children will always arrive at school with different learning needs, better early education will increase the number of kindergartners who are ready to become successful readers.

Only by rejecting business as usual and facing up to these many challenges can we take advantage of the tremendous opportunities to improve child literacy through early care and education. Policymakers and early childhood administrators can work actively to support childcare teachers and to bolster their contributions to reading success.

Resources for early care and education providers may be found in the Reading Resources (Appendix B) section of this book.

Action Steps for Policymakers

Local, state, and national policymakers can improve our systems of early care and education and promote literacy. Policymakers can:

- Develop innovative strategies to adequately fund America's early care and education system. Redesign the current financing system to ensure affordable, high-quality care for children and families and competitive compensation for teachers.

- Broaden expectations for high-quality care to include enhanced early learning environments that promote language skills and literacy.

- Provide high-quality preschool for 3- and 4-year-olds who are at risk for later school difficulties, and examine ways to provide universal preschool.

- Strengthen links between family childcare homes, childcare centers, and public schools to share resources and training.

- Ensure that accreditation and licensing requirements in early care and education incorporate research-based practices that support children's cognitive, language, social, and emotional development, and that build successful readers.

- Develop policies and structures, such as Offices for Young Children, through which state and local authorities can coordinate services in early care and education.

- Create incentives for early childhood programs to use research-based knowledge in program design.

- Where necessary, modify minimum standards for group sizes and adult-child ratios to create better literacy environments for children.

- Support efforts to build an early childhood career ladder, with increased responsibilities and compensation for practitioners with higher qualifications. These efforts should attract and keep the staff who are best at helping children learn.

- Support efforts to improve staff training and ongoing professional development. Coordinate training efforts across programs and sponsoring agencies. Fund scholarships and create incentives to encourage providers to pursue advanced training.

- Use public information campaigns to encourage parents to seek effective childcare that develops language and other pre-literacy skills.

Childcare providers, teachers, directors, and others can actively prepare young children for reading success. Practitioners can:

- Use research-based recommendations and resources to improve literacy environments for children.
- Converse frequently and informally with babies and children to build vocabulary, strengthen concepts, and enhance language skills. Encourage and respond to children when they try to communicate.
- Read to children every day. Encourage children to talk about the story or characters. Read one-on-one with a child when he or she asks.
- Read to infants even before they can speak. Babies love to listen to voices and will associate books with pleasant feelings.
- Encourage volunteers to read with children. Find volunteers through colleges, high schools, community and seniors organizations, religious groups, and businesses.
- Engage children in daily activities to build reading readiness, such as singing nursery rhymes and playing sound, word, and letter games.
- Use the arts to engage young children in the development of language and communication skills.
- Set up a reading and writing area for children. Make sure the area is well lit, with interesting books and writing tools. Include books for and about children with special needs, and books about the children's languages and cultures.
- Encourage parents to read to and with their children, either in English or in their home language. Lend a range of books overnight.
- Make frequent trips to the library. Contact your librarian to plan a guided tour. Ask about bilingual story times or special story hours.
- Seek out continuing education and training in child development and in effective teaching practices. Learn to identify "red flags" that may signal barriers to successful reading.
- Find ways to coordinate training with other early care and education organizations. Joint training may be scheduled at a central site such as a library. Network to share information and resources.

CHAPTER 3

Read to Succeed:
How Schools Can Help
Every Child Become a Reader

We now know that helping all children learn to read by the end of third grade is complex, and that family members, caregivers, and preschool teachers can play significant roles in developing reading readiness.

But clearly schools play the major role in teaching reading. Schools can help us win the war on illiteracy by turning all children who are ready to read into independent readers and giving those children who aren't ready the education they need to succeed.

While older children, teenagers, and even adults can be taught to read with intensive and often costly remediation, the easiest time to learn is during the early elementary years. The primary grades (kindergarten through third) present the best opportunity for each child to become a competent reader.

THE CHALLENGE OF THE PRIMARY YEARS

Roughly half the nation's children learn to read easily regardless of the method of instruction (Lyon, 1997). But as many as 2 in 10 children are considered significantly reading impaired. These children will need intensive instruction to master the complex process of reading (Shaywitz et al., 1990).

But with prevention and early intervention, experts have found, reading failure in the primary grades can be reduced to less than 1 in 10 children (Vellutino et al., 1996; Torgeson et al., 1997; Foorman et al., 1998). Even first-graders who have the greatest reading challenges can reach grade-level reading by the end of second grade with intensive, targeted intervention (Vellutino et al., 1996). This means that more than 9 out of 10 children can become average readers or better.

But many of our children are failing to reach their reading potential. The NAEP 1998 Reading Report Card found that nearly 4 in 10 American fourth-graders are failing to read at the Basic achievement level, having little or no mastery of the reading skills needed for grade-level work. In our highest-poverty schools, nearly 7 in 10 fourth-graders fail to read at the Basic achievement level.

Learning to Read: Not a Moment, But a Process

Experts stress that learning to read and write is not an act, but many steps on a developmental continuum. Preschool and primary school teachers can assess individual children's progress by setting realistic goals and allowing for individual variations. It is appropriate to expect most children to achieve "early reading" by age 7.

Children with learning disabilities, limited English proficiency, or other learning challenges also need high, but achievable goals. These goals should be established by teachers, families, and specialists working together.

Phase 1: Preschool
Awareness and Exploration
Children explore their environment, building foundations for learning to read and write.

Phase 2: Kindergarten
Experimental Reading and Writing
Children develop the basic concepts of print and begin to experiment with reading and writing.

Phase 3: First Grade
Early Reading and Writing
Children read simple stories and write about a meaningful topic.

Phase 4: Second Grade
Transitional Reading and Writing
Children begin to read more fluently and write using simple and more complex sentences.

Phase 5: Third Grade
Independent and Productive Reading and Writing
Children continue to refine reading and writing for different uses and audiences.

Phase 6: Fourth Grade and Up
Advanced Reading

Source: *Learning to Read and Write: Developmentally Appropriate Practices for Young Children—A Joint Position Statement of the International Reading*

Association and The National Association for the Education of Young Children, 1998, (800)424-2460 Full text at:
www.naeyc.org/public_affairs/pubaff_index.htm

THE PERILS OF WAITING TOO LONG

One reason for the disparity between children's capacity to learn and their rates of reading failure is that too few students receive effective aid. Most children don't get special reading help until age 9 or later (Lyon, 1997). This "too little, too late" approach condemns three-quarters of these 9-year-olds to poor reading achievement throughout high school (Shaywitz et al., 1997).

As parents and teachers know, the more often young children fail in reading, the less motivated they are to continue struggling (National Research Council, 1998). This surrender can happen as early as the middle of first grade (Lyon, 1998).

Reading failure can be devastating to a child's self-image. Almost 90 percent of children who have difficulty reading at the end of first grade display similar difficulties in fourth grade (Juel, 1988).

Out of embarrassment, these discouraged readers may try to hide their deficiency, avoid reading aloud, and pass up chances to practice reading at home. As the average student needs to see a word between 4 and 14 times before recognizing it automatically, this limited exposure to words is costly (Lyon, 1997). Without extra practice and intervention, the young student slips further and further behind.

WHAT TEACHERS NEED TO KNOW

The majority of teachers and parents agree that reading is the most important subject for students to learn (Hart, 1994). Disagreements have raged primarily over a different question: How should reading be taught?

The National Research Council made clear in its landmark 1998 report, Preventing Reading Difficulties in Young Children, that we need not choose between one or another method of instruction favored by publishers or politicians. Like the commission that prepared 1983's A Nation at Risk, the National Research Council panel found that a comprehensive approach by well-prepared teachers is far more successful.

To successfully teach reading, the panel found, elementary school teachers must fully understand the structure of the English language, and the similarities and differences between written and spoken language. Teachers need a strong knowledge of child development, including psychology, language, and emergent literacy development. They must keep abreast of the most up-to-date research on reading and be able to use a variety of research-based teaching methods in the classroom.

Teachers need sophisticated training in how to teach young children that spoken language is made up of words, which contain sounds that are represented by letters and groups of letters. They must understand the ways that language conveys meaning, in various social and cultural contexts. Good teachers must be able to diagnose reading problems and respond to them with appropriate interventions. They need to gain feedback from colleagues and to work in an environment that emphasizes literacy (National Research Council, 1998).

GAPS IN THE CLASSROOM

While not exhaustive, this list of pre-requisite skills and knowledge reveals how successful reading instruction requires complex teacher preparation. Teaching reading today is truly a job for an expert (Orton Dyslexia Society, 1997). But researchers at the National Institutes of Health have found that only a tiny fraction of teachers are able to teach reading effectively to children who do not grasp it easily (*New York Times*, 1997).

Some teachers may lack an adequate understanding of the structure of written and spoken English, of the spelling system, or of how these relate to teaching reading (McCutchen et al., 1998). Experienced teachers may still be misinformed about the differences between speech and print (Moats, 1995). Others may need to grasp the fundamental importance of a child's understanding of how units of sound, or phonemes, are represented by letters of the alphabet (National Research Council, 1998).

Gaps may exist in the teacher's training in phonological awareness, or how spoken language has a structure distinct from its meaning. Others may be unaware or misinformed about semantics and what a student must know to comprehend what he or she reads. Few teachers are familiar enough with successful, research-based techniques. Many teachers express frustration with their limitations in helping increasingly diverse students reach their reading potential (Moats, 1995).

Effective Literacy Instruction

Researchers identified nine characteristics shared by outstanding first-grade teachers in five states. In these classrooms, most students were reading and writing at or above first-grade level. The characteristics of these teachers include:

Ability to Motivate High Academic Engagement and Competence
Most students were engaged in academic activities most of the time, even when the teacher left the room.

Excellent Class Management
Teachers in the most effective classrooms managed student behavior, student learning, and instructional aides and specialists well, using a variety of methods.

Ability to Foster a Positive, Reinforcing, Cooperative Environment
These classrooms were positive places. The rare discipline problems were handled constructively. Students received a lot of positive reinforcement for their accomplishments, both privately and publicly, and students were encouraged to cooperate with one another.

Teaching Skills in Context
Word-level, comprehension, vocabulary, spelling, and writing skills were typically taught in the context of actual reading and writing tasks.

An Emphasis on Literature
The students selected books from extensive classroom collections. The teachers read literature and conducted author studies.

Much Reading and Writing
Teachers set aside 45 minutes for language arts, providing long, uninterrupted periods for reading and writing. Both the students and teacher read daily to themselves, to a buddy, to a group, to an adult volunteer, or to the class as a whole. Everyone wrote daily in journals.

A Match between Accelerating Demands and Student Competence
The teachers set high but realistic expectations and consistently encouraged students to try more challenging (but not overwhelming) tasks.

Encouraging Self-Regulation
Teachers taught students to self-regulate, encouraging students to choose appropriate skills when they faced a task rather than wait for the teacher to dictate a particular skill or strategy.

Connections across Curricula
Teachers made explicit connections across the curriculum—providing students with opportunities to use the skills they were learning. Reading and writing were integrated with other subjects.

Source: *National Research Center on English Learning & Achievement, 1998* (http://cela.albany.edu)

INADEQUACIES IN TEACHER EDUCATION

One major cause for the lack of preparation to teach reading is the inadequacy of teacher education. Novice teachers receive little formal education in reading instruction before entering the classroom; most have taken only one course in the subject as undergraduates (Goodlad, 1997). In some teacher colleges, reading is but a part of a single course in English language arts (National Research Council, 1998).

The National Association of State Directors of Teacher Education reports that virtually all states require at least some coursework in reading methods. But few require knowledge of the structure of the English language, the psychology of reading development, or other subjects needed to teach children with reading difficulties. This "overview" approach is inadequate to prepare novice teachers to assist the 50 percent of all students who do not learn reading easily (Moats & Lyon, 1996).

Surveys of college students in teacher education courses have found that the professors often do not demonstrate the most effective instructional techniques, and that the course content is generally more theoretical than practical. These students rarely get the supervised practice time they need to develop effectively as reading teachers (Lyon, 1989).

Sporadic Professional Development

Professional development offerings for teachers already in the classroom are often sporadic and do not compensate for the teachers' lack of preparation in college (National Research Council, 1998). Licensing is often linked to "seat time," or the hours a teacher spends in any course, regardless of its utility. One-shot workshops with little relevance to the classroom are most typical.

Instead, licensing should encourage high-quality, ongoing training in research-based principles, with adequate time for teachers to work in teams and practice new teaching techniques (Darling-Hammond, 1996). The National Research Council panel has created a list of what teachers need to know to successfully teach reading. This list should be the basis of elementary school teacher preparation and professional development across the nation.

Teacher training—whether preservice or inservice—should be based on developing and demonstrating competency. Rigorous and practical preparation should be linked in some way to licensure and credential renewal. Some experts advocate a medical school model for teacher preparation that includes a full year of "residency" in a real school before taking charge of a classroom (Archibold, 1998).

Others stress the advantages of the business school model, using extensive case studies and technology such as videodiscs to view actual classrooms (Risko & Kinzer, 1997). The latter approach connects a college student with the classroom experience, which studies show can improve the student teacher's problem-solving ability and other skills (Risko et al., 1996).

Reading Success Network: The Coach Approach

The Reading Success Network is a national network of schools actively pursuing schoolwide change to propel the reading achievement of every student. Schools join the network and identify a coach, who receives ongoing support, training, and materials, and participates in a Leadership Forum.

Coaches work with classroom teachers to provide powerful instruction in reading that allows all children to succeed, including those at risk of reading failure. Publications, a Web page, and a listserv support teachers, administrators, and parents at local Reading Success schools.

The Reading Success Network is operated by the U.S. Department of Education's Comprehensive Assistance Centers, a network of 15 regional centers designed to improve teaching and learning for all.

Based in California, the network is aligned with Every Child a Reader, the report of the California Reading Task Force, and Teaching Reading, the program advisory.

The network promotes:

- A comprehensive and balanced reading approach
- Continuous student monitoring and modification of instruction
- A proven and rigorous early intervention program
- Clear grade-level standards for student progress
- High-quality print and electronic instructional materials
- Reading as a priority of the school and community
- Continuous and ongoing staff development

Contact:
Janie Gates
(562) 922-6482
Henry Mothner
(562) 922-6343
http://sccac.lacoe.edu/priorities/reading.html

A National, State, and Local Challenge

There is a growing national consensus that standards should be raised for the entire teaching profession. The National Research Council's call for better teacher education and training in reading complements this broader teacher quality agenda.

For example, Education Secretary Riley's call for colleges of education to create more clinical experiences for their students is highly relevant to improving the teaching of reading. As state and national leaders explore better ways to educate and train teachers, the urgent needs of preschool teachers and kindergarten through third-grade reading instructors should be top priorities.

Some states have already strengthened their teacher education programs. Texas requires 70 percent of a teacher college's graduates to pass a certification exam for the institution to maintain its accreditation. Pennsylvania requires prospective teachers to keep a B average in both liberal arts courses and in the subject they seek to teach.

On the local level, most districts are not making up for inadequacies in their teachers' readiness to teach reading. On average, less than .5 percent of school district resources are invested in professional development (Darling-Hammond, 1996).

Opportunities for Improvement

This push for better reading teachers comes at an opportune moment in American education. A surge in student enrollment—the "baby boom echo"—and the retirement of a substantial percentage of older teachers will require the nation to hire 2.2 million teachers over the next 10 years (U.S. Department of Education, 1998). That is equal to hiring every doctor in the United States two and one-half times.

This tectonic shift presents the nation with an unprecedented opportunity to raise the professional standards for teachers. In addition, a recent national poll by Recruiting New Teachers found overwhelming public support for raising teacher standards and providing teachers with more time to keep up with developments in their field (Recruiting New Teachers, 1998).

In fact, time is a precious commodity for both primary school teachers and pupils. To improve reading instruction, teachers must take time to teach children letters and sounds and how to read for meaning. They must give children more time to practice reading and writing, using many types of books and reading materials. They also must take time to maintain children's motivation to read. And teachers need time to give more intensive and systematic individual instruction to those who need it.

Starting School Early

Even highly qualified teachers cannot reach students who are not yet in their classrooms. In nearly half the states, children are not required to attend school until age 7. While 38 states require school districts to offer kindergarten, only 14 states require students to actually attend kindergarten.

Children who have had high-quality preschool and kindergarten experiences have much less difficulty learning to read than children who have not been exposed to early education (National Research Council, 1998).

When all children are enrolled in high-quality early learning programs before entering elementary school, our rates of reading failure surely will go down.

The Reading Excellence Program

In 1998, President Clinton signed the Reading Excellence Act, the most significant child literacy law in three decades. The Reading Excellence Program awards grants to states to improve reading. The program is designed to:

- Provide children with the readiness skills and support they need to learn to read once they enter school.
- Teach every child to read by the end of the third grade.
- Use research-based methods to improve the instructional practices of teachers and others.
- Expand the number of high-quality family literacy programs.
- Provide early intervention for children with reading difficulties.

States compete for $241 million in grants. Successful states hold competitions for local school districts. The first round of grants will be awarded in summer 1999, with local grants to follow. Because low-income children experience reading failure at higher rates than their more affluent peers, the funding is directed toward the state's poorest districts and schools.

(continued)

Contact:
> Dr. Joseph Conaty
> Reading Excellence Program
> U.S. Department of Education
> Washington, DC
> (202) 260-8228
> Fax: (202) 260-8969
> reading_excellence@ed.gov
> www.ed.gov/offices/OESE/REA/index.html

A Whole-School Approach

Principals in Pajamas

Kissing pigs, shaving mustaches, wearing pajamas to school—these are creative ways in which principals at San Diego's Benchley-Weinberger Elementary School have motivated their students to read. Principal Steven Hill believes reading should be fun and challenges the school's 500 students to read a million pages a year. When they meet that goal, they get something special. Hill once shaved off a mustache he'd had for 20 years—on television.

Benchley-Weinberger is an "Achievement through Communications" magnet school. The school's teachers receive specialized training in reading, writing, listening, and observing. The school also utilizes creative community, nonprofit, and private partnerships.

Benchley-Weinberger scores on reading tests are in the top 10 percent in San Diego, and the gap between Blacks, Hispanics, and other students has been reduced.

Contact:
> Steven Hill, Principal
> Benchley-Weinberger Elementary School
> 6269 Twin Lakes Drive
> San Diego, CA 92119
> (619) 463-9271
> tknight@mail.sandi.net

Beyond offering kindergarten, many schools that raise reading achievement develop a schoolwide focus on literacy (National Research Council, 1998). Educators work together to develop comprehensive plans for professional development, assessment, use of technology, and new ways of using instructional time to teach reading and writing skills. Often, they bring literacy experts directly into the planning process. Architects of the most successful schoolwide efforts view research-based classroom instruction as just the foundation.

What else is helpful, besides a well-trained teacher? As stated, research supports devoting more class time to reading and writing (Education Trust, 1998). Students also benefit from one-on-one attention and expert tutoring integrated with classroom instruction (Slavin et al., 1989). Project-based learning that links reading and writing activities is also advantageous (National Research Council, 1998). Many schools measure and monitor students' reading skills to provide immediate, appropriate interventions (Education Trust, 1998). Also, reading and writing are an important part of every subject their students study.

In these successful schools, parents are involved in improving reading in the school and at home. Extra practice time is available through trained, volunteer tutors recruited from colleges, businesses, and retired citizens groups. Community members are viewed as stakeholders in the school's success.

STUDENTS WITH SPECIAL NEEDS

Principles for Success

The Center for the Improvement of Early Reading Achievement (CIERA) identifies research-based principles for improving student reading achievement.

At successful schools:

- Entire school staffs, not just first-grade teachers, are involved in bringing children to high levels of achievement.
- Goals for reading achievement are clearly stated.
- High expectations are shared with all participants.
- Instructional means for attaining these goals are articulated.
- Shared assessments are used to monitor children's progress.

Instructional programs in successful schools have many components, including:

- A range of materials and technology
- A focus on reading and writing
- Parental involvement in their children's reading and homework
- Community partnerships, including volunteer tutoring programs

(continued)

Source: *CIERA 10 Principles*
Full text on-line at
www.ciera.org/resources/principles/index.html

As states and schools work to improve the teaching of reading, special attention must be paid to those children who are likely to require the most help—those who are poor, those who have learning and other types of disabilities, and those with limited English proficiency.

A major insight of the National Research Council's report is that most children with disabilities or disadvantages learn to read in much the same way as other children. They may require much more time and intensive assistance, and benefit from certain environments, materials, and strategies. But what matters most is excellent instruction by qualified teachers who call upon a flexible menu of choices to suit the special needs of each learner.

Good teaching means the ability to address a variety of learning strengths and needs in the same classroom. It means starting with what students already know about reading in any language or format (e.g., Braille or Spanish) and building on and linking that knowledge to an English literacy context. Research-based strategies that are proven in many different populations are helpful in improving instruction for students with special needs. Teachers should always consider whether the research describes effective teaching strategies for students who are similar to their own.

Delays in language development are not unusual among children with disabilities. Children with speech difficulties, such as those with cerebral palsy, may have trouble communicating orally. Children with hearing loss may use seemingly immature language that belies their actual intellectual development. Some mentally disabled children may struggle to express themselves, to understand what is said to them, and to comprehend language in general (Dodge & Colker, 1996).

When teaching children with special needs, teachers should capitalize on each child's individual strengths. If a child has trouble paying attention, the teacher may choose not to finish reading a book. Instead, the teacher might engage the child in conversation, asking questions about the story that require more than a yes or no response. The child may be able to draw a picture or make up a song about the book's characters (Arnold, 1997) to enhance comprehension and maintain motivation.

While not all disabilities and disadvantages are addressed here, many children who experience reading difficulties have the following risk factors: living in poverty, having a learning disability, having limited proficiency in English, or having a hearing impairment.

HIGH-POVERTY SCHOOLS: A STAGGERING CHALLENGE

Because poverty is a very high risk factor for illiteracy (National Research Council, 1998), poor children's rates of reading failure are staggering. The Promising Results report (U.S. Department of Education, 1999) found that 68 percent of fourth-graders in our poorest urban schools failed to read at the Basic level needed for academic success, compared with 38 percent nationwide. Only 1 in 10 fourth-graders at these schools can read at the Proficient level. More than half of all fourth-graders receiving a free or reduced-price lunch (a measure of poverty) read below the Basic achievement level in 1998 (NAEP 1998 Reading Report Card).

Signs of Progress

Despite huge achievement gaps between poor and more affluent students, positive trends are emerging. The 1996 national reading scores of students in high-poverty schools, while still unacceptably low, have improved significantly since 1992 (1996 NAEP Trend Report). For example, in 1996, 9-year-olds attending such schools read nearly a full grade-level better than their counterparts had four years before.

Gains made by the lowest achievers were mainly responsible for the small increase in the nation's average reading score between 1994 and 1998. These students improved about half a grade-level in four years. About 80 percent of these low achievers attend Title I high-poverty schools (U.S. Department of Education, Promising Results, 1999).

A study of three-year achievement trends in 13 large urban school districts with high concentrations of poverty found signs of progress. The number of elementary school students who met district standards for reading proficiency increased in seven districts: Houston, Jefferson County (Louisville), Miami-Dade, New York City, Philadelphia, San Antonio, and San Francisco. The gap between students in the highest- and lowest-poverty schools decreased in four districts: Houston, Miami-Dade, New York City, and San Antonio (U.S. Department of Education, Promising Results, 1999).

Of six states able to provide three-year trend data on students in high-poverty schools, five reported improvements in reading performance: Connecticut, Maine, Maryland, North Carolina, and Texas (U.S. Department of Education, Promising Results, 1999). In Texas, 82 percent of fourth-grade students in the highest-poverty schools scored at or above the proficient level in the 1998 Texas Assessment of Academic Skills, a 15 percent gain from 1996.

These victories offer solid hope that reading achievement can be raised for all students.

Blue Ribbon Schools: How Principals Promote Reading

Innovative principals across the nation are striving to raise reading achievement for all students in their schools. Some take a schoolwide approach by engaging non-teaching staff and teachers from other disciplines. Others are pairing children from different grades to read together. Many are reaching out to parents and the community to support young readers through extended learning time after school and in the home. Creative events and book challenges inspire students and motivate them to read more often. Here are some examples from the National Association of Elementary School Principals:

Schoolwide Focus: At an elementary school in Cape Coral, Florida, teachers, staff, parents, and peers all serve as reading "teachers." As a supplement to classroom instruction, schoolwide activities build reading and writing skills in social studies, science, health, and mathematics. A principal in Washington, Pennsylvania, rescheduled a dozen Title I teachers to reduce class sizes for longer language arts sessions. Many schools are instituting school-wide computer programs and other technology to aid, motivate, and monitor young readers.

Parents: At an elementary school in Boca Raton, Florida, parents support students in friendly competitions between teams to read the most books. Parents are coached to ask comprehension questions about each book before validating its completion, and the local newspaper publishes the pictures of top readers. School murals monitor team progress for all to see. Some schools hold Family Reading Nights each year, with vocabulary word bingo, musical chairs with phonics, computer reading games, and treasure maps for reading comprehension.

Peers: Many schools, such as one in Shreveport, Louisiana, use a "book buddy" system, which pairs an older student with a younger child for extended reading time. This approach can build skills of both learners as it boosts their motivation to read.

Another school in Talladega, Alabama, encourages older students to be "roving readers" by reading aloud before lower grade-level classes to earn certificates of accomplishment. These students build fluency and confidence as they model successful reading for younger pupils.

Community: Schools such as one in Springfield, Illinois, bring tutors into the school for supplemental reading and writing activities. Tutors may be trained through AmeriCorps, senior citizens groups, or colleges in the America Reads work-study program, among others. This approach connects the community at large with young learners who benefit from one-on-one attention to their reading progress. It also provides positive role models for pupils. Some schools, like one in Irmo, South Carolina, partner with the local library to engage elementary students in summer reading with the U.S. Department of Education's free Read*Write*Now! kits.

Fun with Books: A school in Grove City, Pennsylvania, holds an annual event at Halloween, which motivates students to dress up as characters from favorite books and tour senior centers and nursing homes. Teachers also don costumes for this Literacy Parade, which is preceded by oral book reports that develop skills in comprehension and analysis. A Houston, Texas, school uses Scrabble games to build vocabulary. A Coventry, Rhode Island, school sponsors "Reading Month," with a PTA book fair, picnic, presentations of children's original books, and a challenge to choose books over TV. Other principals promise fun rewards for the whole school for exceeding book goals, such as a hot air balloon demonstration, ice cream parties, or seeing the principal eat lunch on the roof.

Source: *National Association of Elementary School Principals, Best Ideas for Reading from America's Blue Ribbon Schools, 1998.*

Contact:
Corwin Press
Thousand Oaks, CA
(805) 499-9774
Fax: (800) 4-1-SCHOOL
www.corwinpress.com

SCHOOLS THAT BEAT THE ODDS

What can schools do to help poor children become better readers? Surveys were taken at schools receiving funds through Title I, the federal program that aims to raise poor students' achievement, especially in reading and math. The surveys reveal certain strategies that are common in high-poverty, high-performing schools.

First, they use standards to design the curriculum, assess student work, and evaluate teachers. Second, they lengthen instructional time in reading. Third, they spend more on professional development. Fourth, they engage parents in their children's education. Fifth, they monitor student progress and get extra help for those who need it. Finally, school staff often are held accountable for their success by the state or district (Education Trust, 1998).

What can teachers do to help poor children become better readers?

Students scored better on reading tests when their teachers felt able to use a variety of assessment tools and to teach diverse groups (U.S. Department of Education, LESCP, 1998). Fourth-graders made better progress in reading when teachers gave them more total exposure to reading and opportunities to talk in small groups about what they read (U.S. Department of Education, LESCP, 1998).

The poorest readers in fourth grade gained in both vocabulary and comprehension skills when teachers gave them reading material of one paragraph or more; reading materials in core subject areas; and opportunities to work on computers, workbooks, and skill sheets. More able readers seemed to benefit from reading aloud (U.S. Department of Education, LESCP, 1998).

Parents as Partners: The Compact for Reading

The *Compact for Reading* is a free guide on how to develop a compact, or written agreement, among families, teachers, principals, and students. The compact describes how all partners can help improve the reading skills of children from kindergarten through third grade, including those with disabilities and with limited English proficiency. Tutors and other community members can also be partners in a *Compact for Reading*.

Research shows that schools with properly implemented compacts raise student achievement higher than similar schools without compacts. Principals reported greater family involvement in homework and more parents reading with children at home. Schools with the greatest need seem to benefit the most (D'Agostino et al., 1998).

The *Compact* guide comes with a School-Home Links Kit to help implement local compacts. Developed by teachers for the U.S. Department of Education, the kit provides 100 reading activities for each grade from kindergarten through third. Three to four times a week, a teacher can provide these easy-to-use activities to families to expand student learning at home and encourage family involvement in reading activities.

Contact
U.S. Department of Education
(877) 4ED-PUBS
www.ed.gov/pubs/CompactforReading

Lessons Learned

More Title I school teachers are applying these lessons, with increasing numbers allowing low achievers to select their own books, read aloud, and talk in small groups about their reading every day (U.S. Department of Education, LESCP, 1998). These teaching strategies are well supported by research chronicled by the National Research Council.

In Massachusetts, a dozen high-poverty, urban elementary schools that apply research-based principles are outperforming other schools in their districts. These schools seek a balance of instructional methods, including literature-based and phonics approaches. Students spend extended time on reading and writing, and teachers work in small groups to focus on pupils' individual needs (Dwyer et al., 1998).

The Summer Reading "Drop-Off"

Successful students have fun during the summer, but they don't take a vacation from reading. Too many students, however, don't exercise their reading muscles during the summer months.

For decades, studies have shown that this summer reading "drop-off" has predictable, negative consequences for student achievement, particularly for disadvantaged children (Hayes & Grether, 1969; Murnane, 1975; Heyns, 1987; Karweit et al., 1994). A Baltimore study found that large differences in achievement between high- and low-income elementary school children were due almost entirely to gains made when school was not in session (Alexander & Entwisle, 1996).

It has long been known that, in high-poverty schools, gains made by poor children during the school year are eroded or erased during the summer, leaving them once again behind their better-off peers in the fall (Pelavin & David, 1977). Students in high-poverty schools make faster progress in reading achievement during first grade than their more affluent peers. Sadly, however, this reading growth slows more than that of their peers the following summer (Rock, 1993). Students in high-poverty schools do not return to the higher rate of growth that they showed in first grade. Instead, they progress at a reduced rate of growth throughout the second grade (Karweit et al., 1994).

Disadvantaged students who don't spend their summers reading and learning are at the greatest risk of skill erosion (Alexander & Entwisle, 1996). Energetic summer reading programs, including tutoring and mentoring by adults, can help disadvantaged students improve their academic skills (Reisner et al., 1989;

Olsen, 1979). Tutoring can also boost students' motivation and attitudes toward reading (Cohen et al., 1982), an advantage for those who find reading difficult (National Research Council, 1998).

The U.S. Department of Education promotes summer reading for all children through the Read*Write*Now! program. The program offers creative tools and materials for adults to help children practice and enjoy reading outside the classroom.

Read*Write*Now! is but one of many summer reading promotions taking place across the country, from baseball parks to book camps to Story-Mobiles. When more children spend the summer honing their reading skills rather than losing them, teachers will not have to play catch-up each fall. More students will read at grade-level from the first bell.

Summer Reading—Share the Fun!

The America Reads Challenge at the U.S. Department of Education has free materials to keep more children reading during the summer and throughout the year.

The Read*Write*Now! Activity Poster, available in English and Spanish, includes a colorful illustration on the front and a set of fun activities on the back. The activities include writing a book review and having it published on the America Reads Web site.

The Read*Write*Now! Basic Kit helps pair young children with adult partners for shared summer reading activities. Each child pledges to read for 30 minutes each day, and the adult pledges to join the child at least once each week. The child also obtains and uses a library card and learns new vocabulary words weekly. The kit's activities are appropriate for babies through sixth-graders, and include a certificate of accomplishment. (This kit is available on-line at: www.ed.gov/Family/RWN/Activ97.)

The Read*Write*Now! Tip Sheet for Developing a Community Reading Program is for librarians, teachers, camp counselors, and community leaders. The booklet offers straightforward suggestions on how to start a summer or after-school reading program. It is available in English and Spanish.

Contact

U.S. Department of Education
(877) 4ED-PUBS
www.ed.gov/inits/americareads

LEARNING DISABILITIES

Approximately 5 percent of all children in public schools are identified as having a learning disability (Lyon, 1996), and the vast majority of learning-disabled children—as many as 80 percent—experience their primary difficulties in learning to read (National Research Council, 1998).

But some children with learning disabilities are not recognized by their school system. Experts believe the actual prevalence of learning disabilities is between 5 and 10 percent (Interagency Committee on Learning Disabilities, 1987.)

While schools are four times more likely to identify a reading disability in boys, research shows the disability is equally common among girls (Shaywitz et al., 1990). In some studies, a reading disability has been documented in about 20 percent of school-age children (Shaywitz et al., 1996).

Early, Intensive Intervention

Most children who are identified with significant reading disabilities in the third grade are still reading below grade-level in high school (Shaywitz et al., 1997). For interventions to succeed, all children at risk for reading failure should be identified and helped before age 9 (Lyon, 1996).

As many as two-thirds of reading-disabled children can become average or above-average readers if they are identified early and taught appropriately (Vellutino et al., 1996; Fletcher & Lyon, 1998).

Those with the most challenging reading disabilities need even more help. From 2 to 6 percent of children may not learn to read well, even with early reading interventions (Vellutino et al., 1996; Torgeson et al., 1997; Foorman et al., 1998). These children should be carefully evaluated to determine the nature of their disability and the impact the disability has on their learning. They may require more highly specialized reading programs, which include special education and related services (Council for Exceptional Children, 1997).

Disability or Difficulty?

A child with a reading disability and one with reading difficulty can be hard to tell apart, though their problems have different roots.

A reading disability seems to result primarily from the brain's struggle to process the sounds of speech as distinct from their meanings (Liberman & Shankweiler, 1991; Rack et al., 1992). This ability, called phonological awareness, is critical to understanding that words are made up of sounds that are represented by letters of the alphabet. The segments of speech sounds, called phonemes, are the building blocks of syllables and words. Cracking this code helps would-be readers recognize words on the page (National Research Council, 1998).

Due to a limited exposure to books, children with a reading disability must overcome both an inadequate vocabulary and insufficient background knowledge to understand the meaning of what is read (National Research Council, 1998).

Children with a reading difficulty due to limited language exposure, poor instruction or other causes may also lack the vocabulary and background knowledge needed to read for meaning, as well as word recognition skills such as phonological and phonemic awareness.

Both kinds of poor readers can suffer from low motivation associated with early reading failure (National Research Council, 1998).

Early remediation of all children who are at risk for reading failure could significantly reduce the number of children mislabeled as learning disabled. This, in turn, could reduce the need of some children for ongoing intervention and permit greater focus of resources on the children who are acutely disabled (Fletcher & Lyon, 1998).

With national assessments showing 25 to 40 percent of American school children unable to read well enough to succeed in school, strategic interventions for all poor readers are a national imperative.

The El Paso Collaborative for Academic Excellence

This community-wide effort to raise student achievement is based on the belief that all children can learn, if given the tools and encouragement to do so. Based in El Paso, Texas, the collaborative aims to improve teaching and learning from pre-kindergarten through university.

Two-thirds of children in El Paso schools come from low-income families, and half enter first grade with only limited English, making them high risks for reading failure. Yet in only five years, the achievement gap between White students and Black and Hispanic students has been cut by almost two-thirds.

The collaborative includes businesses, local government, University of Texas-El Paso (UTEP), El Paso Community College, superintendents from three large school districts, and a grassroots organization. This group plays a major role in redesigning and evaluating the University's teacher preparation program and helping provide field experiences for prospective teachers.

UTEP has completely revised its teacher preparation programs. Faculty from the Colleges of Liberal Arts, Science, and Education are involved in teacher preparation. The College of Education has moved to a clinical, field-based model of teacher preparation, with University students remaining with the same schools for as long as three semesters. The dean of Education likens it to a teaching hospital program. The schools are committed to school reform, redesigning professional development, integrating technology, and building greater outreach to neighborhoods. Most students enrolled in the college and the schools are Hispanic.

Participating schools are given mentors who coach other teachers in improving instruction. UTEP faculty and outside experts offer institutes for school teams in reading, writing, and other core subjects. Technology is introduced early, with every first-grader obtaining an e-mail account. Parent centers offer instruction and engage families.

This project has attracted funding from the U.S. Department of Education, the Texas legislature, The National Science Foundation, The Pew Charitable Trusts, and other private foundations.

Contact:
> M. Susana Navarro
> The El Paso Collaborative for Academic Excellence
> Education Building, Room 413
> University of Texas at El Paso
> El Paso, TX 79968-0683
> (915) 747-5778
> www.epcae.org

LIMITED ENGLISH PROFICIENCY

Children with limited English proficiency are those who speak a language other than English at home. For that reason, they may not speak, understand, read, or write English at the same level as their peers who have English as a first language. The limited-English-proficient population in this country has grown and changed dramatically. There are currently more than 3.4 million English language learners enrolled in kindergarten through grade 12 in this country (Macias, 1998), speaking more than 200 languages other than English (U.S. Department of Education, 1998). Close to 75 percent of all students acquiring English speak Spanish as their first language (Fleischman & Hopstock, 1993).

Most limited-English-proficient students are in the elementary grades, and approximately 40 percent of these students were born in the United States (Fleischman & Hopstock, 1993). Many are poor, and more than one-third of Hispanic students attend high-poverty schools (U.S. Department of Education, 1997). English language learners in the primary grades are twice as likely to be poor compared with their English-speaking peers (Moss & Puma, 1995). Three out of four students with limited English at all grade levels qualify for free or reduced-price lunches by living near or below the poverty line (Fleischman & Hopstock, 1993).

But students acquiring English are diverse in many other ways. Not only do they speak many different languages, but they also come from a large variety of cultures. These students also have different educational experiences: some students have a strong academic foundation and schooling in their native language, while others have received little or no schooling. The lack of any strong literacy or academic background, in addition to the challenge of learning to read in a second language, puts many English language learners, particularly those in high poverty, at risk for developing reading difficulties.

These students' reading difficulties may be manifested in one or more ways. They may have difficulty connecting the sounds of language to their written representation. They may have trouble comprehending what they read. Also, they may not be motivated to read.

The Role of Parents

We know that foundations of early literacy development begin in infancy, with positive interactions between caregivers and babies. These include conversations around books, storytelling, songs, rhymes, word games, and other family activities. This kind of language and literacy development engages babies and young children in communication that provides the basis for later reading success.

Parents of young children with limited English proficiency may need extra encouragement to engage in some of these activities. Their own English language skills may be limited, or they may hesitate to use their native language at home, assuming that it will not help their children succeed in school. Some parents whose culture emphasizes speaking to children in a directive style may benefit from coaching to try a more conversational style. This practice gives parents another way to nurture their child's language skills and vocabulary development (Espinosa & Lesar, 1994).

Some parents who don't speak English are less likely to expose their children to early literacy experiences than English-speaking parents (Liontos, 1992).

In general, mothers whose first language is not English are less likely to read to their children regularly (U.S. Department of Education, 1994). Some of these parents may hold back out of respect for the role of schools and teachers in educating their child (Espinosa, 1995).

Many low-income parents face additional, logistical barriers that make time scarce for book reading, library visits, and early language development. This combination of factors can cause many children from homes with limited English to enter kindergarten behind their peers in language and literacy skills (Espinosa, 1995).

Aiding Literacy Development

We know that a strong base in any language provides the foundation for reading success (Cummins, 1979; 1989). And surveys show that most parents who speak languages other than English, such as Hispanics, place a high value on education (De La Rosa & Maw, 1990). Thus, parents should be encouraged to talk with and read to their children in their native language. Hearing stories read aloud in their first language exposes children to the sounds of written words in a familiar context (Nathenson-Mejia, 1994). Books also can be read aloud by grandparents, older siblings, and other family members.

Parents as Teachers

Parents with little experience reading to their children may be more comfortable starting out with storytelling and writing activities (Landerholm et al., 1994). Traditions of oral storytelling can ease a parent into language and literacy-building activities. Children and parents can create homemade books that transcribe family stories and cultural legends in their home language (Nathenson-Mejia, 1994). Illustrated by the child, these books can be re-read often to strengthen family bonds as well as reading skills.

When low-income, language-minority parents see themselves as teachers, their children benefit. Researchers have found that when parents whose English is limited engage their children in reading, storytelling, problem-solving, and varied learning activities, the children enjoyed above-average academic success (Ebener et al., 1997). Also, when non-English-speaking parents were coached in communicating and reading to their children, practicing in class as well as at home, their children scored significantly higher on reading attitude tests (Cervantes et al., 1979).

Librarians can help non-English-speaking parents select native language books for children and even order new titles based on families' interests. Culturally appropriate community outreach will be required to increase the motivation of these families to use the library regularly.

Preschool Opportunities

Studies that show the advantages of quality preschool programs in preparing children for school success have significance for children whose home language is not English, such as Hispanics. However, only 39 percent of Hispanic 3- to 5-year olds, compared with 65 percent of Blacks and 57 percent of Whites, enroll in early childhood programs (U.S. Department of Education, 1996).

Many Hispanic families cannot afford private preschools (Schwartz, 1996). Yet even when income is not a barrier, Hispanic parents have historically preferred family care for their youngest children. Nearly half of Hispanic mothers stay home to raise their children, and many who work choose relatives over center-based care (Fuller et al., 1994). In the home, Hispanic parents are more likely than White parents to regularly teach their children letters, numbers, words, songs, and music. They are less likely, however, to read or tell stories regularly, or visit the library (U.S. Department of Education, 1994).

Many non-English-speaking families also live in poverty. For most low-income children, high-quality preschools build up the social, emotional, physical, or cognitive skills that may have been underdeveloped in the home (Schwartz, 1996). For youngsters with little or no English spoken at home, preschool also offers valuable exposure to English (Kagan, 1995).

Some communities are identifying these benefits to non-English-speaking parents and building bridges between families and preschools (Lewis, 1993; Blakes-Greenway, 1994). Early childhood professionals can form partnerships with parents, to build on home and community strengths and link the home language with that of the school (U.S. Department of Education, 1998).

But many early childhood professionals need additional training to address the needs of young second-language learners (U.S. Department of Education, Office of Bilingual and Minority Language Affairs, 1998). Training should be provided in early literacy development, second language acquisition, family and community involvement, and diverse linguistic and cultural settings. This base of skills and knowledge can enable early childhood teachers to provide for children's special needs while building on their strengths.

The FLASH Program for Parents with Limited English

The Families Learning at School & Home Program (FLASH) is designed to assist Florida parents of different languages and cultures. Its twin goals are to build children's literacy skills and get parents more involved in their children's schools.

FLASH targets limited-English-proficient Hispanic and Haitian parents and caregivers of students in kindergarten through grade 6 in Dade and Broward County Public Schools. It is a joint project between the school districts and Florida International University's College of Education.

FLASH has four main strategies. First, it aims to improve the literacy skills of families. Second, it aims to increase their proficiency in English. Third, it gives parents and caregivers specific skills and knowledge to enable them to play a more active role in their children's education. And fourth, FLASH works to improve the academic skills of the parents' children, who are learning English as a second language. Evaluations of FLASH are encouraging. Parents showed significant gains in knowledge about the school and its functions. Parent involvement in school-related activities increased significantly, including time spent participating in school activities, volunteering at school, and helping children with homework. FLASH was recognized as an Academic Excellence Program in 1995 by the U.S. Department of Education's Office of Bilingual Education and Minority Language Affairs, which helped fund the program.

Contact:
Dr. Delia C. Garcia
Florida International University
Department of Foundations and Professional Studies
(305) 348-2647

Ms. Wally Lyshkov
Assistant Principal
Dade County Public Schools
(305) 385-4255

English Language Learners in School

The National Research Council's panel found that school-age children with limited English should learn to understand and speak English before learning to read in English. Therefore, initial reading instruction is most effective in a student's first language. If feasible, teachers should speak and use books and other materials in the student's first language (National Research Council, 1998).

Children who can read in any language are readers. There is no need to repeat the entire process of reading instruction if a child simply needs to learn

English. Therefore, a teacher must assess the student's reading skills and abilities in the primary language, and help him or her transfer those abilities to reading in English.

This is more easily accomplished if the teacher speaks the child's language. However, a skilled teacher who does not understand the child's primary language can still learn much about the child's reading abilities by observing him or her reading text in that language and by connecting with community resources.

DEAF AND HARD-OF-HEARING CHILDREN

Toward Universal Newborn Screening

The National Center for Hearing Assessment and Management (NCHAM) was established in 1995 at Utah State University to promote the earliest possible detection of hearing loss and the best possible techniques for assisting people with hearing loss.

With funding from federal, state, and private sources, the center conducts research, develops training materials, provides training and technical assistance, and disseminates information about early identification and management of hearing loss.

Only one in five newborns is screened for hearing impairment. More than 500 hospitals offer these screenings, and five states operate universal hearing screening programs. NCHAM aims to maintain momentum toward universal newborn hearing screening.

Contact
> Karl White
> NCHAM
> Utah State University
> 2880 Old Main Hall
> Logan, UT 84322
> (435) 797-3584
> Fax: (435) 797-1448
> nchamhelp@coe.usu.edu
> www.usu.edu/~ncham

Hearing loss occurs in 3 of every 1,000 births (Utah State University, 1999). Even a slight impairment can hurt language development and academic achievement. This issue is of growing concern, as deaf and hard-of-hearing babies and toddlers are not consistently identified early in life and provided access to language and communication (Padden & Ramsey, 1998). Children with hearing loss in just one ear are 10 times as likely as children with normal hearing to be held back a grade in school (Utah State University, 1999).

Early Detection

The average age of identification of hearing loss in the United States is 2 years, with milder losses at times not detected until a child enters school (Commission on Education of the Deaf, 1988).

The implications are especially significant, since language acquisition begins at birth and progresses very rapidly during the first three years of life. Deprived of critical language learning opportunities, many children with unidentified hearing loss experience disruptions in social, emotional, cognitive, and academic growth.

Research has shown that identification of hearing loss and appropriate intervention before a baby is 6 months old can significantly improve language and cognitive development (University of Colorado, Boulder, 1999). Children who are identified with hearing loss this young can enter first grade as much as one to two years ahead in language, cognitive, and social skills, compared with children identified at a later age (Utah State University, 1999).

The issue is not the ability to learn—deaf and hard-of-hearing children have as much capacity to read and write as their non-deaf peers. Recent research has found that one factor contributing specifically to reading success is, not surprisingly, earlier detection of deafness. Early detection leads to earlier placement in educational programs that offer the best reading instruction for deaf and hard-of-hearing children (Padden & Ramsey, 1998).

A major obstacle faced by children with hearing loss is the lack of the speech foundation on which reading usually rests (McInerney et al., 1998).

The U.S. Department of Education has noted in its Deaf Policy Guidance letter (1992), "[T]he communication nature of the disability is inherently isolating, with considerable effect on the interaction with peers and teachers that make up the educational process. . . Even the availability of interpreter services in the educational setting may not address deaf children's needs for direct and meaningful communication."

Strategies for Success

Studies have found that early reading strategies can involve learning to match sign language to words in print (Andrews & Mason, 1986; Withrow, 1989). More recent research suggests that, while deaf children may focus on visual strategies during early reading development, as reading skills develop, they use other strategies as well (Padden & Hanson, 1999).

Therefore, children with hearing loss may need different kinds of reading instruction as their skills develop. This may include an emphasis on spelling rules and phonological awareness. Deaf children can benefit from exposure to large amounts of written text to build vocabulary and comprehension.

Technology can also play an important role, through the captioning of television programs and videos, computer-assisted real-time captioning, assistive listening devices, and computer software.

The skill of teachers in assessing children's strengths and limitations and in building individual strategies shapes successful reading instruction. This is true whether addressing students with special needs or turning marginal readers into good readers.

Resources for educators and administrators may be found in Reading Resources, Appendix B of this book.

Action Steps for Policymakers

Policymakers can have a great impact on the success of schools in raising reading achievement for all students. Policymakers can:

- Support colleges and universities in revising the reading instruction curriculum so that it focuses not only on theory but also on practical applications of reading development principles.
- Ensure that prospective teachers have balanced instruction that provides foundations in a wide range of research-based approaches to reading.
- Require college students preparing to be teachers to have extended learning experiences in diverse classrooms prior to graduation.
- Provide the training, support, and materials for all teachers in kindergarten through third grade to become more proficient in reading instruction.
- Provide incentives for teachers to pursue master's-level training to become reading specialists.

- Encourage the community to support ongoing, intensive, high-quality professional development for teachers as a way to improve reading instruction.

- Create new avenues through which to circulate new research findings on reading instruction quickly and effectively.

- Provide teachers with assessments to gauge reading skills and to aid in the design and implementation of effective, individualized reading intervention.

- Devise incentives for teacher education programs to seek national accreditation.

- Support the effective instruction of limited-English-proficient students. Ensure that these students have language-appropriate books and other materials.

- Require college students preparing to be teachers to take the time to practice research-based techniques and to get feedback from master teachers.

- Develop performance-based assessments for the initial licensing of teachers that require prospective elementary school teachers to demonstrate their ability to teach reading.

Action Steps for Educators

Teachers, principals, superintendents, and other school personnel have a direct impact on student reading gains. In addition to local initiatives, educators and administrators can consider the following:

- As early as possible, assess each child's developing reading ability and determine appropriate interventions.

- Support high-quality professional development for teachers in research-based instruction and allow sufficient time for teachers to coach and support each other.

- Seek opportunities to consult with knowledgeable and experienced reading specialists to discuss school-wide strategies for literacy improvement on an ongoing basis.

- Implement research-based strategies to promote a schoolwide focus on literacy, including allocating extended blocks of time to reading and writing in the early grades.

- Find ways to increase one-on-one reading between children and adults by recruiting volunteers or re-deploying staff members during the school day, after school, and during the summer.

(continued)

- Develop relationships with community organizations and private industry for aid in offering high-quality professional development.

- Promote independent reading, at least 30 minutes a day, by providing students and parents with specific reading assignments, age-appropriate reading lists, and home assignments linked to class work that involve family members.

- Teach children whose first language is not English to read in their native language if instructional guides, learning materials, and locally available proficient teachers are available.

- Encourage parents to stay involved in their children's education. Encourage open communication between home and school to enhance a child's progress and success. Consider initiating a specific compact on reading between schools and families.

- Contact local libraries, literacy groups, houses of worship, businesses, and community members to provide at-risk children with high-quality, after-school, and summer learning opportunities that support and encourage literacy development.

CHAPTER 4

Every Child a Reader: How Citizens, Public Leaders, and Communities Can Help

Many Americans are energized by the challenge of helping all children learn to read. Committed citizens and public officials are attacking the problem head on, from the nation's capital to statehouses to city halls, from libraries to pizza chains to ballparks.

Their work is informed by mounting research on how to achieve the best results. Activities touch on key issues—training teachers, reading to children, accessing books, and increasing support for parents and childcare providers. There is consensus on the need to touch the lives of children who are the hardest to reach—those who are the least likely to enter school ready to read and the most likely to complete third grade as poor readers.

Businesses, nonprofit organizations, sports teams, newspapers, and local, state, and federal governments are sponsoring programs aimed at winning the war on illiteracy. Many such programs have been profiled in Section III: "Ideas at Work" later in this book. This chapter spotlights more examples of Ideas At Work from a variety of organizations taking strategic action to ensure that all children become good readers. These additional programs are but a fraction of the good work being done from coast to coast.

NATIONAL LEADERSHIP
America Reads

The U.S. Department of Education's America Reads Challenge calls on every American to do what he or she can to help a child become a successful reader. America Reads encourages parents and caregivers to read and talk daily to children from infancy. America Reads advocates research-based college training and high-quality professional development for teachers. America Reads also encourages community efforts to recruit and train reading tutors to supplement classroom reading instruction.

America Reads promotes local literacy partnerships between parents, schools, libraries, childcare centers, universities, businesses, and nonprofit groups. It also disseminates reading research and recommends further study. Since its launch in January 1997, nearly 300 organizations, from libraries and religious groups to schools and businesses, have stepped forward to join The President's Coalition for America Reads.

America Reads unites schools, libraries, and youth and community groups to sponsor summer and after-school reading programs across the country. In 1999, nearly 2 million Read*Write*Now! Activity Posters were distributed, in English and Spanish, to enlist parents, grandparents, schools, and communities to help keep children reading during the summer. The Read*Write*Now! Tip Sheet, in English and Spanish, offers ideas for starting a community reading program.

Financial Aid for Tutors

Through the Federal Work-Study program, more than 22,000 college students at 1,100 colleges and universities earned financial aid by serving as reading tutors in the 1997-98 academic year. Many more participated in the 1998-99 academic year. By 2000, almost all of the 3,300 colleges, universities, and trade schools receiving federal work-study funds were expected to have a reading tutor program.

The Higher Education Act of 1998 included additional funding for the Federal Work-Study program that will allow more college students to earn financial aid as reading tutors. Schools and community groups can contact their local college or university financial aid office to ask about placements for work-study tutors at virtually no cost.

Contact:
>America Reads Challenge
>U.S. Department of Education
>400 Maryland Avenue, SW
>Washington, DC 20202-0107
>(202) 401-8888
>Fax: (202) 401-0596
>To order publications: (877) 4ED-PUBS
>americareads@ed.gov
>www.ed.gov/americareads

Corporation for National Service

The Corporation for National Service (CNS) is a major partner with America Reads. AmeriCorps members operate America Reads tutoring programs and recruit and train volunteers nationwide. In just five years, AmeriCorps members have taught, tutored, and mentored more than 2.2 million children.

In addition to AmeriCorps, thousands of Americans participate in reading improvement programs through AmeriCorps*VISTA, Senior Corps, Foster Grandparents, Seniors In Schools, Retired and Senior Volunteer Program, and Learn and Serve America. AmeriCorps members also organize 45,000 community volunteers in elementary school reading programs.

Contact:

Jeffrey Gale
Corporation for National Service
1201 New York Avenue
Washington, DC 20525
(202) 606-5000, ext. 280
Fax: (202) 565-2789
jgale@cns.gov
www.cns.gov

Training Tutors

The U.S. Department of Education, the Corporation for National Service, and the Regional Educational Laboratories provide training to community literacy leaders and federal work-study tutors.

In 1998, the U.S. Department of Education awarded $3 million to communities in 40 states for ongoing training of 10,000 reading tutors. The $50,000 grants support community partnerships that offer high-quality tutor training to community volunteers, such as senior citizens and employees, and to college students who may earn financial aid by serving as reading tutors. Most local partnerships consist of a university, a school, and a community group.

A 1999 report, So That Every Child Can Read... America Reads Community Partnerships, was created to share the best practices of these projects.

Contact:

Jana Potter
Planning and Program Development
Northwest Regional Educational Laboratory
101 S.W. Main, Suite 500
Portland, OR 97204-3297

(503) 275-0120
Fax: (503) 275-9584
potterj@NWREL.org
www.nwrel.org/cevsc/subcontracts.htm

Even Start

Even Start is a federally funded family literacy program. It helps break the cycle of poverty and illiteracy by improving educational opportunities for the nation's low-income families with young children. Since its modest beginnings in 1989, Even Start grew to more than 730 projects by 1998.

Approximately 40,000 families participate in Even Start projects across the nation. More than 90 percent of participating families have incomes substantially below the poverty level, and 85 percent of the parents have neither a high school diploma nor a GED. Even Start families represent a wide spectrum of racial and ethnic backgrounds.

Even Start views literacy as a legacy to be passed down through a family. The project has three interrelated goals. First, through parenting education, it helps parents become full partners in the education of their children. Second, through early childhood education, it assists children in reaching their full potential as learners. Third, through adult basic education, it provides literacy training for parents. Each component builds upon the other, creating a composite that is more powerful and enduring than any single piece.

Contact:
Patricia McKee
U.S. Department of Education
400 Maryland Avenue, SW
Washington, DC 20202-6132
(202) 260-0826
Patricia_McKee@ed.gov
www.ed.gov/offices/OESE/CEP/programs.html

ACTION IN THE STATES

State leaders are making great strides to improve reading achievement. Many state literacy efforts focus on early care and education, early intervention, and teacher quality. States also seek to involve parents and citizens to extend learning time beyond the classroom. Iowa and South Carolina are reducing class size in kindergarten through third grade for basic skills instruction, particularly in reading. Many are placing a premium on applying the most successful, research-based ideas.

Recently Enacted State Laws

More than 20 states have enacted reading improvement laws since 1997. (See statute summaries in Appendix D.) State timetables for results range from the 1998-99 school year through 2004.

Early Care and Education

To provide quality early childhood services, Colorado's Early Education and School Readiness Program funds initiatives to help achieve readiness goals for at-risk children. The funds support accreditation efforts of early childhood care centers and professional development for early childhood teachers and care-givers. Utah, too, is designing programs for childcare centers to work with and train volunteers to create an environment that fosters reading growth. South Carolina's First Steps initiative will provide subsidies for childcare that prepares children to enter school ready to learn.

Early Assessment and Intervention

To ensure that children are reading at grade-level and that schools intervene if they are not, Arizona, Colorado, Connecticut, Idaho, Indiana, Oklahoma, and Texas—to name a few—have enacted legislation to create assessment and intervention programs in the early grades. Ohio established a Fourth-Grade Guarantee to require that students read at grade-level before going on to middle school and high school.

Teacher Quality

To improve teacher performance, some states, including Mississippi, New Hampshire, Virginia, and Washington, have funded teacher development and credentialing programs. California's Commission on Teacher Credentialing is required to gauge the skills and abilities of all reading teachers in the primary grades. In 1999, California launched professional development institutes to provide reading instruction training to 6,000 primary school teachers.

Also in 1999, South Carolina's Governor's Institute for Reading offered research-based professional development to kindergarten through third grade teachers. Idaho recently required new teachers to pass an exam based on new literacy standards for certification. Idaho also requires kindergarten through eighth-grade teachers to complete three credits in state-approved reading instruction for recertification every five years.

Parental Involvement

Arizona, Colorado, Oregon, and other states are encouraging parental involvement through programs that teach parents how to help their children in reading. The Texas Reading Initiative directs information and resources to parents, in addition to schools and communities.

Extended Learning Time

Launched in 1999, a California initiative offers four hours of instruction per day to children in kindergarten through fourth grade when school is not in session, including summertime. Virginia's Literacy Passport requires students who fail literacy tests to receive after-school or summer school instruction. Washington and Ohio sponsor large tutoring programs that match thousands of trained volunteers with elementary school student who need extra help and encouragement.

Statewide Efforts

Many statewide programs are tackling the challenge of illiteracy in diverse and creative ways. Here are a few examples from across the nation.

Delaware: Delaware Reading Is Fundamental Initiative

Launched in 1998 by Delaware First Lady Martha S. Carper, the Delaware Reading Is Fundamental (RIF) Initiative aims to bring literacy services and free books to young children and their families. Supported by the state Department of Education, corporations, and foundations, the initiative serves every first-grader in public school and every preschool child enrolled in Head Start, Even Start, or the Parents as Teachers program. Over five years, this statewide, first-in-the-nation project will reach about 80,000 children.

The initiative serves first-graders through RIF's intensive Running Start program. Almost 100 percent of 9,000 first-graders met their reading goals as each child read (or had read to him or her) 30 books in 12 weeks. The preschool program provides reading readiness activities for the classroom and home, read-aloud modeling for parents and caregivers, and children's books to take home. More than 3,500 children received three new books in 1998.

A University of Maryland study of the project found an increase in the quality of first-grade classroom libraries, in students' motivation to read, in students' reading achievement, and in the quality and quantity of home literacy practices (Gambrell, 1999).

The second year was launched by Mrs. Carper with community reading rallies, reading recognition programs, public service announcements, and other motivational events. The First Lady also will lead the spouses of the nation's governors in a national campaign for child literacy for one year.

Contact:
    Peggy Dee
    Delaware Department of Education
    Gifted & Talented, Reading, and Service-Learning
    (302) 739-4885, ext. 3110

Ohio: OhioReads

Ohio's Fourth-Grade Guarantee requires all school districts to assess students' reading skills at the end of first, second, and third grades. If students fail, they are offered extra help. Beginning in 2001, fourth-graders who fail in reading will not be promoted.

Recently, the scope of the challenge was laid bare when 53 percent of all fourth-graders failed the reading section of the state proficiency test. So Governor Bob Taft does more than serve as figurehead for the new OhioReads program. He also serves as a weekly tutor for a Columbus third-grader.

Taft has called for a corps of 20,000 volunteer tutors from Ohio businesses, the public sector, service organizations, colleges and universities, senior citizens, parents, and the general community. The Ohio legislature unanimously supported $25 million for the OhioReads initiative. In addition to tutor recruitment, funds will support public school needs, such as professional development for teachers and community grants for after-school and summer reading programs.

The private sector was quick to respond to the governor's challenge. The Limited, a clothing retailer based in Columbus, immediately offered $250,000 to help 400 employees tutor kindergarten children in local schools. OhioReads was launched in September 1999.

Contact:
    Sandy Miller
    OhioReads
    Office of the Governor
    77 S. High Street, 30th Floor
    Columbus, OH 43215-6117
    (614) 466-0224
    www.ode.ohio.gov/www/ohioreads/ohioreads.html

South Carolina: First Steps

South Carolina was 1 of just 10 states or jurisdictions where fourth-graders showed improvements on the NAEP reading assessments between 1994 and 1998. In 1999, Governor Jim Hodges secured $20 million from the legislature for South Carolina First Steps, an early childhood program. The program aims for all children to enter school healthy and ready to learn.

"Gov. Hodges' First Steps initiative is designed to provide children and their parents with access to high-quality preschool education, parenting education, and family literacy programs," said State School Superintendent Inez Tenenbaum. "It will help our students build the academic foundation they need for success."

Modeled on North Carolina's successful Smart Start program, First Steps will be community-based: it aims to unite state and local agencies, churches, parents, teachers, and businesses to identify and address children's needs.

Hodges also secured funding to continue to lower class size in primary schools so that no kindergarten through third-grade teacher has more than 17 students. The governor's proposal for a new Reading Institute was also approved by the legislature. The Institute will research the best ways to teach reading, provide extensive training for elementary school reading teachers, and monitor results annually.

Hodges is also asking the parents of every South Carolina public school child to sign a new "Compact with Our Children" at the beginning of each school year. This pledge calls for teachers, parents, and students to share the responsibility for children's education and to live up to high standards. Parents pledge to:

- Read to young children.
- Encourage older children to read to themselves.
- Provide a quiet, well-lit study area at home.
- Ensure regular and punctual school attendance.
- Provide adequate rest, food, and a healthy environment.
- Support school activities by volunteering, visiting the classroom, and attending parent-teacher conferences.

Contact:
Jim Ray, Deputy Superintendent
Division of District and Community Services
South Carolina Department of Education
1429 Senate Street
Columbia, SC 29201
(803) 734-8492

Utah: Utah Reads

In 1998, Governor Michael Leavitt launched Utah Reads, a literacy campaign to ensure that all Utah students are reading at grade-level by the end of the third grade. In March 1999, the legislature approved funds for local school districts to develop personalized instruction plans for readers in first through third grades. Funds were also approved for community-based literacy efforts.

Staff development on early literacy success is available to all preschool teachers and childcare providers. Professional development for elementary school teachers includes the use of informal tests to assess and monitor students' progress in reading. Utah Reads is training principals on early literacy issues and research-based classroom practices.

A community volunteer tutoring program is being developed with a link to Utah's Promise. The goal is to have 12,000 struggling readers at or above grade-level by the end of third grade. Utah communities are identifying volunteers and training them to tutor children in local schools. In some schools, older students tutor younger children. Utah Reads provides grants for purchases of new books for tutoring sessions.

The Utah reading initiative also promotes family involvement. First Lady Jacalyn Leavitt leads the "Read to Me" campaign, which aims to help parents understand the importance of reading aloud to their children. Public service announcements will be broadcast, and a literacy resource kit will be given to parents of newborns.

"This is the cornerstone of my budget," Leavitt said. "I've made a decision to make literacy one of my highest priorities as governor. Reading is the most fundamental skill for success in learning. Literacy is not just a school or government responsibility. It starts with parents at home."

Contact:
> Dr. Janice Dole
> Utah Reads
> Utah State Office of Education
> (801) 538-7823
> jdole@usoe.k12.ut.us
>
> Read to Me
> (877) ALL-READ
> www.governor.state.ut.us/firstlady/

Local Efforts

Local communities are expanding their efforts to improve children's reading abilities. Popular grassroots initiatives include summer reading programs, book drives, tutoring sessions, and events featuring professional sports teams. Here are examples of local literacy projects.

Atlanta: Fast Break for Reading

The Atlanta Hawks basketball team sponsors Fast Break for Reading, a program now in more than 100 schools. Players and dance team members join mascot Harry the Hawk at school assemblies to promote reading. Students who complete the program win tickets and discount vouchers. In 1998, students collectively read 18,500 books, earning 2,600 tickets valued at $92,000.

Contact:

> Gena Gatewood
> Fast Break for Reading
> (404) 827-3800
> www.NBA.com/hawks/comm_affairs.html

Boston: ReadBoston

Nearly 50 percent of Boston's third-graders do not read at grade-level. Under the leadership of Mayor Thomas M. Menino and Superintendent Thomas W. Payzant, ReadBoston unites families, schools, and the community to help all Boston's children become able readers by third grade. Support includes research and referral help, workshops, financial assistance, reading tutors, and books for children.

A major thrust of the campaign is to promote more effective reading instruction in elementary schools. The Primary Literacy Project's list of seven essential elements of strong reading programs has been formally adopted by the school system. More than $7 million in new public and private funding has been allocated to improve reading instruction. Reading programs such as Success for All and the Early Learning Literacy Initiative are being implemented in at least 75 percent of the city's elementary schools.

The Boston Public Schools is intensifying its efforts to promote literacy. All second-graders at risk of reading failure are attending month-long summer sessions and will receive extra instruction in reading throughout the school year.

ReadBoston's focus has expanded to include family involvement. Home visiting programs, preschools, community agencies, and schools work with ReadBoston to develop practical strategies to engage families in helping their children become ready to read. In 1999, more than 6,000 families participated in home reading programs throughout the city. Recent community initiatives include giving 250,000 new books to children and placing 1,000 volunteers and work-study students in schools and community settings.

Contact:
Margaret Williams, Executive Director
ReadBoston
43 Hawkins Street
Boston, MA 02114
(617) 635-READ or (617) 918-5282
Fax: (617) 918-5475
www.cityofboston.com/readboston

Seattle: The Stanford Book Fund

In honor of Seattle's school superintendent, the late John Henry Stanford, the Seattle community rallied to re-supply the school system's libraries. Organized by the Alliance for Education in 1998, the Stanford Book Fund raised $600,000 from more than 2,000 community and business partners to buy a new book for every child in the public school system. This is in addition to $300,000 raised by Stanford himself from private donors for new library books.

The Seattle-based rock group Pearl Jam donated $78,000 from a benefit concert and encouraged radio station promotions that raised even more. The Seattle Sonics and the Washington State Lottery donated $100 for every three-point shot scored by Sonics guard Hersey Hawkins. Other major donors included Microsoft, The Ackerley Group, Boeing, and PEMCO. An anonymous donor gave $100,000.

In 1999, the first delivery of 31,175 books was presented to 100 school libraries. Each book bears a special Stanford Book Fund sticker with its namesake's quote: "The most important gift we can give our children is the gift of reading."

Contact:
Jacque Coe
Alliance for Education
500 Union Street
Suite 320
Seattle, WA 98101-2332
(206) 205-0329
Fax: (206) 343-0455
www.alliance4ed.org

Morgantown, West Virginia: Energy Express

Energy Express is a six-week summer reading program that seeks to feed the minds and bodies of children in parts of West Virginia. It aims to meet twin challenges: the erosion of skills that makes summertime costly for new readers and the nutritional decline faced by students accustomed to receiving free meals at school.

College students are trained to serve as mentors for children in rural, low-income communities. Mentors provide free books and exciting learning experiences to keep children reading. Activities include shared reading, writing, drawing, and other creative arts projects. The mentors also provide two nutritious meals each day, ensuring that children can focus on feeding their imaginations.

Energy Express partners with AmeriCorps to help support the hundreds of West Virginia college students who serve as mentors. It focuses on developing strong partnerships at the local level between schools, parents, communities, and state agencies and organizations.

Contact:

Ruthellen Phillips
Energy Express
West Virginia University
407 Knapp Hall
P.O. Box 6031
Morgantown, WV 26506-6031
(304) 293-2694
Fax: (304) 293-7599
rphillip@wvu.edu

Everybody's Business

Many diverse businesses are making extraordinary efforts to help more children succeed in reading. Here is a sampling of literacy efforts in the private sector.

Pizza Hut: Tasty Rewards

Pizza Hut's BOOK IT! National Reading Incentive Program rewards young readers with free pizza, along with recognition buttons, stickers, all-star reader medallions, and praise. In its fourteenth year, BOOK IT! enrolls about 22 million students in more than 895,000 classrooms in nearly 56,000 elementary schools in all 50 states. In addition, Pizza Hut provides free pizzas for any child who completes the U.S. Department of Education's Read*Write*Now! summer activity program, a contribution worth millions of dollars.

Contact:
> BOOK IT! Program
> P.O. Box 2999
> Wichita, KS 67201
> (800) 426-6548
> www.bookitprogram.com

Time Warner: It's Time to Read

Time Warner's nonprofit Time to Read is the largest corporate volunteer literacy program in the United States. Five thousand Time Warner employees and community members volunteer each week to tutor 20,000 children, adolescents, and adults in reading.

With Time to Read, learners use magazines such as Sports Illustrated for Kids, TIME and People to develop lifelong reading and learning strategies that they can use in school, on the job, and at home. By making reading interesting and fun, Time to Read promotes literacy skills that are relevant to the learners' lives. More than 1 million volunteer hours are donated annually in 100 cities, at a cost of $175 per learner, for sponsor, tutor, learner, and training materials.

Every division of Time Warner participates in the program. Home Box Office, Time Inc., Time Warner Cable, Turner Broadcasting System, Warner Bros., and Warner Music Group all sponsor programs in their local communities where employees volunteer.

Contact:
> Virginia McEnerney
> Time to Read
> Time Warner Inc.
> (212) 484-6404
> Fax: (212) 484-6417
> www.timewarner.com/ttr

Scholastic, Inc.: More Books for Children

Scholastic Inc. has long supported community literacy programs through book donations and a discount book program. At the President's Summit for America's Future in 1996, Scholastic committed to donating more than 1 million books to national, state, and local literacy organizations that support the America Reads Challenge. In 1998, Scholastic exceeded that goal by donating 1.76 million books to programs such as Born to Read, Reach Out and Read, Reading Is Fundamental, Rolling Readers, Jumpstart, Toys for Tots, and First Book, among others.

Through the Sizzling Summer Books program in 1999, Scholastic distributed 250,000 free books to students in the District of Columbia. Every public elementary school child was allowed to select three age-appropriate Scholastic books for summer reading.

In addition, Scholastic participates in national literacy events such as Read Across America Day. Scholastic offers special discounts, challenge grants, and fundraising packages to assist literacy programs in becoming more self-sufficient.

Contact:
Julie Kreiss
Scholastic Inc.
Literacy Initiatives
(212) 343-6472
jkreiss@scholastic.com

Civic Journalism

America's newspapers are playing a major role in creating a nation of readers. Here is an example of what a newspaper can do to help more children learn to read.

The Los Angeles Times: **Reading by 9**

The majority of third-graders in Southern California read below grade-level. In 1999, *The Los Angeles Times* announced its five-year Reading by 9 campaign that seeks to help 1 million children in the five-county area of greater Los Angeles achieve grade-level reading. *The Times'* extraordinary commitment will involve virtually every division of the company, as well as community, business, civic groups, media partners, and literacy groups. *The Times* estimates it will invest more than $100 million in the effort.

In partnership with the U.S. Department of Education, *The Los Angeles Times* published hundreds of thousands of copies of *The Compact for Reading*, a guide and activity kit to link families and schools to improve student reading gains. The publication has been widely distributed at the local and national level.

Reading by 9 aims to have 6,000 trained reading tutors and literacy volunteers helping children in schools across Southern California. The campaign will donate 1 million new books to kindergarten through third-grade classrooms. A broadcast and print public service campaign will promote the importance of reading.

As *Times Mirror* CEO Mark Willes has stated, "Failure to teach our children to read is a catastrophe of epic proportions. But it is not inevitable. We can, in fact, teach them to read, and to read well, and shame on us if we don't."

Contact:

Jan Berk
Los Angeles Times Reading by 9
Times Mirror Square
Los Angeles, CA 90053
(877) READBY9
(213) 237-3039
Readingby9@latimes.com
www.latimes.com/readingby9/

The Nonprofits: A Pro-Literacy Tradition

Hundreds of nonprofit organizations are working throughout the United States to help children read well. Nonprofit organizations are providing tutors for children, organizing book drives, and assisting teachers and families. Here is a small sample of these efforts.

Association for Library Service to Children

The Association for Library Service to Children (ALSC), a division of the American Library Association, serves children from birth to age 14 and their families and caregivers.

ALSC is a major partner with the U.S. Department of Education's America Reads Challenge in promoting summer reading. ALSC helped create the new Read*Write*Now! Activity Poster for kids and Tip Sheet for adults to start a community reading program. Virtually all of America's 16,000 public libraries have summer reading programs. Over the past 20 years, preschoolers have been added to summer reading efforts through "Read to Me" programs, where children receive recognition for books read to them by parents, older siblings, and caregivers.

Story hours for preschoolers and school-age children flourish in almost every local library. Librarians also offer staff development and training to teachers and childcare workers. ALSC encourages librarians to form partnerships with schools, museums, Head Start centers, healthcare providers, churches and synagogues, and other community groups. Librarians and community health centers are reaching out to new and expectant parents on the importance of reading daily to their child through national programs like Born to Read.

ALSC is also a partner with many public television programs that promote reading and literacy.

Contact:

> Susan Roman
> Executive Director
> American Library Association/Association for Library Services to Children
> 50 East Huron Street
> Chicago, IL 60611-2795
> (800) 545-2433, ext. 2162

> Born to Read
> (800) 545-2433, ext. 1398
> www.ala.org/alsc

Reading Is Fundamental

Reading Is Fundamental (RIF) is the nation's largest nonprofit children's literacy organization, serving 3.5 million children annually at 17,000 locations. In recent years, RIF's volunteer corps has grown nearly 10 percent, to 240,000. RIF involves children in reading-related activities, encourages families to participate in their children's education, and enables children to select free books.

RIF partnered with Scholastic Inc. to donate 250,000 books to District of Columbia schoolchildren for summer 1999 reading. By 2000, RIF had placed 200 million books in the hands and homes of America's children.

Among its many innovative programs, RIF has a partnership with the Mississippi State Department of Health called Healthy Start/Smart Start. Rather than using candy or tote bags as incentives for immunizations of small children, state health clinics are distributing books. Every child who is immunized receives a free book, and any accompanying siblings are also offered a book. Volunteers read with patients and coach parents on the importance of reading. Up to 60,000 poor children could be reached annually.

Contact:

> Margaret Monsour
> RIF Inc.
> 600 Maryland Avenue, SW
> Suite 600
> Washington, DC 20024
> (877) RIF-READ
> www.rif.org

Phi Theta Kappa: Honorable Service

Phi Theta Kappa, the International Honor Society of the Two-Year College, has chosen the America Reads Challenge as its service project. Phi Theta Kappa has thousands of chapters whose members are working in their communities to help all children learn to read. Phi Theta Kappa members serve as tutors, organize book drives, and raise funds for literacy organizations.

For example, Phi Theta Kappans at Tulsa Community College in Oklahoma created the Readers and Leaders series at a local elementary school. Tulsa's mayor, local celebrities, and athletes read children's stories to emphasize the role that reading had played in their successes. The speakers also donated the books to the school library.

Contact:
 Jennifer Westbrook
 Director of Chapter Programs
 Phi Theta Kappa Center for Excellence
 1625 Eastover Drive
 Jackson, MS 39211
 (800) 946-9995, ext. 532
 www.ptk.org/sprogram/amreads/amreads_intro.htm

Action Steps for Organizations

Every member of the community has something to offer a child. Community groups can:

- Encourage the staff of your organization or the members of your group to volunteer as tutors to read with children. Contact literacy programs and offer volunteers. Encourage release time to allow staff to meet with students.

- Start an after-school or summer community reading program. Provide transportation for children and tutors. Offer your organization's resources or building as a safe site in which the program can take place. Work with your local school to coordinate your efforts.

- Donate children's books to an early childhood center or parent-child play group. Organize members to read to children each week.

- Sponsor trips to the local library. Provide transportation or escorts. Assist those with special transportation needs such as a wheelchair lift.

(continued)

- Involve families in local reading efforts. Conduct community outreach in stores, clinics, and communities of faith. Use the print, radio, and TV media. Take information about local reading programs into the schools. Involve families whose children have special needs.

- Work with reading specialists from your school system, college, or library to obtain training. Request assistance from your school district's special education office for volunteers working with students who have learning challenges.

- Hold an essay or speech contest among local children on the topic of "How Reading Has Made a Difference in My Life." Offer a small prize related to literacy, such as a reference book or a bookstore gift certificate.

- Cooperate with other community organizations and school staff on reading activities for students. Contact other reading programs and school staff for guidance.

- Find high-quality books for a wide age range that reflect the interests of children in your community. Offer these in the form of book lists or donate actual books to your local reading program. Offer to supplement the reading with related activities.

Action Steps for Universities

Higher education communities are making significant contributions to improving child literacy.

Administrators can:

- Help recruit and train Federal Work-Study students, community service volunteers, faculty, and staff as reading tutors. Increase the percentage of work-study slots that are reserved for reading tutors.

- Open classrooms to literacy programs when they are not in use. Link literacy programs with efforts to raise student expectations and pathways to college.

- Sponsor an on-campus summer reading program for elementary school children. Involve the local library.

Faculty can:

- Develop training materials for reading tutors. Offer training to students, community members, and families.

- Develop and conduct evaluations of local reading initiatives, and advise others on how to make literacy efforts more effective.

- Include tutoring and mentoring skills in academic programs involving teacher preparation, social service, and human resources.

- Share current research on reading and mentoring with organizers of local reading initiatives.

Students can:

- Ask your financial aid officer how the university plans to institute a reading tutor component to the Federal Work-Study program by 2000. Recruit work-study students, and staff, faculty, and student volunteers to fill tutoring positions.

- Volunteer to read with or to a child at a local school.

- Use student newspapers, radio, television stations, campus electronic bulletin boards, and other on-line information sources to promote involvement in America Reads.

Staff can:

- Enlist all staff to read with their own children and grandchildren. Distribute high-quality reading materials.

- Build bridges to family literacy organizations for your staff members to strengthen their literacy skills and upgrade their education and training.

Action Steps for Employers

Employers are significant stakeholders in the community and have the resources to make a real difference in the education of children. Employers can:

- Encourage employees who are parents and grandparents to read and write with their children and grandchildren.

- Encourage customers to read and write with their children. Set up a supervised reading area for children while they wait for their families to shop. Place children's books and children's magazines in lounge areas or waiting rooms. Place word games on placemats to encourage reading and writing.

- Establish a lending library in the workplace so employees can take books and other reading materials home to their children.

(continued)

- Set up high-quality, educational preschools and childcare centers at or near work sites. Set up an educational after-school program for your employees' children. Include a well-stocked selection of books.

- Allow employees to use paid time each month to volunteer as reading tutors at local schools or childcare centers. In partnership with reading specialists at your local school or college, support tutor training. Consider adding a multilingual component to your tutoring program.

- Help build coalitions to coordinate literacy efforts in the private sector. Contact your local newspapers, school districts, and other businesses to create district or regional efforts.

- Provide books, videos, consultants, and other resources to schools. Refurbish school libraries and reading centers to serve as the center of the school's literacy activities. Help schools modernize their teaching materials and equipment, including those to help children with special needs.

- Start a community reading program. Provide space at your workplace. Provide transportation for students and tutors. Encourage your employees to volunteer.

- Support after-school and summer school programs. Often employers can play a key role in bringing together schools and other community and cultural resources to start or expand programs.

SECTION II

YOU CAN MEET THE CHALLENGE: SIMPLE THINGS YOU CAN DO TO HELP

You can help meet the America Reads Challenge, a national, grassroots literacy effort to help all children read well and independently by the end of third grade.

Everyone has something important to contribute to the America Reads Challenge. You can change the life of a child by reading daily to your own child, by serving as a tutor in your community to another child, or by joining together with other members of your community to start or expand a local literacy program.

Here you will find suggestions for simple things you can do to help meet the America Reads Challenge. You can help as a parent, school, librarian, concerned citizen, community organization, university, employer, or as a member of the media.

We hope you will join the millions of people in the United States who are already helping to meet this Challenge by working with children in reading and other language skills. Whether you help as an individual, or join with others, every contribution toward this effort makes a difference in the future of our children.

YOU CAN MAKE A DIFFERENCE!

CHAPTER 5

Simple Things Families Can Do

Read to and with your children for 30 minutes every day. It is very important to read out loud to your children before they start school. Help your children to read with you. Ask them to find letters and words on the page and talk with your children about the story.

Talk with infants and young children before they learn to read. Talk with your children all day long, using short, simple sentences. Talking with them even before they can speak will help them later when they learn to read and write.

Help your children to read on their own. Reading at home helps children do better in school. Have lots of children's books in your home and visit the library every week. Help your children get their own library cards and let them pick out their own books.

If your child has a developmental delay, your child may find reading frustrating. Have books on tape in your home. Borrow or buy a tape player that is easy to work. If you cannot find recordings of your child's favorite books, you or a family member could make recordings of them for your child to listen to while looking at the books.

Help your child to see that reading is important. Suggest reading as a free-time activity. Make sure your children have time in their day to read. Set a good example for your children by reading newspapers, magazines, and books.

Set up a reading area in your home. Keep books that interest your children in places where they can easily reach them. As your children become better readers, make sure that you add harder books to your collection.

Give your children writing materials. Children want to learn how to write and to practice writing. Help them learn by having paper, pencils, pens, or crayons for them in your home. Help your children write if they ask you. If your child has a special learning or physical need, regular pens and pencils may not be the best choice. Ask your pediatrician or people who work with your child at school or at the childcare center to suggest other writing materials your child can use.

Read and write with your children in their native language. Practicing their first language will help your children learn to read and write English.

Talk with your children as you do daily activities together. When you take your children places, talk with them about what you are doing and ask them questions. If your child cannot hear, use whatever form of communication your child usually uses.

Ask your children to describe events in their lives. Talking about their experiences makes children think about them. Giving detailed descriptions and telling complete stories also helps children learn about how stories are written and what the stories they read mean.

Restrict the amount and kind of TV your children watch. Watch educational TV programs with your children that teach letter sounds and words or give information about nature and science.

Keep track of your children's progress in school. Visit your children's classrooms to learn how your children are doing in school and how you can help your children become better students. Ask about the school's reading program and where your children need help.

Become a learning partner/reading tutor to a child in your neighborhood or from your local elementary school. Volunteer to read with or to a child for 30 minutes a week for at least eight weeks. Take the child to the library to get him or her a library card.

Help start a community reading program. A good way to begin is to help set up an America Reads Challenge: READ*WRITE*NOW! program. Offer to volunteer as a reading tutor or serve as a community contact/coordinator for the program. Call 1-800-USA-LEARN for America Reads Challenge: READ*WRITE*NOW! materials.

CHAPTER 6

Simple Things Childcare Providers Can Do

Read to infants even before they are able to talk. Make books part of your one-on-one time with babies. Although they don't always understand exactly what you are saying, babies love to listen to voices. Over time, babies will associate pleasant feelings with books and reading.

Set up a reading area. Create a colorful or cozy space where children can read or you can read to them. Make sure the area is well lit and that interesting books are placed where children can easily see and reach them. Include books for children with special needs. The space does not need to be very large. It is more important that it is well defined and that children feel comfortable using it. Plan time when children can look at books on their own.

Read to children every day. Read with small groups, share illustrations, and change your voice to make stories come to life. Also, read one-on-one with children when they ask you to or when you want to share a book. Use these times to encourage children to talk about the story and characters and to share their ideas.

Encourage volunteers to read with children. Identify children who need extra help in reading and contact volunteer groups at nearby colleges, high schools, community organizations, religious groups, businesses, or senior centers. Include children with special needs. In addition to reading with volunteers, children can draw pictures about the characters in the book or make up stories of their own. After listening to the child's story, volunteers might print or type the story for the child to keep.

Read with children about their native culture. Children often respond well to stories about their own cultures. This practice also exposes other children to cultures different from their own. In addition, offer books without words so children can make up their own stories to go with the pictures.

Encourage families to read with children. Support family reading times by allowing children to borrow books overnight or for a few days. Sign up for programs that provide free or inexpensive reading materials. Also, encourage families who speak languages other than English to read with their children in their native language. This will help children learn to write and read English as well.

Teach children rhymes, songs, and poems. Make up stories about children in the group and include their names in familiar songs. Ask families to help you learn songs, poems, and stories in the children's home languages.

Talk with young children about their own lives. Make a special effort to talk with infants and babies. Responding to their cooing and babbling as if you understand them helps them learn about language. As children grow older, encourage them to join you in conversation and be interested in what they have to say. Giving details, descriptions, and telling stories not only helps children learn how stories are written and what they mean, but it also builds vocabulary and communication skills. Do not focus on correcting grammar; instead, model correct grammar yourself.

Plan a field trip to the library. Contact your local library to arrange a guided tour that explains how children can use the library. Learn about the library's services for young children. Ask about bilingual story times, special story hours for childcare programs, and workshops for caregivers. Discuss how children and families can obtain and use their own library cards.

Help start a community family reading program. A good way to begin is to help set up an America Reads Challenge: READ*WRITE*NOW! program. Consider inviting families to attend reading and parenting discussions. Make sure these gatherings are held at a time when family members can attend. When necessary, send information home about these programs in the family's native language.

CHAPTER 7

Simple Things
Schools Can Do

SCHOOL PERSONNEL AND STAFF

Start a schoolwide or community reading program. Two good ways to begin are to set up an America Reads Challenge: READ*WRITE*NOW! program or to sponsor an after-school AmeriCorps project. Identify students who need extra help in reading. Keep your school open in the evenings and on weekends to provide a safe site for children and tutors. Encourage older students to volunteer as reading tutors and reading teachers to help train tutors. Ask your librarian to identify appropriate reading materials. Ask your school district's special education office to provide special training for volunteers working with students with disabilities. When children complete the program, reward them with a special activity such as a field trip.

Encourage family members to get involved in teaching and learning reading skills and raising standards. Let families know what they can do at home to help children become better readers, so that their children can read independently and well by the end of third grade. Send home periodic progress reports on each child with suggestions on how families can help their children improve.

Publish a multilingual school newsletter. Take advantage of your school's ethnic diversity. Encourage multilingual teachers, families, and students to help. If you do not have a multilingual population, encourage your school's language clubs to contribute.

TEACHERS

Rigorously teach reading and writing skills and the core academic subjects. Focus reading activities on developing higher-order thinking skills as well as on basic skills. Compare your reading curriculum and materials with those of the most successful schools and the best state standards.

Set high expectations for your students and encourage families to do the same. If you expect a lot from your students, they will work to meet your expectations and expect more of themselves. Consult with appropriate school or district staff on how to extend high expectations to include students with learning challenges and special needs.

Encourage students to read at home with their families. Provide suggested age-graduated children's book lists to families. Families are often unsure of the level at which their child reads; book lists can help them choose books of appropriate difficulty, and provide examples of high-quality children's books. Develop a rewards system for students who take books home, read with their families, and report back on the books they have read.

Plan a field trip to the local library. Contact the head librarian to arrange for a guided tour and explanation of how students can use the library. Have all students sign up for their own library cards during this visit. If any of your students have visual, hearing, or learning disabilities, tell the librarians before the visit so that they can make the necessary accommodations. Ask about special resources such as books on tape, sign-language interpreters, books in Braille or large print, and accessibility for wheelchairs.

Encourage students to go to the school library and to the local library after school. Such visits will help develop a link in the child's mind between free time and reading. Work with the school librarian or media specialist to place a collection of age-appropriate books on topics of high interest to your students in a special area.

Use interesting community settings to stimulate reading and writing. Organize students and their families to conduct an oral history project, a history or case study of their school, or a neighborhood project that involves collecting local stories or recipes for a community cookbook.

Have students frequently work in groups. Group work allows students with varying levels of literacy and language proficiency to both gain from and contribute to each other's learning. Rotate group members regularly to ensure that students work with all of their classmates.

Encourage the academic achievement of students with limited English proficiency. Include books in the native languages of students in the classroom library. Obtain or develop appropriate native language materials and technology for classroom use. Provide daily opportunities for students to read and write in both their first and second languages.

ADMINISTRATORS

Encourage your teachers to work together to teach reading and writing across all the subjects. Encourage them to develop interdisciplinary courses. Provide opportunities for special educators to share with general educators effective strategies for working with students who have learning challenges. Introduce challenging reading and writing activities and provide technology to engage all students.

Offer extended learning time for students after school and in the summer to increase reading opportunities. Keep your school open beyond regular school hours and in the summer as a community learning center. Organize volunteer reading partners to come in during those times and read with your students. Request assistance from your school district's special education office to provide training for volunteers working with students who have learning challenges.

Establish a family literacy program. Provide literacy, parenting, and early childhood education programs for language-minority families and other families with literacy needs and their children. Devote a PTA meeting on how to become a reading tutor and to inform parents of effective methods of reading with their children. Send home information about these programs in the family's native language, where necessary.

Implement systematic and routine homework schedules. Help families know what to expect of their children regularly and how to monitor assignments. Ensure that all teachers regularly assign challenging homework. Develop and send home a sheet of suggestions for families about how to help their children with their schoolwork.

Provide high quality staff development in second-language acquisition and bilingualism. Students with limited English proficiency experience greater success in school when their teachers understand the role of the first language in literacy learning. Encourage teachers to become familiar with the native language of their students.

CHAPTER 8

Simple Things
Librarians Can Do

Learn more about the America Reads Challenge. Call 1-800-USA-LEARN for fliers on the America Reads Challenge and READ*WRITE*NOW! and provide them to the public. Contact your local READ*WRITE*NOW! program and see how your library can help.

Work with local partners to start a community reading program. One good way to begin is to set up an America Reads Challenge: READ*WRITE*NOW! program. Identify quality reading materials for the program. Look into providing materials in Braille, large-print texts, books on tape. Use communication specialists such as sign-language interpreters. Establish structured learning time at the library to give children who need extra help opportunities to become successful readers. Volunteer to train tutors or serve as a community coordinator. Offer the library as a safe site for the community program. Promote a special sign-up day for children to come in and get their own library cards.

Help children learn how to use the library's resources effectively. Provide free orientation sessions on how to use the library. Encourage local businesses and community groups to donate computer hardware and software, then offer special sessions for children to be trained in the use of the computer.

Help parents who cannot read or have low-level literacy skills. Offer tutoring services to those who cannot read or who have low-level literacy skills. Contact your local school, church, or neighborhood organization to find a tutor.

Expand your library's resources, particularly computers and children's software programs. Let families and children know that the Internet offers them a wealth of free information. Offer free introductory sessions on how to use these resources. Include equipment and software for children with physical and learning disabilities.

Ask your local schools how you can help them improve students' reading. Contact your local schools and offer to give short library presentations in the classrooms. Ask how the library can help meet the needs of children with disabilities.

Increase opportunities for preschoolers and their childcare workers to visit the library. Invite groups of preschoolers from local childcare centers to attend special reading programs at the library. Offer recognition to children who have read (or listened to) a certain number of books. Let caregivers know that they should encourage families to visit the library with their children.

Help motivate all children to read for enjoyment. Identify children's favorite subjects and direct them to books, magazines, book/cassette kits, videos, computer software, and other library resources. Make the necessary arrangements for special resources to enable children with special needs also to read for enjoyment.

Work with local parent groups to establish a parent or grandparent corps of volunteer reading tutors. Identify a volunteer coordinator, reading specialist, teacher, or librarian to plan and develop procedures for recruitment and service. Contact the local PTA, senior center, or Retired and Senior Volunteer Program office to recruit volunteers. Consider helping children with learning challenges and special needs. Provide the training tutors will need when working with these students. Ask your local Foster Grandparent Program to provide senior citizen mentors with this training.

Collect and distribute information that will help families improve their children's reading skills. Circulate America Reads Challenge: READ*WRITE*NOW! materials and encourage similar efforts in the community. Display and provide suggested book lists for children of a wide age range.

CHAPTER 9

Simple Things Grandparents, Seniors, and Concerned Citizens Can Do

Become a learning partner/reading tutor to a child in your neighborhood or from your local elementary school. Volunteer to read with or to a child for 30 minutes a week for at least eight weeks. Take the child to the library to get him or her a library card.

Start a community reading program. One good way to begin is to help set up an America Reads Challenge: READ*WRITE*NOW! project. Volunteer to serve as a tutor or a community coordinator. Contact your local senior centers, Retired and Senior Volunteer Program office, Foster GrandParents Program, retirement homes, and other community groups to recruit tutors. Work with local schools to set up matches between community members and children.

Ask your public librarian how you can help at your local library. Offer to volunteer after school in the children's section, reading stories or helping children pick out books. Offer to develop a program or support an existing summer reading program at the library.

Encourage community businesses and nonprofit organizations to help support community reading programs. Establish contacts by visiting local businesses and organizations. Encourage them to donate supplies and to allow their employees time off to volunteer in local schools. Make sure the supplies they donate meet the needs of children who have special learning or physical challenges by including materials such as books in Braille, large-print texts, and books on tape.

Develop a monthly program at your library, school, or community center in which seniors discuss their oral histories with children. Speak with local retirement homes and senior centers to enlist seniors who would be willing to tell children a highlight of their life stories. Arrange for a location where the program can be held, and advertise it.

Be supportive of school, community, and state efforts to meet high reading academic standards. Let your neighbors know the importance of reading and meeting the President's America Reads Challenge. Make an effort to stay informed about your local school's reading programs and current issues.

CHAPTER 10

Simple Things Community, Cultural and Religious Organizations Can Do

Encourage the staff of your organization or the members of your group to volunteer as tutors to read with children. Contact literacy programs already in place through local schools, libraries, or other community groups and offer volunteers from your organization to support their work. Offer release time to allow staff to meet with students.

Start a community reading program. One good way to begin is to set up a summer America Reads Challenge: READ*WRITE*NOW! program. Encourage your members or staff to volunteer as tutors. Provide transportation for children and tutors. Offer your organization's building as a safe site in which the program can take place.

Work with preschool children. Donate children's books to an early childhood center, mothers' day out program, or parent/child play group. Organize a program in which members volunteer to read to children in these programs each week.

Sponsor trips to the local library. Help provide transportation or escorts for neighborhood children during weekly trips to the library. Ask whether any children have special transportation needs such as a wheelchair lift and try to link them with an escort who can meet those needs.

Get families involved in local reading efforts. Parental involvement has a crucial impact on children's academic achievement. Take information about local reading programs into the school. Encourage families whose children have special needs to participate in local reading efforts.

Think of ways your organization's expertise can help make stories come alive for students. By adding music, movement, or improvisation, performers can help students respond to and better understand a story. Develop a weekly storytelling hour at your organization, using your members' individual talents.

Help train other volunteers. Work with reading specialists from your school system or an America Reads Challenge: READ*WRITE*NOW! program to obtain training for your volunteers. Request assistance from your school district's special education office to provide training for volunteers working with students who have learning challenges.

Help students write their own stories and produce them in book or dramatic form. Students may develop more interest in reading the stories of others once they have tried writing themselves. Organize an event for the students to read or perform their written work.

Hold an essay or speech contest among local children on the topic of how "Reading Has Made a Difference in My Life." These stories can reinforce the benefits of learning to read and help set high reading standards. Offer a small prize related to literacy, such as a reference book or a bookstore gift certificate.

Cooperate with other community organizations and school staff on reading activities for students. Rarely can one organization or individual "do it all." Contact other community organizations that have different expertise from your own. Ask for and offer help to improve and expand your reading activities. Contact other reading programs and school staff for guidance.

Find quality books for a wide age range that reflect the interests of children in your community. Offer these in the form of book lists or actual books to your local reading program. Offer to supplement the reading with related activities.

CHAPTER 11

Simple Things
Universities Can Do

STUDENTS

Ask your financial aid adviser if your university has officially signed on to the America Reads Challenge. Colleges have been asked to voluntarily invest significant portions of their Federal Work Study dollars toward tutoring children in reading.

Volunteer to read with or to a child at a local school. Visit your university's community service center or contact the volunteer coordinator to be matched with a child. If your campus does not have these resources, call the local elementary school and ask whether you can be matched with a child who needs a learning partner. Find out what opportunities are available through your local YMCA/YWCA, Girl Scout, Learn and Serve America, and AmeriCorps programs.

Get the local associations and organizations on your campus involved in literacy/mentoring community service projects. Contact organization presidents to discuss ways in which the organization may be able to contribute to existing literacy projects or to initiate a project. Encourage members of groups you belong to, to volunteer as reading tutors.

Use student newspapers, radio and television stations, campus electronic bulletin boards, and other on-line information sources to promote student involvement in the America Reads Challenge. Provide notices about school or local literacy projects to the person in charge of advertising; include in the notice a request for volunteers and a contact name and phone number for those who are interested.

Work with local precollege youth organizations such as Boys and Girls Clubs or the YMCA/YWCA. Talk with the heads of local precollege youth organizations to discover how students at your university can act as learning partners or mentors to their members. Post flyers on campus to inform students about the program and encourage them to participate.

FACULTY

Use your expertise to develop training materials for reading tutors. The President of the American Association of Colleges of Teacher Education and the Secretary of the U.S. Department of Education are encouraging colleges of education to help prepare tutors to help children meet the President's America Reads Challenge. As you develop materials, request that colleagues in special education contribute strategies for training tutors of children with special needs.

Develop and conduct evaluations of local reading initiatives. Work with these initiatives to develop and conduct evaluations of their programs. Advise them on how they can use the evaluation findings to become more effective.

Share current research on reading and mentoring with organizers of local reading initiatives or conduct new research in this field. Many local literacy groups are eager for research that will support and help guide their work. Contact local reading programs and literacy groups to discover areas where research is needed.

Offer training on how to become an effective reading partner to interested students, community members, and families. Use your skills as an educator to help others develop effective mentoring skills and habits. Develop a training guide. Post information and sign-up sheets on campus and at your local library and school to inform the community and attract interest.

Include tutoring/mentoring skills and service learning opportunities in academic programs involving teacher preparation, social service, and human resources. Incorporate becoming a learning partner into your syllabus. Part-time student volunteer tutoring activities can provide enrichment to education, social services, psychology, and English classes. Match students in these programs with local schoolchildren to give your students one-on-one experience as mentors.

ADMINISTRATORS

Assign and train Work-Study students as reading tutors. Increase the percentage of Work-Study slots that are reserved for reading tutoring. The Secretary of Education has waived the matching requirement for students serving as reading tutors to preschool and elementary schoolchildren. This 100 percent federal funding of Federal Work-Study reading tutors facilitates the participation of postsecondary institutions in the America Reads Challenge. Contact the local school's reading specialist or a local community-based organization such as Boys and Girls Clubs, YMCAs/YWCAs, Girl Scouts, and AmeriCorps projects to help develop an effective training program for Work-Study students.

Include reading tutoring/mentoring as an option for students participating in community service projects. Encourage your campus community service center or volunteer coordinator to develop a partnership with the local school so students can serve as learning partners or tutors to schoolchildren.

Provide space for local reading programs. Open classrooms or lecture halls to literacy programs on weekends and other times when they are not in use. Encourage students to volunteer as assistants.

Sponsor an on-campus summer reading program for elementary school-children. Invite professors and qualified students to teach sessions. Contact the community library and local reading programs to encourage their participation.

Make campus computer resources available to local families and their children. Open campus computer clusters to the public during off-times. Offer free orientation sessions for people who have never used the Internet before. Provide a list of educational sites related to reading.

CHAPTER 12

Simple Things Employers Can Do

Encourage parents/employees to read and write with their children. Give children's books to employees who have worked overtime to thank them for time away from their families and to encourage them to read with their children. Copublish America Reads Challenge: READ*WRITE*NOW! materials for distribution to your employees' children or schools with whom you have a partnership arrangement.

Encourage your customers to read and write with their children. Set up a supervised reading area for children while they wait for their families to shop. Place children's books and children's magazines in lounge areas or waiting rooms. Place word games on placemats to encourage reading and writing.

Establish a lending library in the workplace so that employees can take books and other reading materials home to their children. Contact the local library to obtain suggested children's book lists. Ask employees to donate books and books on tape that their children have outgrown.

Set up high-quality, educational preschools and day care centers at or near work sites. Set up a program of educational, supervised activities for your employees' school-age children. Include a well-stocked collection of children's books and encourage childcare providers to read to the children daily.

Advocate family-centered policies. Urge employees (parents and others) to use flex-time or give them extra time off to volunteer as tutors for children at local schools. Allow employees to use some paid time each month to serve as a learning partner to a child.

Develop a program to bring children to your work site for tutoring. Bringing children to the work site for tutoring gives them a safe place to go after school hours, helps improve their schoolwork, and makes mentoring and tutoring convenient for employees. Provide support for training reading tutors both in schools and in the workplace. Contact your local school district's special education department for assistance on how to address and support the training of tutors for students with special needs.

Establish and support bilingual tutoring and classroom programs. If your business already has a tutoring program, think about adding a bilingual component. If it does not, consider starting a bilingual program. Encourage bilingual employees to volunteer as reading tutors and purchase bilingual teaching and reading materials for them.

Establish a national program for employees to tutor, mentor, and allow children to shadow model employees. Encourage each affiliate, franchise, or company branch to get involved with its local schools by tutoring or mentoring students. Allow students to shadow workers for a day to understand how the skills they learn in school will someday be used in the workplace.

Develop public service announcements for newspapers, billboards, television, and radio that can help spread the message on the importance of reading. Help get the whole community involved in their local schools. Reach out to community members who do not have children. Everyone has a skill to offer from which children can benefit.

Support funding for leadership development and team-building among school district staff, school board members, community leaders, and families. Sponsor workshops to help the community set goals for its children and their schools. Bring in reading specialists and teachers to explain the most effective ways to increase literacy skills.

Help build coalitions to coordinate literacy efforts in the private sector. Contact your local newspapers, school district, and other businesses to create district or regional efforts to improve reading skills among children. Establish a relationship with local schools to determine where your help is needed most.

Provide books, videos, consultants, and other resources to schools. Contact your local school's administrators to determine which resources are most needed. Rebuild or refurbish school libraries so that they become the center of the school's literacy activities. Help to guarantee that schools have the most modern teaching materials, computers, books, and videos. Ask the school administrator about whether there is a need for your company to provide special materials/equipment for children with special needs.

Start a community reading program. One good way to begin is to set up an America Reads Challenge: READ*WRITE*NOW! program. Provide space in your office building for the program's operations. Provide transportation for children and tutors. Encourage your employees to volunteer as tutors.

CHAPTER 13

Simple Things the Media Can Do

Highlight successful reading programs. Cover stories about literacy events sponsored by schools, libraries, AmeriCorps projects, and communities and successful participants in them. Feature individual success stories and "unsung tutoring heroes." Provide information on how others can get involved.

Provide free newspapers for school use. Train teachers on how to use the newspaper in the classroom. Start a Vacation Donation program allowing subscribers on vacation to donate their unread issues to schools.

Start a Community Volunteer Alert Program. Publicize a weekly listing of volunteer programs in need of tutors. Provide contact names and numbers.

Help your community learn how to help children read better. Publicize tips such as those listed in this booklet and information about how to get involved with local reading programs. Promote literacy resources available in the community for families.

Keep families and the community informed about local student performance. Publicize school reading test scores and school efforts to reach high standards. Highlight a "student of the month" from an area school who has excelled academically in language arts or reading.

Sponsor literacy-focused events such as a Get a Library Card Day, Read-A-Thons, Book Drives, or Essay Contests. Contact your local library or literacy program for information about existing programs you can support and for help in organizing such events. Publicize a monthly calendar of these events and a short item about the outcome of each.

Support local literacy programs by donating advertising space. Produce a community public service announcement in support of reading. Publicize recommended reading lists for books that families can read with children of different ages.

SECTION III

IDEAS AT WORK

INTRODUCTION

We are witnessing a time of unparalleled activity to get more children on the road to reading. An unprecedented pro-literacy movement, focused on children under age 9, is sweeping through thousands of communities across the nation. A common strategy has emerged for reading success: we must start early by preparing young children to read, and we must finish strong by providing excellent instruction and community support in the primary grades.

Recent Momentum

Under Secretary Richard W. Riley, the 1992–2000 administration made child literacy a top education priority. In 1998, The National Research Council produced Preventing Reading Difficulties in Young Children, a blueprint for action to create a nation of readers.

Congress passed the Reading Excellence Act, the boldest child literacy law of the past thirty years, which awarded its first grants in 1999. Governors and legislatures in the majority of states are taking decisive action to combat illiteracy, with more than 20 states passing new laws in recent years. Many mayors of cities with stubborn illiteracy rates are tackling the challenge head-on, as are public leaders in smaller communities.

Newspapers, businesses, libraries, sports teams, community service groups, employees, college students, and volunteers of all ages are stepping forward to tutor children, work with parents, provide books, and support schools. This crusade is reshaping our view of the reading challenge. No longer can we simply point fingers at schools for failing to teach children to read. Every parent, caregiver, teacher, and citizen has a role to play to spark dramatic improvement in reading.

Key Players

What can be done to prepare more children for reading success? First, families can maximize the benefits of parent-child communication from birth. Second, caregivers and preschool teachers can be trained and given resources to stimulate emergent literacy. Third, children deserve well-trained teachers who understand reading development, who can pinpoint problems, and who can address them effectively.

In addition, entire communities can rally around their children for literacy success. This means more partnerships between schools and communities. It means greater engagement of private enterprise, colleges, universities, and cultural groups. It means more volunteers and more opportunities for legions of mentors and tutors.

By expanding our view of who contributes to students' reading success, we are increasing opportunities for millions of Americans to endow our children with this lifelong skill. If we succeed in engaging this untapped pool of adults, the results will revolutionize education in this country.

Ideas at Work

This collection highlights examples of activities to help all children become good readers. It expands upon ideas presented in Section I of this book, "Start Early, Finish Strong." These projects and programs are but a fraction of the good work being done from coast to coast, and are offered here to provide inspiration and to show the diversity of opportunities to take action.

Many of these programs have joined the Coalition for America Reads, which is open to any organization that acts to help a child become a good reader. We encourage you to contact these and other programs to ask questions, to share ideas and resources, and to strengthen the network of support for our children. The momentum is with us for a breakthrough in student reading achievement. We can win the war on illiteracy, if every American does what he or she can to help a child.

Contact:

Carol H. Rasco, Director
America Reads Challenge
U.S. Department of Education
For questions and comments: (800) USA-LEARN
For free publications: (877) 4ED-PUBS
America Reads staff: (202) 401-8888
Fax: (202) 401-0596
Americareads@ed.gov
www.ed.gov/americareads

CHAPTER 14

National Leadership

The call for a national crusade to ensure that all children can read engaged individuals and organizations. It also launched and strengthened federal initiatives and programs to raise student reading achievement and prepare young children to learn to read.

AMERICA READS CHALLENGE

The U.S. Department of Education's America Reads Challenge calls on every American to do what he or she can to help a child become a successful reader. America Reads encourages parents and caregivers to read and talk daily to children from infancy. For teachers, America Reads advocates research-based college training and high-quality professional development. America Reads also encourages community efforts to recruit and train reading tutors to supplement classroom reading instruction.

America Reads promotes local literacy partnerships between parents, schools, libraries, childcare centers, universities, businesses, and nonprofit groups. It also disseminates reading research and recommends further study. Since its launch in January 1997, nearly 300 organizations, from libraries and religious groups to schools and businesses, have stepped forward to join The President's Coalition for America Reads.

America Reads unites schools, libraries, and youth and community groups to sponsor summer and after-school reading programs across the country. Nearly 2 million Read*Write*Now! Activity Posters have been distributed, in English and Spanish, to enlist parents, grandparents, schools, and communities to keep children reading during the summer. The Read*Write*Now! Tip Sheet, in English and Spanish, offers ideas for starting a community reading program.

Through the Federal Work-Study program, more than 22,000 college students at 1,100 colleges and universities earned financial aid by serving as reading tutors in the 1997–98 academic year. Many more participated in the 1998–99 academic year. By 2000, almost all of the 3,300 colleges, universities, and trade schools receiving federal work-study funds had a reading tutor program.

The Higher Education Act of 1998 included additional funding for the Federal Work-Study program that will allow more college students to earn financial aid as reading tutors. Schools and community groups can contact their local college or university financial aid office to ask about placements for work-study tutors.

Contact:
> America Reads Challenge
> U.S. Department of Education
> 400 Maryland Avenue, SW
> Washington, DC 20202-0107
> (202) 401-8888
> Fax: (202) 401-0596
> To order publications: (877) 4ED-PUBS
> Americareads@ed.gov
> www.ed.gov/americareads

America Reads/New York University

New York University (NYU) was one of the first universities to join the America Reads work-study program in 1997. Under the leadership of its president, NYU now has the largest America Reads work-study program in the nation. More than 700 work-study tutors serve in 61 New York City public elementary schools, reaching thousands of schoolchildren through 6,500 hours of service per week.

NYU America Reads tutors also work in the district's summer school programs and as camp counselors in the "Break Away Camps" sponsored by the chancellor of the New York City schools. The counselors tutor in reading as part of their duties.

One NYU tutor, Pablo, taught a first grader named Yesenia, who had problems with basic letter sounds, to read in English. "Now that Yesenia can read beginner books all the way through, she won't stop demanding that I teach her to read in Spanish," wrote Pablo. "She wants to be the first person in her class to be able to read in two languages! Last year, for my work-study job, I handed out ping-pong balls at an NYU game room. America Reads is a work-study job that is a lot more challenging and more rewarding."

NYU will launch the America Counts program, assigning work-study tutors to help children struggling with math.

Contact:
Sharon Slotnick
America Reads/America Counts
New York University
25 West 4th Street - Room 322
New York, NY 10012
(212) 998-2097
sms1@is3.nyu.edu

America Reads Tutor Training

The U.S. Department of Education, the Corporation for National Service, and the Regional Educational Laboratories provide training to community literacy leaders and federal work-study tutors.

In 1998, the U.S. Department of Education awarded $3 million to communities in 40 states for ongoing training of 10,000 reading tutors. The $50,000 grants support partnerships that offer high-quality tutor training to community volunteers, such as senior citizens and employees, and to college students who may volunteer or earn financial aid by serving as reading tutors. Most local partnerships consist of a university, a school, and a community group.

A 1999 report, *So That Every Child Can Read...America Reads Community Partnerships*, was created to share the best practices of these projects. It is available online at no charge through the Northwest Regional Educational Laboratory.

Contact:
Jana Potter
Planning and Program Development
Northwest Regional Educational Laboratory
101 S.W. Main, Suite 500
Portland, OR 97204-3297
(503) 275-0120
Fax: (503) 275-9584
potterj@NWREL.org
www.nwrel.org/cevsc/subcontracts

The Compact for Reading: Parents As Partners

The Compact for Reading is a guide on how to develop a compact, or written agreement, among families, teachers, principals, and students. The compact describes how all partners can help improve the reading skills of children from kindergarten through third grade, including those with disabilities and with limited English proficiency. Tutors and other community members can also be partners in a Compact for Reading.

Research shows that schools with properly implemented compacts raise student achievement higher than similar schools without compacts. Principals reported greater family involvement in homework and more parents reading with children at home. Schools with the greatest need for reading progress seem to benefit the most.

The Compact Guide comes with a School-Home Links Kit to help implement local Compacts. Developed by teachers for the U.S. Department of Education, the kit provides 100 reading activities for each grade from kindergarten through third. Three to four times a week, a teacher can provide these easy-to-use activities to families to expand student learning at home and encourage family involvement in reading activities.

The Compact for Reading is published in cooperation with *The Los Angeles Times* Reading by 9 campaign and available free from the U.S. Department of Education.

Contact:
> U.S. Department of Education
> (877) 4ED-PUBS
> www.ed.gov/pubs/CompactforReading

The Comprehensive School Reform Demonstration Program

The Comprehensive School Reform Demonstration (CSRD) Program, launched by the U.S. Department of Education in 1998, will help raise student achievement by assisting public schools across the country in implementing effective, comprehensive school reforms. Through CSRD, approximately 2,500 schools will receive competitive grants from their states to adopt comprehensive reforms that help students reach high standards in reading, math, and other areas of identified need. The legislation requires each participating school to receive at least $50,000 of CSRD assistance annually.

These reforms must be based on reliable research and effective practices. They address virtually all aspects of a school's operations, including curriculum and instruction, student assessment, teacher professional development, parent involvement, and school management. Successful reforms also take advantage of high-quality assistance from outside partners experienced in school-wide reform.

Contact:

Comprehensive School Reform Demonstration Program
(202) 205-4292
compreform@ed.gov
www.ed.gov/offices/OESE/compreform

The Corporation for National Service

The Corporation for National Service is a major partner with America Reads. AmeriCorps members operate America Reads tutoring programs and recruit and train volunteers nationwide. In just five years, AmeriCorps members have taught, tutored, and mentored more than 2.2 million children.

In addition to AmeriCorps, thousands of Americans participate in reading improvement programs through AmeriCorps*VISTA, Senior Corps, Foster Grandparents, Seniors In Schools, Retired and Senior Volunteer Program, and Learn and Serve America. AmeriCorps members also organize 45,000 community volunteers in elementary school reading programs.

Contact:

Jeffrey Gale
Corporation for National Service
1201 New York Avenue
Washington, DC 20525
(202) 606-5000, ext. 280
Fax: (202) 565-2789
jgale@cns.gov
www.cns.gov

Even Start

Even Start is a federally-funded family literacy program. It helps break the cycle of poverty and illiteracy by improving educational opportunities for the nation's low-income families with young children. Since its modest beginnings in 1989, Even Start grew to more than 730 projects by 1998.

Approximately 40,000 families participate in Even Start projects across the nation. More than 90 percent have incomes substantially below the poverty level, and 85 percent of the parents have neither a high school diploma nor a GED. Even Start families represent a wide spectrum of racial and ethnic backgrounds.

Even Start views literacy as a legacy to be passed down through a family. The project has three interrelated goals. First, through parenting education, it helps parents become full partners in the education of their children. Second, through early childhood education, it assists children in reaching their full potential as learners. Third, through adult basic education, it provides literacy training for parents. Each component builds upon the other, creating a composite that is more powerful and enduring than any single piece.

Contact:
Patricia McKee
U.S. Department of Education
400 Maryland Avenue, SW
Washington, DC 20202-6132
(202) 260-0826
Fax: (202) 260-7764
Patricia_McKee@ed.gov
www.ed.gov/offices/OESE/CEP/programs.html

Head Start

Head Start, a federally funded grant program, was launched in 1965. Through age-appropriate activities, the program has helped more than 15 million young children develop the social competence that fosters language and literacy skills, such as listening, speaking, reading, and writing. In 1998, 830,000 children ages 3 to 5, and their families, were served in all 50 states. Ninety percent of Head Start lead teachers have a Child Development Associate credential, a degree in early childhood education, or a state certificate to teach.

A major priority for Head Start is to involve parents in the education of their children. More than 800,000 parents volunteer annually, and about 30 percent of Head Start staff are parents of either current or former students of children enrolled in the program.

Head Start also promotes family literacy. It seeks to:

■ Develop the skills of parents and staff in providing language-rich opportunities to children

- Increase families' access to materials and activities that develop literacy
- Support parents in their role as a child's first teacher
- Assist parents in addressing their own literacy needs

The Early Head Start program, for low-income families with infants and toddlers, aims to enhance children's development in all areas, including language and literacy. In 1998, more than 200 Early Head Start centers served 39,000 youngsters in 50 states, the District of Columbia and Puerto Rico. In 1999, more than 100 new centers served 4,000 additional children. The 1992-2000 administration proposed doubling in five years the number of babies and toddlers reached by Early Head Start.

Contact:
U.S. Department of Health and Human Services
Head Start
www.acf.dhhs/programs/opa/facts/headst.htm

National Head Start Association
(703) 739-0875
www.nhsa.org

National Institute for Literacy

The National Institute for Literacy (NIFL) serves as a resource for the entire literacy community. A joint project of the U.S. Departments of Education, Labor, and Health and Human Services, NIFL focuses primarily on adult and family literacy. In 1998, NIFL received a $5 million grant from the Reading Excellence Program to disseminate literacy information.

LINCS, the Institute's technology initiative, is a cooperative electronic network of major literacy resources and organizations. LINCS is America's only national information retrieval and communication system for adult literacy.

Contact:
National Institute for Literacy
1775 I Street NW
Suite 730
Washington, DC 20006-2401
(800) 228-8813
(202) 233-2025
Fax: (202) 233-2050
www.nifl.gov

A National Summit on Reading

U.S. Education Secretary Richard Riley convened the first National Reading Summit in September of 1998. The Summit brought together policymakers and education leaders from 50 states and territories to disseminate the findings of the National Research Council's report, *Preventing Reading Difficulties in Young Children*. Riley also challenged each state to do more to improve child literacy.

States are now able to share best practices and model programs with each other and compare policies regarding teacher preparation and certification, standards for professional development, spending on early childhood and literacy, and other cutting edge issues.

Contact:
National Reading Summit
U.S. Department of Education
(202) 401-8888
Fax: (202) 401-0596
www.ed.gov/inits/readingsummit

Partnership for Family Involvement in Education

Education Secretary Riley launched The Partnership for Family Involvement in Education (PFIE) in 1994 to bring together employers, educators, families, religious groups, and community organizations to improve schools and raise student achievement.

More than 5,000 organizations are currently members of the Partnership, from every state in the country. Employers include Hewlett-Packard, Mattell, Walt Disney, TEXACO, HBO, IBM, NBC, MTV, Scholastic, Bristol-Meyers Squibb, Eastman Kodak and AT&T. Community groups include Boys and Girls Clubs, the Children's Defense Fund, YMCAs, PTAs, and Girls Scouts of the USA. Religious group members represent a variety of faiths. Many different kinds of schools are members.

The Partnership has several important roles. First it strengthens family-school partnerships through good communication and mutual responsibility for children's learning. Second, it encourages adoption of family- and student-friendly business practices. Third, it provides before- and after-school learning activities for children. Fourth, it makes effective use of facilities, schools, community buildings, and churches for children and families. And fifth, PFIE gives parents the resources, training, and information they need to help children learn, and teachers and principals the tools they need to engage families.

Contact:
> Partnership for Family Involvement in Education
> U. S. Department of Education
> 400 Maryland Avenue, SW
> Washington, DC 20202-8173
> (800) USA-LEARN
> Fax: (202) 205-9133
> partner@ed.gov
> www.pfie.ed.gov

PBS: Ready To Learn

Ready To Learn Television is a large network of public television stations. Supported by the U.S. Department of Education, the Ready To Learn program funds hands-on workshops to train child care workers, families, and teachers to connect PBS children's television programming with language, literacy, reading, and other learning activities.

The number of participating stations grew from 48 in 1995 to 122 at the end of 1998. This gives Ready To Learn the potential to reach 90 percent of the nation. To date, Ready To Learn training has reached more than 120,000 parents and more than 97,000 early childhood teachers and other professionals.

Ready To Learn stations collaborate with local partners, such as Head Start, Even Start, the PTA, libraries and museums. In addition, the project publishes a quarterly magazine in English and Spanish and distributes books to children.

Contact:
> Jean Chase
> PBS
> Ready To Learn Program
> 1320 Braddock Place
> Alexandria, VA 22314
> (703) 739-5000
> www.pbs.org/kids/rtl

Prescription For Reading Partnership

Championed by Hillary Rodham Clinton when she was first lady, Prescription for Reading is a national partnership led by Reach Out and Read, Born to Read (of The American Library Association), Scholastic, and First Book. Launched in 1997, the program challenges booksellers, publishers, libraries, hospitals, pediatricians, health centers, and others to work together to ensure that infants and toddlers who visit doctors have access to books and are read to regularly.

Among the partnership's accomplishments are:

- An increase from 150,000 to 750,000 children served by Reach Out and Read.
- An increase from 500 to 4,500 doctors and nurses trained to "prescribe" reading.
- Contributions made by Scholastic and First Book of more than 235,000 books.
- Distribution of more than one million books by participating doctors.

In support of this program, Mrs. Clinton launched Reach Out and Read programs in Baltimore; Chicago; Washington, DC; and New York City.

Contact:

Nicole Rabner
Prescription for Reading
Office of the First Lady
The White House
Washington, DC 20500
(202) 456-7263

Reading Excellence

In 1998, President Clinton signed the Reading Excellence Act, the most significant child literacy law in three decades. The Reading Excellence Program awards grants to states to improve reading. The program is designed to:

- Provide children with the readiness skills and support they need to learn to read once they enter school.
- Teach every child to read by the end of the third grade.
- Use research-based methods to improve the instructional practices of teachers and others.
- Expand the number of high-quality family literacy programs.
- Provide early intervention for children with reading difficulties.

States compete for $241 million in grants. Successful states hold competitions for local school districts. The first round of grants will be awarded in summer 1999, with local grants to follow. Because low-income children experience reading failure at higher rates than other students, the funding is directed toward the state's poorest districts and schools.

Contact:
Dr. Joseph Conaty
Reading Excellence Program
U.S. Department of Education
400 Maryland Avenue, SW
Room 5C-141
Washington, DC 20202-6200
(202) 260-8228
Fax: (202) 260-8969
reading_excellence@ed.gov
www.ed.gov/offices/OESE/REA/index.html

Teacher Quality Enhancement Grants

This new $75 million federal program aims to boost student achievement in
reading and other subjects through improvements in teacher quality. State
Grants support comprehensive statewide reforms to improve teacher quality,
including systemic change to state teacher licensure policies and practices.
Partnership Grants bring about fundamental change and improvement in traditional teacher education programs. Teacher Recruitment Grants reduce short-
ages of qualified teachers in high-need school districts. All grants are
competitive.

Contact:
Ed Crowe
U.S. Department of Education
(202) 260-8460
teacherquality@ed.gov
www.ed.gov/offices/OPE/heatqp

Title I Funding

Funds under Title I of the Elementary and Secondary Education Act provide
$8 billion in support for elementary and secondary education. The goal is to
improve teaching and learning for students who live in low-income areas and
who are at risk of failing to meet challenging state standards. Of more than
eleven million children served by Title I, 37 percent are in first, second, or
third grade, and most receive extra help in reading.

Title I funds also assist children of migrant workers and families with low literacy, as well as students with other educational barriers such as limited English,

disabilities, delinquency, neglect, and homelessness. Title I aims to help all children reach high standards.

Local schools use more than 90 percent of Title I funds for instruction and instructional support, such as salaries for teachers and aides to help children improve in reading or mathematics. Funds also may be used for professional development, early childhood programs, family literacy, evaluation, and parental involvement efforts. Additional federal funding is available to some Title I schools under the Reading Excellence Act, targeting professional development and tutoring in reading, as well as assistance with kindergarten transition and family literacy.

Contact:

U.S. Department of Education, Office of Compensatory Education
(800) USA-LEARN
www.ed.gov/offices/OESE/CEP/programs.html

21st Century Community Learning Centers

The 21st Century Community Learning Centers were a key component of the 1992-2000 administration's effort to keep children safe and help them learn after school. With the strong support of the Charles Stewart Mott Foundation, approximately 250,000 children participate.

About $200 million supports 1,600 Community Learning Centers in more than 460 communities in 49 states. These funds help schools stay open longer and establish or expand after-school and summer programs for children. The Centers provide academic enrichment, tutors and support; artistic, sports, and cultural activities; opportunities for children to participate in service learning and community development projects; nutritional and health services; access to technology and telecommunications; and activities to promote parent involvement and lifelong learning.

Contact:

21st Century Community Learning Centers
U.S. Department of Education
(800) USA-LEARN
21stCCLC@ed.gov
www.ed.gov/offices/OERI/21stCCLC/

U.S. Department of Labor Certification in Child Development

The U.S. Department of Labor's Bureau of Apprenticeship and Training (BAT) is taking a collaborative approach to credentialling child care providers. Through BAT's partnership with the state of West Virginia's apprenticeship program, candidates who take four semesters of college courses and get 4,000 hours of on-the-job training receive certification from the U.S. Department of Labor as a Child Development Specialist.

Hundreds of providers have graduated from the program, and many hundreds more are actively pursuing completion of the requirements. Florida, Minnesota, and Maine have followed suit, with Maine requiring six semesters of college courses.

The program draws on core teams of educators, health professionals, parents, and employers. The system creates a career ladder for child care providers who earn their salaries while in the program and receive incremental wage increases as their skills, abilities, and knowledge increase. Research shows that appropriate training can enhance a caregiver's ability to develop children's literacy and language skills.

Employers report almost no turnover among participating providers, and the providers report high satisfaction with their careers. Plans are underway to launch similar projects in 10 more states.

Contact:
Dana Daugherty
U.S. Department of Labor
Bureau of Apprenticeship and Training
Child Care Development Specialist Registered Apprentice Program
200 Constitution Avenue, NW
Washington, DC 20210
(202) 219-5921
www.doleta.gov/bat

CHAPTER 15

Action in the States

State leaders are making great strides to improve reading achievement. Most state literacy efforts aim to ensure children are reading at grade level, to improve teacher performance, to provide high-quality early care and education, and to encourage parental involvement. Many are placing a premium on using the most practical and successful research-based ideas.

Many governors pledged to take strong action to improve reading achievement. Some governors used their State of the State addresses to promote their ideas for such improvement. Here are examples of some of these governors' proposals, in their own words.

EXCERPTS ON READING
FROM STATE OF THE STATE ADDRESSES
Alabama
Governor Don Siegelman

"We will continue teacher training with the Alabama Reading Initiative. Teachers will attend intensive seminars to learn how to identify children with reading problems and how to teach every child to read better. Since using the reading initiative, the Verner Elementary School in Tuscaloosa reports that 64 percent—nearly two-thirds—of their students are reading a full year above their grade-level. We will provide $4 million for this program, and I pledge to take this program statewide during my term as governor."

Arizona
Governor Jane Dee Hull

"I propose an additional $20 million over the next two years for kindergarten through third grade for reading improvement. I want to work with you to ensure we target these resources. I do not want them eaten up by the administrative bureaucracy. I want them used to provide smaller classes and instruction for students who need additional classroom help."

California

Governor Gray Davis

"I am, to be specific, proposing $444 million in new spending for measures to improve the reading skills of our children, to enhance the quality of our teachers, and to institute tough standards of performance and accountability for each of our 8,000 schools. I call this program READ: Raising Expectations, Achievement, and Development. It represents a significant down payment on the future of our children.

"As you know, reading is the gateway skill for all California students. Unfortunately, our schools rank at or near the bottom of all states as measured by the results on the National Assessment for Education Progress.

"To attack this intolerable problem, I will call on you to allocate $186 million for reading improvement programs, including $75 million specifically targeted for Intensive Reading Instruction Academies for pupils. I also will create a Reading Call to Action Campaign designed to get people interested in reading, as well as special programs for English language learners to help accelerate the teaching and mastery of English. In addition, we will publish and distribute preschool reading development guidelines, and we will provide funding for elementary schools to expand classroom libraries.

"My budget also will include funds for a Governor's Reading Awards Program which will provide competitive cash grants to the top 400 schools whose students read the most books designated in the California Reading Lists. This will help us ensure that every child in California public schools is a competent reader by the end of the third grade.

"For the first time, I will ask community colleges to create teaching and reading development partnerships with elementary and secondary schools. And I intend to train more paraprofessionals to become teachers and to waive credential fees for all new teachers."

Delaware

Governor Tom Carper

"Students in grades 3, 5, 8, and 10 will take challenging tests—called assessments—in reading, writing, and math. Students in grades 3 and 5 whose reading-comprehension tests well below our standard must attend summer school and hone their reading skills. Students whose reading skills improve sufficiently will move on to the next grade. Those who do not will repeat the same grade with a curriculum that focuses on reading.

"Similar requirements apply to both reading and math in the eighth and tenth grades. The focus on these two subjects is critical because, beginning with the class of 2002—this year's freshmen—Delaware students must demonstrate that they have mastered our rigorous standards in order to receive a high school diploma. If they fail to meet Delaware standards in reading or math by the end of the twelfth grade, they may attend commencement exercises with the class of 2002. They may even receive a certificate of completion. But let me be clear: those students will not receive a diploma from the State of Delaware."

Idaho

Governor Dirk Kempthorne

"We must continue our focus on children as they reach school age. Reading is the most basic and most important skill for the education of our children and is my highest priority for our public schools. Therefore, I have identified the funds for a comprehensive reading program aimed at grades 1, 2, and 3 in the total amount of $5.5 million.

"I want to acknowledge the tremendous effort of the Legislative Interim Committee on Reading and the work they have done. Their recommendations must be a part of what you and I, in collaboration with the State Board of Education and the Superintendent of Public Instruction, determine the final product will look like. But the funds are identified and that $5.5 million is to be utilized, and we are to get on with this, so that all children by third grade will be reading at grade-level, and no one, I repeat, no one is left behind.

"...we all have to be working together. If you cannot read by third grade, how can you be successful in the rest of your career in school? You cannot. So this is a priority.

"I have acknowledged that teaching is a calling. To some, when you suggest a financial incentive, they would say, 'That's their job. That's what they are supposed to be doing.' I appreciate that. But I also believe in the principles of good competition and reward. So, I am recommending good financial incentives for those teachers and schools that become the models of successful reading programs. I will also recommend financial incentives for teachers who attain national certification."

Illinois

Governor George Ryan

"Third—reading. Back to basics. We are talking about literacy. The first step on any path to opportunity. My budget asks that we increase reading grants by

$10 million and early childhood and summer bridge programs by $16 million. No child will be left behind. Our goal should be nothing less than an Illinois where, by the end of the third grade, every child can read at that level."

Indiana

Governor Frank O'Bannon

"Full-day kindergarten, reading by third grade, school security, and expanded school report cards and accountability. All necessary investments to ensure that the first generation of the new millennium is the best educated in Hoosier history.

"Now, elementary school will always pose special challenges for some students, even when they are well prepared. What happens to children who need extra help learning to read? Unfortunately, we know what happens to those who do not get help. Right now, nearly one-third of all third-graders cannot pass the ISTEP Plus reading test. That is an appalling statistic. And a poor reader at age 8 is more likely to drop out by 16. Tonight, I ask your support for a comprehensive, statewide reading assessment to find, and assist, those second-graders who need more help."

Maryland

Governor Parris Glendening

"...it is just common sense that the best way to ensure our children master the basics of reading and math is to increase the amount of individual attention they receive in these core subjects. And that is why we will reduce class size for reading in first and second grade and for math in seventh grade. Our formula for continuing to improve education is simple: more classrooms, plus additional, qualified, certified teachers, equals smaller class size. And smaller class size for early reading and math means a better education for every child.

"In order to make this journey successful, we must ensure the best possible beginning. Mastering the fundamentals of reading and math is critical to success in education."

Michigan

Governor John Engler

"...I propose, for all Michigan high school graduates who master reading, writing, math, and science, that we reward your achievement. Each of you will receive a Michigan Merit Award—a $2,500 scholarship that can be used for further study at a Michigan school of your choice. It is important we reward students who play by the rules, study hard, achieve on their tests, and meet high standards. And we should inspire even more to raise their performance. You are Michigan's future, and we will invest in you.

"I have a message for students in those critical middle school years. Your studies are important, too. I further propose that all of you who pass your seventh and eighth-grade MEAP tests in reading, writing, math, and science be awarded $500. Then, when you successfully complete high school, your total Michigan Merit Award will be $3,000. Every student is eligible to participate—every student—whether attending public school, private school, or home school.

"...being Michigan's number one budget priority does little good if our children still cannot read. That is why our reading readiness initiative will be expanded to include summer school. The launch of the READY (Read, Educate, and Develop Youth) program was successful. The goal this year is to make this reading readiness kit available statewide to parents of our young children. The goal of our strategy—for every child to be a good reader no later than the end of third grade. We cannot stress the importance of this enough. If you cannot read, you will not succeed. Yes, reading is fundamental.

"I am grateful to the many volunteers and mentors from all corners of Michigan who have answered the call to help our children read. Their efforts are fulfilling the dream of America's Promise, the volunteer campaign so ably led by General Colin Powell. So tonight, for putting volunteer power to work, helping our children in schools and communities, I salute our volunteers, our Michigan Community Service Commission, and its chair and my favorite appointee—First Lady Michelle Engler."

Oklahoma

Governor Frank Keating

"Let us, more importantly of all, this was a recommendation in our summit, stop social promotion. Cathy and I last year participated with a lot of parents in teaching reading to seniors in high school here in Oklahoma City. Seniors who could not read beyond a fifth-grade level. There were 200 of them. How have we come to this point? We spend $5,000 a year for every one of those students, times 12 years—$60,000 we spend on this youngster who cannot read beyond a fifth-grade level. Stunted for life. It is going to be difficult for that individual or any of these individuals to find productive work. We have to address it."

Rhode Island

Governor Lincoln Almond

"Reading is the gateway to the whole world of knowledge. Reading sets the foundation for academic success. For access in the workplace. For success in all of our endeavors. Tonight, I ask that we focus our energies on the goal that all children be proficient in reading by the fourth grade. We can achieve this objective by working together.

"I will be pushing an aggressive set of initiatives to make this goal a reality. First, we must give teachers the tools they need to help our students meet required reading standards. Teachers must have knowledge of the best practices and approaches to help children learn to read. That is why I am calling for $500,000 targeted to improve professional development in reading. I am also establishing a Teacher Preparation Task Force to help make recommendations on teacher training at the college level with a special emphasis on reading. I am proud to announce that Sally Dowling, who chairs the Board of Higher Education, will head up this task force. I look forward to the many positive results that will come from this effort. We must also enhance funding for reading specialists to assist local school districts with reading programs.

"Additionally, I will be asking the Board of Regents to assure that the strategic improvement plans now required of all school districts include specific plans to strengthen reading skills. The City of Pawtucket has a reading program that has been developed by the school department and the teachers. At the Baldwin School, teachers are training teachers to enhance the way children learn to read. They are focusing on the early grades, and they are also teaming up with parents. We are already seeing the positive results of their efforts. Test scores at Baldwin on reading and writing are up. That is proof positive that creating a development plan for reading has a far-reaching impact upon student performance.

"One of the most rewarding aspects of my job is having the opportunity to visit schools and read to our children. It is fun, and it is enjoyable. It also reminds me of the days when my children were young, and I would read to them. To all parents, let me just say that if you read to your children, they will excel in school. That is a proven fact. In the coming months, Marilyn and I will be promoting a public awareness campaign to encourage parents to inspire their children to become good readers."

South Carolina

Governor Jim Hodges

"Of all the goals I hope to realize during my term in office, nothing would give me greater personal satisfaction than to see our current kindergarten students complete the third grade as good readers. Reading skills form the foundation for all other learning. That foundation must be in place by the end of the early grades. That is why I am proposing a Governor's Institute of Reading. The Institute will bring to South Carolina the nation's leading reading experts, promote reading through grants to local schools, provide the best professional development for reading teachers, and promote a world-class collaborative reading effort. We need to teach our children that the most valuable possession a kid can have is not a new pair of Nike's or a Game Boy—it is a library card."

Utah

Governor Mike Leavitt

"...number one in that [improvement] continuum is reading. While many of our test scores are improving, reading scores in our fourth and fifth grades are declining. They are now below the national average. So we will embark on a program to reverse downward momentum, and we will put it in place early. Eighty percent of all children who have not attained the appropriate reading level by the end of the third grade never catch up. That is a sobering statistic considering that reading is the key to success in every area of learning, and reading failure is almost completely preventable. I propose that every first-, second-, and third-grader be tested. If students are not reading at grade-level, this state should provide them with an additional 30 days of school in summer classes no larger than seven students.

"I propose that every tenth-grade student be given a basic skills exam to test in the areas of reading, writing, math, and technology. Demonstration of these skills must become a prerequisite for receiving a high school diploma. Students who fail can take the exam again in the eleventh grade and again in the twelfth. But if their class graduates and they have not passed, they will not receive a diploma—only a certificate of completion. The door will always be open for a certificate holder to come back at any point to master the basic skills and trade up for a diploma. A diploma must be a meaningful guarantee of competence, not just a verification of attendance.

"In addition to supplementary instruction, I propose dramatic increases in the level of training we provide teachers who teach reading. I recommend age-appropriate materials be provided to assist children who lag behind. And I propose an aggressive campaign to give new parents information so they can help prepare their children for reading long before they start school.... I also call upon our communities to join together in partnership. We need volunteers to go into our schools, take a child by the hand, and help him or her through this stage of critical learning. All will be worth the investment of time and money because the cost of solving our education problems is minuscule compared to the cost of doing nothing."

Virginia

Governor Jim Gilmore

"My budget provides an additional $5.3 million to restore full funding for the Early Reading Initiative. The Early Reading Initiative assesses the literacy needs of children in kindergarten and the first grade and corrects reading problems immediately. This is a solid program that works."

Washington

Governor Gary Locke

"But the most important thing our schools need is us—citizens of our state. Teachers cannot do it all. They need our time, our support, and our consistent involvement. In the past six months, the Washington Reading Corps has begun to make good on the promise of greater parent and citizen involvement in schools all across our state. Today, over 9,000 volunteers have spent time helping 19,788 children master the skill of reading. But many more children who need this help are still not getting it. So I call on all parents and citizens to be more involved in our schools, to help our children learn to read, and to help our schools be the best in the nation.

"It is my passionate belief, as it was the belief of Governor Rogers 100 years ago, that a relentless focus on creating avid readers will do a 'vast and incalculable good' and that it will help to 'raise the character of the future men and women of this state to a higher plane.'"

Wisconsin

Governor Tommy Thompson

"We started talking about education tonight with our newborns, so let us end with our adults. Join me in helping low-income adults learn to read through a new $4 million literacy initiative targeted at low-income families. In America's Education State, everyone should be able to read. Let us make it happen."

RECENTLY ENACTED STATE LAWS

More than 20 states have enacted reading improvement laws since 1996. State timetables for results continue through 2004. Many of these laws focus in the areas of early care and education, assessment and intervention, teacher quality, parental involvement, and extended learning time. The following section summarizes some examples of state legislative activity in reading for children in grade 3 and younger.

Early Care and Education

To provide quality early childhood services, Colorado's Early Education and School Readiness Program funds initiatives to help achieve readiness goals for at-risk children. The funds support accreditation efforts of early childhood care centers and professional development for early childhood teachers and caregivers. Utah, too, is designing programs for childcare centers to work with and train volunteers to create an environment that fosters reading growth. South Carolina's First Steps initiative will provide subsidies for childcare that prepares children to enter school ready to learn.

Early Assessment and Intervention

To ensure that children are reading at grade-level and that schools intervene if they are not, Arizona, Colorado, Connecticut, Idaho, Indiana, Oklahoma, and Texas—to name a few—have enacted legislation to create assessment and intervention programs in the early grades. Ohio established a Fourth-Grade Guarantee to require that students read at grade-level before going on to middle school and high school.

Teacher Quality

To improve teacher performance, some states, including Mississippi, New Hampshire, Virginia, and Washington, have funded teacher development and credentialing programs. California's Commission on Teacher Credentialing is required to gauge the skills and abilities of all reading teachers in the primary grades. In 1999, California launched professional development institutes to provide reading instruction training to 6,000 primary school teachers. South Carolina's Governor's Institute for Reading will offer research-based professional development to kindergarten through third-grade teachers.

Idaho recently required new teachers to pass an exam based on new literacy standards for certification. Idaho also requires kindergarten through eighth-grade teachers to complete three credits in state-approved reading instruction for re-certification every five years.

Parental Involvement

Arizona, Colorado, Oregon, and other states are encouraging parental involvement through programs that teach parents how to help their children in reading. The Texas Reading Initiative directs information and resources to parents, in addition to schools and communities.

Extended Learning Time

A California initiative offers four hours of instruction per day to children in kindergarten through fourth grade when school is not in session, including summertime. Virginia's Literacy Passport requires students who fail literacy tests to receive after-school or summer school instruction. Washington and Ohio sponsor large tutoring programs that match thousands of trained volunteers with elementary school students who need extra help and encouragement.

STATEWIDE EFFORTS

Many statewide programs are tackling the challenges of illiteracy in diverse and creative ways. Here are some examples from across the nation.

Alabama
The Alabama Reading Initiative and Reading Alabama

The Alabama Reading Initiative is a statewide movement that aims to improve reading instruction and achieve 100 percent literacy among students. It targets reading achievement on three fronts: beginning reading, expanding reading power, and effective intervention.

The program began with 600 teachers at Literacy Demonstration Sites, and will expand over a four-year period. Colleges of teacher education serve as trainers and mentors to the sites, providing advanced training to 100 teacher educators.

The school sites agreed to five criteria:

- A goal of 100 percent literacy
- A 10-day faculty training program
- Adjustments in reading instruction
- Modeling effective reading instruction for other schools
- Outside evaluation

The initiative received its first state funding—$6 million—in 1999. The program also receives contributions from businesses, professional organizations, and government. Participating schools are reporting increases in the number of books read and progress among struggling readers.

Contact:

Tony Harris
State of Alabama Department of Education
Gordon Persons Building
P.O. Box 302101
Montgomery, AL 36130-2101
(334) 242-9950
Fax: (334) 242-2101
tharris@sdenet.alsde.edu
www.alsde.edu

Reading Alabama

Reading Alabama is a not-for-profit joint venture whose partners are the executive branch of Alabama State Government, the Alabama state and local school systems, and private industry. One hundred eighty businesses and foundations have joined the effort, contributing $5 million.

Reading Alabama raised matching funds to place Writing to Read, a computer-assisted program, in the majority of Alabama's school systems. State legislators purchased Writing to Read labs for schools in their districts. More than 3,000 teachers have been trained, and nearly 70,000 children have participated.

"Our students' test scores have clearly indicated that reading is our greatest weakness," asserts State Superintendent Ed Richardson. "Only about 23 percent of our students in grades three through eleven read above average. Writing to Read is an effective tool for helping us attack the problem at its root, in the earliest grade levels, and it's a great example of what can happen when all the stakeholders come together to solve a problem."

Contact:

Heather Coleman
State of Alabama Department of Education
Gordon Persons Building
P.O. Box 302101
Montgomery, AL 36130-2101
(334) 242-9700
hcoleman@sdenet.alsde.edu

California
California Reading Initiative and California Reads

The NAEP 1998 Reading Report Card found that 52 percent of California's fourth-graders have little or no mastery of the reading skills needed for grade-level work. The California Reading Initiative, launched in 1996, aims to improve the reading performance of California students in kindergarten through grade 12. The goals are that all students will learn to read at grade-level by the end of third grade and will be able to read and understand grade-level materials through graduation.

The first several years focused primarily on improving the capability of teachers to provide a balanced and comprehensive reading program. More than 90 percent of California's kindergarten through third-grade teachers participated in professional development that focused on the elements of a comprehensive early reading program. Professional development offerings were expanded to teachers of grades four through eight. Training in reading instruction was also offered to primary school teachers who were new to a district, and for teachers who provide reading instruction in grades four through twelve. School and district administrators were encouraged to participate in professional development activities alongside teachers.

Two benchmark documents published by the California Department of Education continue to form the basis for the Initiative. Both documents, *Every Child a Reader*, the report of the Superintendent's Task Force on Reading, and *Teaching Reading*, the Reading Program Advisory, describe a rationale and a research base for a balanced and comprehensive approach to the teaching of early reading. This approach incorporates:

- A strong literature, language, and comprehension program with a balance of oral and written language
- An organized, explicit skills program that includes phonemic awareness, phonics, and decoding skills to address the needs of the emergent reader
- Ongoing diagnosis that informs teaching, and assessment that ensures accountability
- A powerful early intervention program that provides individual tutoring for children at risk of reading failure

Contact:
California Reading Initiative
Reading and Mathematics Policy and Leadership Office
721 Capitol Mall, 4th Floor
Sacramento, CA 95814
(916) 657-5140
www.cde.ca.gov/cilbranch/eltdiv/

California Reads

California Reads is a partnership between the California State Department of Education, the Eisenhower State Grant program and the nonprofit group Books and Beyond. California Reads calls upon tutors, volunteers, and families to support schools and help every child read well and independently by the end of third grade. *Building the Bridge: California Reads* provides a model to help schools develop individual action plans so that every child becomes a reader. It can be used as a schoolwide program, as a grade-level or individual classroom program, and in after-school programs; public libraries; and tutoring programs.

Using a home-school-community approach, with the school as its core, California Reads seeks to:

- Give teachers greater knowledge about current research on reading and writing
- Establish links between teachers, parents, and community members
- Provide parents with a better understanding of how children learn to read and write
- Help parents reinforce classroom instruction in the home
- Provide opportunities for tutors to work for 30-45 minutes a week to support student learning

California Reads focuses on both year-round and summer programs and encourages schools to build community partnerships that support strong interaction between tutors and students.

Contact:
> Books and Beyond
> 309 N. Rios
> Solana Beach, CA 92075
> (619) 755-6319
> Fax: (619) 755-0449
> booksbey@sbsd.sd.k12.ca.us
> www.sbsd.k12.ca.us/sbsd/specialprog/BB/calreads.html

Connecticut
Summer Reading Challenge and Early Reading Success

Since 1996, the State of Connecticut has made reading improvement in the early grades a top priority, including a coordinated campaign to boost community involvement and the commitment of state financial resources. Connecticut fourth-graders had the highest scores in the nation on the 1998 NAEP reading assessment.

Governor John Rowland's 1998 summer reading program reported a membership of over 100,000 students. The Summer Reading Challenge is underway, with bookmarks, reading journals, posters, book lists and other tools to boost participation. Students are encouraged to use the library, read every day, and talk about what they read with friends and family members.

Early Reading Success grants are made available to schools to fund local efforts to improve reading skills at the kindergarten through third-grade level. School Readiness grants are available to targeted school districts to promote the development of quality preschools and family resource centers. About $2.5 million was invested for 1999. The rationale is simple: starting early can pay big dividends down the road.

The Connecticut Legislature also approved a law requiring each local school district to develop a three-year reading plan to improve the reading skills of students in the early grades.

As the Governor said, "This renewed emphasis on reading is one of the most targeted investments we've made in our schools, and the future of our children, in more than a decade. By emphasizing reading we are acknowledging how important it is to concentrate on the fundamentals to make sure every child in Connecticut develops a solid foundation for life-long learning. A child who can read well at an early age is a child who is prepared to succeed."

Contact:
Thomas Murphy
Connecticut State Department of Education
P.O. Box 2219
Hartford, CT 06145
(860) 566-5677
thomas.murphy@po.state.ct.us
www.state.ct.us/sde

Delaware
Delaware Reading Is Fundamental Initiative
Launched in 1998 by Delaware First Lady Martha S. Carper, the Delaware Reading Is Fundamental (RIF) Initiative aims to bring literacy services and free books to young children and their families. Supported by the state Department of Education, corporations, and foundations, the initiative serves every first-grader in public school and every preschool child enrolled in Head Start, Even Start, or the Parents as Teachers program. Over five years, this statewide, first-in-the-nation project will reach about 80,000 children.

The initiative serves first-graders through RIF's intensive Running Start program. Almost 100 percent of 9,000 first-graders met their reading goals as each child read (or had read to him or her) 30 books in 12 weeks. The preschool program provides reading readiness activities for the classroom and home, read-aloud modeling for parents and caregivers, and children's books to take home. More than 3,500 children received three new books in 1998.

A University of Maryland study of the project found an increase in the quality of first-grade classroom libraries, in students' motivation to read, in students' reading achievement, and in the quality and quantity of home literacy practices.

The second year was launched by Mrs. Carper with community reading rallies, reading recognition programs, public service announcements, and other motivational events.

The First Lady also will lead the spouses of the nation's governors in a national campaign for child literacy for one year.

Contact:

> Peggy Dee
> Delaware Department of Education
> Gifted & Talented, Reading, Service-Learning
> (302) 739-4885, ext. 3110

> Elyse Tipton
> Reading Is Fundamental
> (202) 287-3220
> www.rif.org

Maryland
Maryland Reading Network

During the 1996-1997 school year, a committee of classroom teachers and reading supervisors joined with representatives from institutions of higher education and created a network of professional educators from Maryland's school systems.

The purpose of The Maryland Reading Network is to extend understanding of how reading is learned and to provide models of effective reading programs. Each school system in Maryland selects three participants for their network team: a staff development specialist in reading from the central office level, a school level administrator, and a reading resource or other teacher from the same elementary school.

Each team creates a plan for a balanced reading program at participating elementary schools, which become observation sites for exemplary reading instruction. School-level administrators provide training for all members of the school community regarding the reading program in the school. Central office representatives provide system-wide staff development in reading and provide assistance and support in reading to teachers in participating schools.

Contact:

Dr. Mary Jo Comer
Specialist in Language Arts Assessment
Maryland Reading Network
200 West Baltimore Street
Baltimore, MD 21201
(410) 767-0343
mcomer@msde.state.md.us
www.msde.state.md.us/factsndata/factsheets/fact33.html

North Carolina
Smart Start and Reading Together

North Carolina is one of only five states or jurisdictions that had significant gains in fourth-grade reading skills from 1992-1998, according to the 1998 NAEP Reading Report Card. "North Carolina's schools are making dramatic progress, and our students, our teachers, our educators and our parents deserve the credit," said Governor Jim Hunt. "We're on the right course, because we've kept our focus on what works: making sure our children get a Smart Start, supporting our teachers, making our schools safer, and helping our students achieve their very best."

During his first term as governor, Hunt placed teaching assistants in primary school classrooms to provide more one-on-one instruction in reading. His class size reduction efforts in kindergarten through third grade have allowed for individual instruction in reading and other basic subjects. In 1992, the state revised its elementary and middle school reading curriculum to make it more challenging. North Carolina also implemented an accountability program, the ABCs of Public Education.

The Smart Start project uses early childhood education to enhance the literacy skills of young children before they enter kindergarten. Launched by Gov. Hunt in 1993, Smart Start targets children from birth through age five and their families. It is a locally-driven initiative supported by public and private funds. Studies by the Smart Start Evaluation Team show that children who received Smart Start services were better prepared when they entered school.

Scores on kindergarten assessment tests were higher for children who received Smart Start services. Smart Start has won the Ford Foundation's Innovation in Government Award.

North Carolina also employs other programs, such as Reading Together, which trains fifth-grade students to be reading tutors for first-grade students. The North Carolina Teacher Academy offers professional development in reading and literacy to teachers each summer. The governor's after-school program, SOS (Support Our Students), provides tutoring and mentoring to middle-grade students.

Contact:
> Smart Start/North Carolina Partnership for Children
> 1100 Wake Forest Road, Suite 300
> Raleigh, NC 27604
> (919) 821-7999
> Fax: (919) 821-8050
> www.smartstart-nc.org
>
> Dan Farsaci
> Reading Together
> University of North Carolina at Greensboro
> (336) 334-3480

Ohio
OhioReads

Ohio's Fourth-Grade Guarantee requires all school districts to assess students' reading skills at the end of first, second, and third grades. If students fail, they are offered extra help. Fourth-graders who fail in reading will not be promoted.

The scope of the challenge was laid bare when 53 percent of all fourth-graders failed the reading section of the state proficiency test. So Governor Bob Taft does more than serve as figurehead for the new OhioReads program. He also serves as a weekly tutor for a Columbus third-grader.

Taft has called for a corps of 20,000 volunteer tutors from Ohio businesses, the public sector, service organizations, colleges and universities, senior citizens, parents, and the general community. In 1999, the Ohio legislature unanimously supported $25 million for the OhioReads initiative. In addition to tutor recruitment, funds will support public school needs, such as professional development for teachers and community grants for after-school and summer reading programs.

The private sector was quick to respond to the governor's challenge. The Limited, a clothing retailer based in Columbus, immediately offered $250,000 to help 400 employees tutor kindergarten children in local schools.

Contact:
> Sandy Miller
> OhioReads
> Office of the Governor
> 77 S. High Street, 30th Floor
> Columbus, OH 43215-6117
> (614) 466-0224
> www.ode.ohio.gov/www/ohioreads/ohioreads.html

South Carolina
First Steps, Reading Institute, and Compact with Our Children

South Carolina was one of just 10 states or jurisdictions where fourth-graders showed improvements on the NAEP reading assessments between 1994 and 1998. In 1999, Governor Jim Hodges secured $20 million from the legislature for South Carolina First Steps, an early childhood program. The program aims for all children to enter school healthy and ready to learn.

"Gov. Hodges' First Steps initiative is designed to provide children and their parents with access to high-quality preschool education, parenting education, and family literacy programs," said State School Superintendent Inez Tenenbaum. "It will help our students build the academic foundation they need for success."

Modeled on North Carolina's successful Smart Start program, First Steps will be community-based. It aims to unite state and local agencies, churches, parents, teachers, and businesses to identify and address children's needs.

Hodges also secured funding to continue to lower class size in primary schools so that no kindergarten through third-grade teacher has more than 17 students. The governor's proposal for a new Reading Institute was also approved by the legislature. The Institute will research the best ways to teach reading, provide extensive training for elementary school reading teachers, and monitor results annually.

Hodges is also asking the parents of every South Carolina public school child to sign a new "Compact with Our Children" and at the beginning of each school year. This pledge calls for teachers, parents, and students to share the responsibility for children's education and to live up to high standards.

Parents pledge to:

- Read to young children.
- Encourage older children to read to themselves.
- Provide a quiet, well-lit study area at home.
- Ensure regular and punctual school attendance.
- Provide adequate rest, food, and a healthy environment.
- Support school activities by volunteering, visiting the classroom, and attending parent-teacher conferences.

Contact:

    Jim Ray, Deputy Superintendent
    Division of District and Community Services
    South Carolina Department of Education
    1429 Senate Street
    Columbia, SC 29201
    (803) 734-8492

Texas

Texas Reading Initiative

Texas has made reading a top education priority. The goal is to have all students read at grade-level by the end of third grade and continue to read at grade-level. Governor George W. Bush laid out four steps to achieve this goal: (1) early intervention, (2) resources for help, (3) teacher academies/ professional development, and (4) school accountability.

Currently, schools are required to use a reading inventory to identify whether kindergarten through second-grade students are progressing in reading. Those who fall behind are provided accelerated reading instruction, as well as possible summer school, extended-day programs, or tutorials. Up to $670 in state money is available, per student, to provide accelerated instruction.

Teachers have the opportunity to participate in summer reading seminars that will focus on the science of reading and the methods of instruction for correcting reading problems. Kindergarten teachers began training in the summer of 1999, followed by first-grade teachers in 2000 and second-grade teachers in 2001. The state pays participating teachers a stipend and absorbs $1,200 per teacher in professional development costs.

Third-grade students must pass the reading section of the Texas Assessment of Academic Skills (TAAS) starting in 2003 to be promoted to fourth grade. If a student fails in his or her first attempt, there will be a second opportunity. Upon a second failure, a grade placement committee comprised of the student's parents, teacher, and principal is formed to determine the instruction needed before the third administration of the TAAS. A third failure will result in retainment.

"Children who never master reading will never master learning," said Gov. Bush. "Many will drop out of school. As uneducated adults, they face a life of frustration and failure on the fringes of society. Large numbers turn to crime and wind up in prison. Many others eventually join the welfare rolls. In study after study the empirical evidence is deafening: You cannot succeed if you cannot read."

Contact:

Robin Gilchrist
Assistant Commissioner for Statewide Initiatives
Texas Education Agency
1701 North Congress Avenue
Austin, TX 78701
(512) 463-9027
www.tea.state.tx.us/reading

Utah
Utah Reads and Read to Me

Governor Michael Leavitt launched Utah Reads, a literacy campaign to ensure that all Utah students are reading at grade-level by the end of the third grade. In March 1999, the legislature approved funds for local school districts to develop personalized instruction plans for readers in first through third grades. Funds were also approved for community-based literacy efforts.

Staff development on early literacy success is available to all preschool teachers and child care providers. Professional development for elementary school teachers includes the use of informal tests to assess and monitor students' progress in reading. Utah Reads is training principals on early literacy issues and research-based classroom practices.

A community volunteer tutoring program is being developed with a link to Utah's Promise. The goal is to have 12,000 struggling readers at or above grade-level by the end of third grade. Utah communities are identifying volunteers and training them to tutor children in local schools. In some schools, older students tutor younger children. Utah Reads provides grants for purchases of new books for tutoring sessions.

The Utah reading initiative also promotes family involvement. First Lady Jacalyn Leavitt leads the Read to Me campaign, which aims to help parents understand the importance of reading aloud to their children. Public service announcements will be broadcast, and a literacy resource kit will be given to parents of newborns.

"This is the cornerstone of my budget," Leavitt said. "I've made a decision to make literacy one of my highest priorities as governor. Reading is the most fundamental skill for success in learning. Literacy is not just a school or government responsibility. It starts with parents at home."

Contact:
> Dr. Janice Dole
> Utah Reads
> Utah State Office of Education
> (801) 538-7823
> jdole@usoe.k12.ut.us
>
> Read to Me
> (877) ALL-READ
> www.governor.state.ut.us/firstlady

Vermont
Vermont Parent/Child Centers

The Vermont Parent/Child Centers are a network of sixteen community-based, non-profit organizations serving all of Vermont. The focus of each Center is to provide support and education to 15,000 families with very young children. The goal is to give families a healthy start and act to prevent problems such as illiteracy. Services include home visits, early childhood services, parent education, parent support, on site services, playgroups, information and referral, and community development.

Centers work with Head Start, chambers of commerce, health care providers, state agencies, literacy programs, and others. They serve a primarily rural population. The Addison County Parent/Child Center works to build school readiness in babies, toddlers and preschoolers through playgroups, story hours, and bookmobiles. Playgroups are available to disabled children in mainstream settings.

Home visits allow Center staff to help parents learn activities to stimulate their young children's development. A focus on family literacy allows the Center to help a whole family by improving a parent's reading skills.

Contact:

Sue Harding
Addison County Parent/Child Center
P.O. Box 646
Middlebury, VT 05753
(802) 388-3171
acpcc@sover.net
www.sover.net/~acpcc/index.html

Washington
Washington Reading Corps

Governor Gary Locke launched the Washington Reading Corps in 1998 with an $8 million budget from the state legislature. With more than 11,000 volunteer tutors, the Washington Reading Corps has helped 22,000 elementary students improve their reading skills. Nearly 200 schools now participate. The programs also use AmeriCorps and VISTA volunteers who tutor children and work with the community.

Locke created the Reading Corps in response to the low number of students (48 percent) who met the fourth-grade reading standard on the first Washington Assessment of Student Learning in 1997. In 1998, nearly 56 percent of fourth-grade students met the reading standard. In 1999, the legislature indicated its approval by fully funding the program for two years.

"While the test scores are on the rise, we still have a long way to go," Locke said. "The Reading Corps is working, and we must continue to support its goal to help every student become a good reader.

"We need to bring together children who are learning to sound out words with volunteers who will listen to them and praise them when they do it right," Locke said. "That's how a lifetime of success gets started, and how a lifetime of failure and frustration is averted."

Nearly $100,000 in private donations to the Reading Corps purchased books for low-income children to practice reading at home. A private donation of $100,000 helped sponsor a statewide conference in September 1999 at the University of Washington. The conference focused on reading and tutoring approaches, volunteerism, and community involvement.

Contact:
Washington Reading Corps
515 15th Avenue, Southeast
P.O. Box 43134
Olympia, WA 98504-3134
(800) 323-2550
(360) 902-0653
Fax: (360) 902-0414
http://www.readingcorps.wa.gov
www.readingcorps.wa.gov

Wisconsin
Mother Goose, Family Literacy, and Library Outreach

Championed by Governor Tommy Thompson and First Lady Sue Ann Thompson, the state of Wisconsin began to widely distribute baby books in September 1998. Up to 70,000 newborns are receiving a copy of "My First Little Mother Goose" from Wisconsin publisher Golden Books. The next phase of the project will include older babies and toddlers who have been adopted.

Mrs. Thompson was instrumental in the creation of the Governor's Office for Family Literacy, a program aimed at organizing and coordinating all resources in order to reach more people and more families. An avid reader and former elementary school teacher, Mrs. Thompson promotes reading to children at least 15 minutes a day before the age of five.

Under a Wisconsin grant program, librarians are reaching out to promote a love of reading. Librarians use small grants—from $500 to $1000—to offer new literacy opportunities to preschoolers in child care. Libraries purchase new sets of books for rotation among child care homes and centers. Library outreach workers visit sites for special story hours, to engage children, and to model reading aloud for caregivers. Other libraries offer workshops for child care providers on how to read with young children and develop emergent literacy skills.

Contact:
Barbara Manthei, Director
Literacy and Lifelong Learning
State of Wisconsin
(608) 266-9709
barbara.manthei@gov.state.wi.us

CHAPTER 16

Local Efforts

Local communities are expanding their efforts to improve children's reading abilities. Popular grassroots initiatives include summer reading programs, book drives, tutoring sessions, and events featuring professional sports teams. Here are some examples of local literacy projects.

Baltimore

SuperKids Camp and Baltimore Reads

In Baltimore, Mayor Kurt L. Schmoke created a 1998 summer reading camp that linked the city library, *The Baltimore Sun* newspaper, the Ravens football team, and other organizations. Team Read '98 got 9,400 children to read nearly 58,000 books over the summer and gave Ravens souvenirs as prizes. SuperKids Camp, America Reads, Summer VISTA, Baltimore READS, and Parks and People Foundation involved another thousand third-graders in an intensive summer reading camp.

Baltimore continues its partnership with SuperKids Camp to reach 3,000 children in 1999. Another 1999 summer reading camp is run as a partnership between The Village Learning Center, Baltimore READS Reading Edge, and the Margaret Brent Elementary School.

The city is also partnered with the Enoch Pratt Free Library. Young summer readers who read at least eight books will receive fun prizes.

Contact:
    Maggi Gaines, Director
    Baltimore READS
    5 East Read Street
    Baltimore, MD 21202
    (410) 752-3595
    contact@baltimorereads.org
    www.baltimorereads.org

Birmingham
Birmingham R.E.A.D.S.

In Alabama, Birmingham Public Schools Superintendent Johnny Brown has made reading a priority for all students during the school year and the summer. Teachers, principals, school district office staff, parents, community members, business partners, librarians, college and university partners, religious leaders, city leadership, and employees are all an integral part of Birmingham R.E.A.D.S. Birmingham students from kindergarten through grade twelve are required to participate in 90 minutes of reading daily.

Birmingham students' enthusiasm for reading continues when school is out— Birmingham children read 307,675 books during the summer of 1998. In 1999, more than 5,000 students participated in summer school and 2,500 more were involved in other learning activities such as Camp Birmingham, with ten campsites that focus primarily on reading.

Every schoolchild is provided with an age-appropriate summer reading list of 30 books. Three hundred students ages 14 to 15 received summer jobs to serve as America Reads Challenge Learning Partners. Also, the Birmingham Public Library has partnered with the schools to offer creative summer reading programs.

Contact:
> Dr. Peggy Sparks
> Birmingham Public Schools
> P.O. Box 10007
> Birmingham, AL 35203
> (205) 543-4763
> Fax: (205) 581-5003
>
> Dr. Abbe Boring
> (205) 581-8676
> aboring@bhm.k12.al.us

Boston
ReadBoston

Nearly 50 percent of Boston's third-graders do not read at grade-level. Under the leadership of Mayor Thomas M. Menino and Superintendent Thomas W. Payzant, ReadBoston unites families, schools, and the community to help all Boston's children become able readers by third grade. Support includes research and referral help, workshops, financial assistance, reading tutors, and books for children.

A major thrust of the campaign is to promote more effective reading instruction in elementary schools. The Primary Literacy Project's list of seven essential elements of strong reading programs has been formally adopted by the school system. More than $7 million in new public and private funding has been allocated to improve reading instruction. Reading programs such as Success for All and the Early Learning Literacy Initiative are being implemented in at least 75 percent of the city's elementary schools.

The Boston Public Schools intensified its efforts to promote literacy in 1999. All second-graders at risk of reading failure are attending month-long summer sessions and will receive extra instruction in reading throughout the school year.

ReadBoston's focus has expanded to include family involvement. Home visiting programs, preschools, community agencies, and schools work with Read-Boston to develop practical strategies to engage families in helping their children become ready to read. In 1999, more than 6,000 families participated in home reading programs throughout the city. Recent community initiatives include giving 250,000 new books to children and placing 1,000 volunteers and work-study students in schools and community settings.

Contact:

> Margaret Williams, Executive Director
> ReadBoston
> 43 Hawkins Street
> Boston, MA 02114
> (617) 635-READ or (617) 918-5282
> Fax: (617) 918-5475
> www.cityofboston.com/readboston

Charlotte, North Carolina
Bright Beginnings

Bright Beginnings is a public pre-kindergarten program in North Carolina's Charlotte-Mecklenburg Public Schools. Focused on literacy, the program provides 4-year-olds with a literacy-rich, resource-rich, full-day school experience. Each school day is constructed around four 15-minute literacy circles, where teachers engage children in reading and literacy activities.

The school district has developed its own pre-kindergarten curriculum, content standards, and performance expectations that set high goals for every child. Pre-kindergarten standards have been developed in the areas of social and personal development, language and literacy, mathematical thinking, scientific thinking, social studies, the creative arts, physical development, and technology.

Supported mainly through federal Title I funds, the program currently serves more than 1,900 children. Plans call for reaching all 4,000 children in the school district who need high-quality preschool experiences to get ready for school.

The district collaborates with Head Start, special education, and other public and private partners. All teachers are early childhood specialists with at least a four-year degree, and are certified to teach by the state.

Bright Beginnings serves only eligible children who are selected according to federal funding guidelines. An initial program evaluation shows promising outcomes.

Contact:

Tony Bucci, Ellen Edmonds, or Barbara Pellin
Charlotte-Mecklenburg School District
Bright Beginnings Pre-K Screening Office
401 S. Independence Blvd., Suite 526
Charlotte, NC 20204
(704) 379-7111
www.cms.k12.nc.us/k12/curricul/prek/index.htm

El Paso, Texas
El Paso Collaborative for Academic Excellence

This community-wide effort to raise student achievement is based on the belief that all children can learn, if given the tools and encouragement to do so. Based in El Paso, Texas, the collaborative aims to improve teaching and learning from pre-kindergarten through university.

Two-thirds of children in El Paso schools come from low-income families, and half enter first grade with only limited English, making them high risks for reading failure. Yet in only five years, the achievement gap between White students and Black and Hispanic students has been cut by almost two-thirds.

The collaborative includes businesses, local government, University of Texas-El Paso (UTEP), El Paso Community College, superintendents from three large school districts, and a grassroots organization. This team plays a major role in redesigning and evaluating the University's teacher preparation program and helping provide field experiences for prospective teachers.

UTEP has completely revised its teacher preparation programs. Faculty from the Colleges of Liberal Arts, Science, and Education are jointly involved in teacher preparation.

The College of Education has moved to a clinical, field-based model of teacher preparation, with University students remaining with the same schools for as long as three semesters. The dean of Education likens it to a teaching hospital program. The schools are committed to school reform, redesigning professional development, integrating technology, and building greater outreach to neighborhoods. Most students enrolled in the college and the schools are Hispanic.

Participating schools are given mentors who coach other teachers in improving instruction. UTEP faculty and outside experts offer institutes for school teams in reading, writing, and other core subjects. Technology is introduced early, with every first-grader obtaining an e-mail account. Parent centers offer instruction and engage families.

This project has attracted funding from the U.S. Department of Education, the Texas legislature, The National Science Foundation, The Pew Charitable Trusts, and other private foundations.

Contact:

M. Susana Navarro
Executive Director
The El Paso Collaborative for Academic Excellence
Education Building, Room 413
University of Texas at El Paso
El Paso, Texas 79968
(915) 747-5778
www.epcae.org

Gallup, New Mexico
Al Chinii Baa

Al Chinii Baa, meaning, "For Our Kids " in the Navajo language, is a cross-age tutoring and mentoring program focused on reading skills of kindergarten through third-grade students in the Gallup, New Mexico area. Tutoring is provided by specially trained fourth- through twelfth-graders, parents, and volunteers. In support of the America Reads initiative, Al Chinii Baa has received a three-year grant through Learn and Serve America, part of the Corporation for National Service. The program serves more than 200 students.

Sponsored by the National Indian Youth Leadership Project, those who volunteer also take part in weekend instruction designed to build teamwork through camping, rock climbing, rappeling, canoeing, and other activities. Group sessions also give the volunteers an opportunity to learn and practice the skills needed to tutor in reading, such as how to use puppets in storytelling and literature activities.

Four elementary schools, the junior high and high school in Gallup take part in this program. A teacher at each school, provided with a stipend, is designated as a facilitator.

Contact:
National Indian Youth Leadership Project
814 South Boardman
Gallup, NM 87301-4711
(505) 722-9176
Fax: (505) 722-9794
waldenco@ix.netcom.com
www.cia-g.com/~niylp/index.htm

Houston
Houston READ Commission

The Houston READ Commission is a broad-based coalition of more than one hundred community-based literacy providers and adult education programs. The coalition is united in its efforts to achieve the goal of 100 percent literacy set by Mayor Lee Brown. In addition to adult and family literacy, the Commission is a partner in child literacy efforts through Houston Reads to Lead!, a volunteer initiative involving libraries, churches, the Girl Scouts, community-based organizations, and schools.

The summer program is one of the largest sessions organized each year. During the summer of 1998, Houston Reads to Lead! reached 10,000 children. The Houston Independent School District was the largest partner, implementing the U.S. Department of Education's Read*Write*Now! program in many elementary schools. In 1999, 13,000 children and parents participated.

Houston Reads to Lead! met its goal in 1999 of recruiting 20,000 learning partners, part of a pledge made to America Reads and America's Promise. The city will celebrate with a Summer Festival of Reading sponsored by AMC Theatres and Southwest Bell.

Houston Reads to Lead! 1999 reading season has included WNBA's Most Valuable Player, Cynthia Cooper of the Houston Comets, as its spokesperson. Cooper appears in public service announcements on Houston-area television stations. As Cooper says, "The key to one's ability in life begins with one's ability to read, to acquire knowledge and understanding."

Contact:
Margaret Doughty
Houston READ Commission
5330 Griggs Road, #75

Houston, TX 77021-3715
(713) 845-2551
info@houread.org
www.houread.org

Summer Reading Resources
Houston Independent School District
Jdean@houstonisd.org
http://www.houstonisd.org/read
www.houstonisd.org/read

Miami
FLASH Program for Parents with Limited English

The Families Learning at School & Home (FLASH) Program is designed to assist Florida parents of different languages and cultures. Its twin goals are to build children's literacy skills and get parents more involved in their children's schools.

FLASH targets limited-English-proficient Hispanic and Haitian parents and caregivers of students in kindergarten through grade 6 in Dade and Broward County Public Schools. It is a joint project between the school districts and Florida International University's College of Education.

FLASH has four main strategies. First, it aims to improve the literacy skills of families. Second, it aims to increase their proficiency in English. Third, it gives parents and caregivers specific skills and knowledge to enable them to play a more active role in their children's education. And fourth, FLASH works to improve the academic skills of the parents' children, who are learning English as a second language.

Evaluations of FLASH are encouraging. Parents showed significant gains in knowledge about the school and its functions. Parent involvement in school-related activities increased significantly, including time spent participating in school activities, volunteering at school, and helping children with homework. FLASH was recognized as an Academic Excellence Program in 1995 by the U.S. Department of Education's Office of Bilingual Education and Minority Language Affairs, which helped to fund the program.

Contact:
Dr. Delia C. Garcia, Director
Florida International University
Department of Foundations and Professional Studies
University Park Campus
Miami, FL 33199
(305) 348-2647

Ms. Wally Lyshkov
Assistant Principal
Dade County Public Schools
(305) 385-4255

Morgantown, West Virginia
Energy Express

Energy Express is a six-week summer reading program that seeks to feed the minds and bodies of young children in parts of rural West Virginia. It aims to meet twin challenges: the erosion of skills that makes summertime costly for new readers and the nutritional decline faced by students accustomed to receiving free meals at school.

College students are trained to serve as mentors for children in low-income communities. Mentors provide free books and exciting learning experiences to keep children reading. Activities include shared reading, writing, drawing, and other creative arts projects. The mentors also provide two nutritious meals each day, ensuring that children can focus on feeding their imaginations.

Energy Express partners with AmeriCorps to help support the hundreds of West Virginia college students who serve as mentors. The project focuses on developing strong partnerships at the local level between schools, parents, communities, and state agencies and organizations.

Contact:
Ruthellen Phillips
Energy Express
West Virginia University
407 Knapp Hall, P.O. Box 6031
Morgantown, WV 26506-6031
(304) 293-2694
rphillips@wvu.edu

Nashville
NashvilleREAD

NashvilleREAD targets children from age three through elementary school, with a focus on first through third grades. The mission of this program is to increase the children's reading skills and to support parents and caregivers in helping their children become proficient readers.

In the summer of 1998, NashvilleREAD reached 1,125 preschoolers in Head Start programs and 2,400 elementary school children in Title I learning programs. Public libraries and community centers in Nashville also provide summer reading activities for Nashville children. Partners who read with children 30 minutes each week include community volunteers, parents, AmeriCorps members, and volunteers supplied by Nashville's Reading Coalition members.

NashvilleREAD continued the program in 21 elementary schools during the 1998-99 school year. NashvilleREAD recruited, trained, and placed more than 200 community Reading Partners in the schools to tutor alongside 27 full-time Reading Coaches.

A June 1999 reading rally kicked off the summer reading season in Nashville. NashvilleREAD, the Public Library System, the Public School System and the privately funded STARFISH project teamed up to keep kids reading while school is out of session. National service members of the Summer VISTA and AmeriCorps programs participate. Parents and other adults are recruited and trained to read to children at least 30 minutes per day for seven weeks of summer fun. Three parent education seminars will focus on reading.

Contact:

Carol Thigpin, Executive Director
NashvilleREAD
1701 West End Avenue, Suite 100
Nashville, TN 37203
(615) 255-4982
NashREAD@aol.com
www.nashvilleread.citysearch.com

New Orleans
New Orleans Reads and
Give Yourself a Break, Get a Library Card

New Orleans Reads is a partnership of the Office of Mayor Marc Morial, the New Orleans Public Schools, the New Orleans Enterprise Community and other business and community-based agencies. Many reading programs are active within Orleans Parish, and the City sponsors two extended-day programs. The Extended-Day Reading Intervention Program targets the lowest performing 15 schools in New Orleans and offers six hours of after-school reading intervention per week. The Safe Harbor Program conducts after-school tutorials in language arts and math four days per week in eight Enterprise Community neighborhoods.

Another popular program is the Mayor Marc H. Morial Give Yourself a Break, Get a Library Card program which issued 145,000 library cards to all Orleans Parish residents through their sewer and water bills.

Contact:

Thelma French
Stacy Simms
New Orleans Reads
1300 Perdido Street, Room 2E04
New Orleans, LA 70112
(504) 565-6414
thelmaf@mail.city.new-orleans.la.us
stacys@mail.city.new-orleans.la.us

Philadelphia
Philadelphia Reads, the 100 Book Challenge, and Power Partners

Philadelphia Reads, under the leadership of Mayor Edward Rendell, is a collaborative effort of the School District and the Free Library of Philadelphia. Philadelphia Reads mobilizes individuals, organizations, institutions, community groups, colleges and universities, and communities of faith to provide time, materials, books, and other resources for in-school, after-school, and summer programs.

Philadelphia's the 100 Book Challenge is based on a simple philosophy: "The more kids read, the better they will read." The twin goals are to turn students into independent readers while developing a love for reading.

But the 100 Book Challenge involves more than each child reading 100 books. Teachers meet one-on-one with each child throughout the school year to start at the right level, check their progress, and provide individual instruction. Students read independently in the classroom for at least 45 minutes per day, and at home for at least 15 minutes per day. Children can choose what books they read according to ability, and are given opportunities to write about the books. All Philadelphia libraries carry program materials to encourage participation.

The 100 Book Challenge provides books for more than 200 classrooms throughout the city. Additionally, Philadelphia Reads supports a coalition of more than 75 community-based organizations by offering recruitment of volunteers, training, books, and computers.

The Philadelphia Eagles Football team provides operating funds for The 100 Book Challenge, and other partners include Student Finance Corporation, VISA, Western Union, and First Union Bank.

Five major law firms have begun the Power Partners program with books and weekly tutoring sessions at their offices. Subaru has donated a van for book drive pick-ups—17,000 books have been distributed to schools and community centers.

Philadelphia Reads is the beneficiary of the Starbucks Corporation's new "Out of the Park, Into the Books" program, which provides $5,000 for a designated reading program in each city where slugger Mark McGwire hits a home run.

Contact:
> Marciene Mattleman
> Philadelphia Reads
> Office of the Mayor
> Municipal Services Building
> Suite 1000
> Philadelphia, PA 19102
> (215) 686-4450
> Fax: (215) 686-4466
> philadelphia.reads@phila.gov

San Jose, California
The Gardner Children's Center

For this bustling childcare center, serving children from 6 weeks old through seventh grade, literacy is the foundation of all learning. Each child is read to daily. Lesson plans are based on "Ten Best Books," which each teacher chooses to ensure that all children learn the joy of reading.

Every classroom has a designated reading area, and both pre-kindergarten and school-age children regularly visit the Biblioteca (the Spanish language library) for story hour and book selection. Teachers aim to make visiting the library a lifelong habit.

The Gardner Children's Center also reaches out to families to promote literacy. At orientation, all parents are given a book in their home language and coached on the importance of reading to and with their children. These messages are reinforced at parent conferences twice a year. A family literacy night is celebrated through a partnership with the local public television station.

Also, parents learn to share literacy activities at home with their children in English and Spanish. Children's books are distributed at the annual health fair. At holiday time, every child enrolled in the program, and each sibling, receives at least one book as a gift. The total environment communicates the value and joy of reading.

Contact:
>Frederick Ferrer, Director
>Gardner Children's Center Inc.
>611 Willis Avenue
>San Jose, CA 95125
>(408) 998-1343
>http://www.gardnerchildrens.com
>www.gardnerchildrens.com

Seattle
The Stanford Book Fund

In honor of Seattle's school superintendent, the late John Henry Stanford, the Seattle community rallied to re-supply the school system's libraries. Organized by the Alliance for Education in 1998, the Stanford Book Fund raised $600,000 from more than 2,000 community and business partners to buy a new book for every child in the public school system. This is in addition to $300,000 raised by Stanford himself from private donors for new library books.

The Seattle-based rock group Pearl Jam donated $78,000 from a benefit concert and encouraged radio station promotions that raised even more. The Seattle Sonics and the Washington State Lottery donated $100 for every three-point shot scored by Sonics guard Hersey Hawkins. Other major donors included Microsoft, The Ackerley Group, Boeing, and PEMCO. An anonymous donor gave $100,000.

In 1999, the first delivery of 31,175 books was presented to 100 school libraries. Each book bears a special Stanford Book Fund sticker with its namesake's quote: "The most important gift we can give our children is the gift of reading."

Contact:
>Jacque Coe
>Alliance for Education
>500 Union Street
>Suite 320
>Seattle, WA 98101-2332
>(206) 205-0329
>Fax: (206) 343-0455
>www.alliance4ed.org

CHAPTER 17

Reading: Everybody's Business

The private sector's interest in literacy is clear: it needs a skilled workforce without high costs to train employees. For the newspaper industry or book publishers, a nation of readers is essential for growth. But less traditional businesses also are taking the challenge. Here is a sampling of literacy efforts in the private sector.

7-ELEVEN: PEOPLE WHO READ ACHIEVE

The Southland Corporation's 7-Eleven chain teamed up with PBS television star Wishbone (courtesy of Lyrick Studios) to recruit college students to serve as reading tutors in local schools during the 1998-99 academic year. 7-Eleven is also a sponsor of Wishbone, the educational television show that promotes reading classic literature to elementary school children.

In the summer of 1998, 5,000 7-Eleven stores launched a national campaign, People Who Read Achieve, to raise $1 million for literacy programs and organizations across the country. In the first year, the national campaign raised more than $677,000 and distributed grants to nearly 400 programs and organizations serving 372,000 children and adults. In-store canisters continue to collect donations.

The campaign is an expansion of a pilot program started in 1989 in 7-Eleven stores in North Carolina; Maryland; Virginia; and Washington, DC. In nine years, the stores in those states awarded more than $2 million to some 800 schools, libraries, and other community organizations dedicated to helping people learn to read. 7-Eleven has high hopes for the expansion of this effort to build a nation of readers.

Contact:
Sharon Neal
Southland Corporation/7-Eleven
People Who Read Achieve
Cityplace Center East
2711 North Haskell Avenue
Dallas, TX 75204
(214) 828-7345
www.7-eleven.com/store/community.html

ABC: CHAMPIONS OF QUALITY CHILDCARE

In response to growing demands on working families for child and elder care, 20 major U.S. companies came together in 1992 to form the American Business Collaboration for Quality Dependent Care (ABC). By 1999, the effectiveness of this alliance inspired 100 regional and local businesses to partner with the original "Champions."

At the start, the ABC targeted most of a $27 million investment toward early childhood projects and school-age care. These funds reached 45 communities in 25 states and the District of Columbia. ABC committed to investing an additional $100 million for 1995-2000.

In partnership with a national campaign to raise awareness of the importance of the first three years of life, ABC has supplied 4,000 *I Am Your Child* Provider Kits to family childcare homes, childcare centers, and informal caregivers. Each kit contains a brochure, video, and CD-ROM to aid understanding of how caregivers and families can play a significant role in brain development in the early years of life. (See *I Am Your Child Foundation* at www.iamyourchild.org/.)

In addition, ABC has introduced a popular North Carolina program, T.E.A.C.H. (Teacher Education and Compensation Helps) Early Childhood Project, into Illinois, New York, Florida, Colorado and Pennsylvania. T.E.A.C.H. supports continuing education and increased compensation for childcare workers. Scholarships for college-level training can improve early care and education by enabling teachers to better develop children's pre-literacy and other skills. ABC's support has helped to leverage state and foundation funding for T.E.A.C.H. expansion.

The 20 Champion companies are Aetna, Allstate Insurance Company, American Express, Amoco, AT&T, Chevron, Citibank, Deloitte & Touche, Eastman Kodak, Exxon, GE Capital Services, Hewlett-Packard, IBM, Johnson & Johnson, Lucent Technologies, Mobil, PriceWaterhouseCoopers, Texaco, Texas Instruments, and Xerox.

Contact:
Betty Southwick
Director of Community Development
American Business Collaboration
(800) 447-0543
www.pewtrusts.com/pubs/misc/childcare/child037.cfm

AMC THEATRES: READ FOR THE STARS

Schoolchildren in 23 states and the District of Columbia who read throughout the summer months can benefit from AMC Theatres popular "Read for the Stars" program. Now in its tenth year, Read for the Stars motivates kids to keep reading when school is out. The theatres reward young readers with special "Kids Pak" refreshments each time a child reads three books. Young readers are also eligible for free movie tickets and VIP recognition as Reading Stars in a theatre auditorium. At the end of the summer, readers are invited to theatre parties where drawings are held to win multimedia computers. Organizers estimate that the Read for the Stars program has encouraged kids to read nearly one million books since the program began in 1989.

Contact:
Marjorie Grant
Read for the Stars
AMC Theatres
106 West 14th Street
Kansas City, MO 64141
(816) 221-4000
mgrant@amctheatres.com
www.amctheatres.com/kids/kids_read.html

HAMBLETON-HILL PUBLISHING: JUST OPEN A BOOK

In Tennessee, a local publishing company was the catalyst for a major effort to ensure that all kindergarten through third-grade public school children in the state have a book of their own. Hambleton-Hill Publishing announced its commitment at Governor Don Sundquist's Summit on Tennessee's Children in June 1998.

Hambleton-Hill worked with other Tennessee businesses and nonprofit organizations to distribute 300,000 books to Tennessee public elementary schools on the same day in early 1999. Their motto: "No child should be unable to read for lack of a book."

Contact:
> Van Hill, President
> Hambleton-Hill Publishing
> Just Open a Book
> 1501 County Hospital Road
> Nashville, TN 37218
> (615) 254-2420

PIZZA HUT: BOOK IT!

Pizza Hut's BOOK IT! National Reading Incentive Program rewards young readers with free pizza, along with recognition buttons, stickers, all-star reader medallions, and praise. In its fourteenth year, BOOK IT! enrolls about 22 million students in more than 895,000 classrooms in nearly 56,000 elementary schools in all 50 states.

In addition, Pizza Hut has provided free pizza for any child who completes the U.S. Department of Education's Read*Write*Now! summer activity program, a contribution worth millions of dollars.

Contact:
> BOOK IT! Program
> P.O. Box 2999
> Wichita, KS 67201
> (800) 426-6548
> www.bookitprogram.com

SCHOLASTIC, INC.

Scholastic Inc. has long supported community literacy programs through book donations and a discount book program. At the President's Summit for America's Future in 1996, Scholastic committed to donating more than 1 million books to national, state, and local literacy organizations that support the America Reads Challenge. In 1998, Scholastic exceeded that goal by donating 1.76 million books to programs such as Born to Read, Reach Out and Read, Reading Is Fundamental, Rolling Readers, Jumpstart, Toys for Tots, and First Book, among others.

Through the Sizzling Summer Books program Scholastic distributed 250,000 free books to students in the District of Columbia. Every public elementary school child was allowed to select three age-appropriate Scholastic books for summer reading.

In addition, Scholastic participates in national literacy events such as Read Across America Day. Scholastic offers special discounts, challenge grants, and fundraising packages to assist literacy programs in becoming more self-sufficient.

Contact:

Julie Kreiss
Scholastic Inc.
Literacy Initiatives
(212) 343-6472
jkreiss@scholastic.com

TIME WARNER: TIME TO READ

Time Warner's nonprofit Time to Read is the largest corporate volunteer literacy program in the U. S. Five thousand Time Warner employees and community members volunteer each week to tutor 20,000 children, adolescents, and adults in reading.

With Time to Read, learners use magazines such as *Sports Illustrated for Kids*, *TIME* and *People* to develop lifelong reading and learning strategies that they can use in school, on the job, and at home. By making reading interesting and fun, Time to Read promotes literacy skills that are relevant to the learners' lives. More than 1 million volunteer hours are donated annually in 100 cities, at a cost of $175 per learner, for sponsor, tutor, learner, and training materials.

Every division of Time Warner participates in the program. Home Box Office, Time Inc., Time Warner Cable, Turner Broadcasting System, Warner Bros., and Warner Music Group sponsor programs in their local communities where employees volunteer.

Contact:

Virginia McEnerney
Time to Read
Time Warner Inc.
(212) 484-6404
Fax: (212) 484-6417
www.timewarner.com/ttr

TOYOTA FAMILIES FOR LEARNING PROGRAM

The National Center for Family Literacy works to improve:

- Parents' basic education skills
- Their parenting skills

- Their children's literacy skills and school readiness
- The overall quality of the parent-child relationship

In 1991, Toyota Motor Corporation funded the National Center for Family Literacy to develop programs in 15 U.S. cities and helped build the momentum for future expansion. They found that adults are more likely to stay enrolled at Toyota Families for Learning sites than in adult-focused literacy programs.

When parents stay in the program, both parents and children reap the benefits. According to the Center's studies, children in the Toyota project made gains at least three times greater than expected based on their pre-enrollment rate of development. Changes in language patterns in the home showed enhanced parent/child interaction. They also found a significant increase in family reading activities—an 80 percent increase in reading books and twice as many trips to the library.

In 1999, more than 100 local program sites were directly linked to the Toyota Families for Learning Program. Building on the strength of this project, Toyota has provided funding to start the Toyota Families in Schools Program. Five school districts have received funding to establish comprehensive family literacy programs in elementary schools. The Toyota Families for Schools Program is expected to help 7,000 parents and children gain the basic skills they need.

Contact:

Becky King
National Center for Family Literacy
325 West Main Street, Suite 200
Louisville, KY 40202
(502) 584-1133, ext. 24
ncfl@famlit.org
www.famlit.org

UNITED COLLEGE PLUS: VOLUNTEERS EARN MILES

In 1998, United Airlines joined with America's Promise to develop a recognition program for college students who volunteer as mentors or tutors for young children. Through United College Plus VolunteerMiles program, college students can earn up to 10,000 Mileage Plus Miles annually from United Airlines for volunteer work, such as tutoring an student in reading. United estimates that this has the potential to create one million hours of volunteer time for organizations such as America Reads.

Contact:
> United VolunteerMiles
> cservice@collegeplus.com
> www.collegeplus.com

GOOD SPORTS

Sports franchises across America are actively supporting children's reading. These creative and highly motivational projects are inspiring thousands of children with the message that reading is important to their futures. Here are some examples of good sports. Other examples may be found under Baltimore READS (Ravens), Houston READ Commission (Comets' Cynthia Cooper), Newspapers Association of America (Grant Hill), Philadelphia Reads (Eagles), Read Across America Day (Shaquille O'Neal), and Seattle (Sonics' Hersey Hawkins).

Individual Leadership

As individuals, sports heroes such as basketball player Grant Hill of the Detroit Pistons, football player John Elway of the Denver Broncos, basketball player Nikki McCrae of the Washington Mystics, and baseball player Cal Ripken Jr. of the Baltimore Orioles all support efforts to improve literacy. Ripken funds multiple literacy efforts and has been known to read with children on the dugout steps in Florida before a spring training game.

Atlanta Hawks: Fast Break for Reading

The Atlanta Hawks basketball team sponsors Fast Break for Reading, a program now in more than 100 schools. Players and dance team members join mascot Harry the Hawk at school assemblies to promote reading. Students who complete the program win tickets and discount vouchers. In 1998, students collectively read 18,500 books, earning 2,600 tickets valued at $92,000.

Contact:
> Gena Gatewood
> Fast Break for Reading
> (404) 827-3800
> www.NBA.com/hawks

Kansas City's 3 Rs Project

College basketball stars also are doing their part to encourage children to read, through Kansas City's 3 Rs Project (Reinforcing Reading and wRiting) and through the Big 12 Conference Women's Basketball Win for KC Reading Challenge.

Students in kindergarten through second grade participate in the 3Rs Project's Saturday reading partner program. Free tickets to the Opening Round of the Big 12 Conference Women's Basketball Tournament, recognition at basketball games as a "Successful Participant in the Reading Challenge," and special celebrity reading sessions are a few of the incentives for students who attend at least six of the Saturday sessions. Third- through eighth-grade students receive prizes for reading at least twelve books during a three-month period. Reading Challenge programs are planned for the other cities of the Big 12 Conference members.

Contact:
> The 3 Rs Project
> Kansas City, MO
> (816) 418-7522

LA Dodgers and Pacific Bell

Pacific Bell and the Los Angeles Dodgers are on the same team, encouraging young children to read. In 1998, Pacific Bell continued its co-sponsorship of a summer reading program operated by the County of Los Angeles Public Library. The program offers children the opportunity to earn tickets to Dodgers games by reading books.

Pacific Bell, with the Library, was also co-creator of the Fiesta Dodgers Essay Contest, an opportunity for youth to read a book in English or Spanish, either based on Hispanic culture or written by an Hispanic author. Students were presented with prizes—including $500 scholarships—at Dodger Stadium in 1998.

In addition, Pacific Bell presented "Bat and Batting Glove Night" at Dodger Stadium where children under 14 were given a free batting glove and a coupon for a bat which could be redeemed at one of 30 participating libraries. Both programs aim to introduce children to the world of public libraries, reading, and baseball.

Contact:
> Dodgers Public Affairs
> Los Angeles, CA
> (323) 224-1435

Roopster Roux and His All-Star Reading Team

The star of the children's book series "The Adventures of Roopster Roux," and his All-Star Reading Team of NBA and WNBA stars, visited 20 cities in 1998 to tout the message that reading is the most important aspect of education. Roopster's adventures center around his ability to read, which saves him from peril. Roopster was joined by A.C. Green of the Dallas Mavericks; Brent Barry of the Miami Heat; Cynthia Cooper of the Houston Comets; and Tammi Reiss of the Utah Starzz.

Parents, children, and families must read more and learn to love reading. With sponsor Wal-Mart, Roopster traveled the country with his reading message.

Contact:
> Eva Hall
> 12600 Bissonnet, Suite A-455
> Houston, TX 70099
> (281) 498-8120
> www.roopsterroux.com

CIVIC JOURNALISM FROM COAST TO COAST

America's newspapers are playing a major role in creating a nation of readers. Many newspapers are actively supporting reading improvement. Some provide special sections for parents and kids, staff coordinators, and school liaisons, or Internet sites and programs for young readers. *The St. Petersburg Times* consults directly with young readers about topics for its weekly sports page called "Short Stops." Here are examples of what newspapers can do to help more children learn to read.

Times Mirror

The Baltimore Sun and *The Los Angeles Times*, both published by media giant Times Mirror Company, are pacesetters for regional daily newspapers. Led by CEO Mark Willes, both papers are taking a comprehensive approach to stubborn child literacy rates in their home areas. As Willes has stated, "Failure to teach our children to read is a catastrophe of epic proportions. But it is not inevitable. We can, in fact, teach them to read, and to read well, and shame on us if we don't."

The Baltimore Sun's **Reading by 9**

The Sun's campaign is a five-year, comprehensive community service program that seeks to inspire a measurable increase in the percentage of nine-year-olds who are able to read at, or above, third-grade level. *The Sun* has dramatically increased news, editorial, and feature coverage on child literacy issues, including an interactive section for parents and children to read together and daily sections for elementary school children to read to themselves. More than 150 *Sun* employees tutor struggling readers in Baltimore City schools, donating 5,000 to 10,000 hours per year.

The Sun also recognizes reading success through an awards program for parents, students, teachers, schools, and librarians. The paper partners with libraries, bookstores, and the local media to sponsor book fairs, book giveaway programs, and a summer reading club. *The Sun's* Newspapers in Education program provides more newspapers to schools for use in the classroom.

Contact:
    Luwanda Jenkins, Program Coordinator
    The Baltimore Sun
    Reading by 9
    (410) 332-6098
    Carol Dreyfuss, Public Relations Coordinator
    (410) 332-6047
    www.baltimoresun.com/readingby9/

The Los Angeles Times' **Reading by 9**

The majority of third-graders in Southern California read below grade-level. *The Los Angeles Times* announced its five-year Reading by 9 campaign that seeks to help 1 million children in the five-county area of greater Los Angeles achieve grade-level reading. *The Times'* extraordinary commitment will involve virtually every division of the company, as well as community, business, civic groups, media partners, and literacy groups. *The Times* estimates it will invest more than $100 million in the effort.

In partnership with the U.S. Department of Education, *The Los Angeles Times* is publishing hundreds of thousands of copies of The Compact for Reading, a guide and activity kit to link families and schools to improve student reading. The publication will be widely distributed.

Reading by 9 aims to have 6,000 trained reading tutors and literacy volunteers helping children in schools across Southern California. The campaign will donate 1 million new books to kindergarten through third-grade classrooms. A broadcast and print public service campaign will promote the importance of reading.

Partners include Bank of America, Sun America, Univision Communications, KLVE radio, Rotary International, Harley-Davidson/Love Ride, La Opinion, Rolling Readers USA, and the Screen Actors Guild.

Contact:
> Jan Berk
> Los Angeles Times
> Reading by 9
> Times Mirror Square
> Los Angeles, CA 90053
> (877) READBY9
> (213) 237-3039
> Readingby9@latimes.com
> www.latimes.com/readingby9

Newspaper Association of America's Newspapers in Education

More than 700 Newspapers in Education projects are cultivating young readers through the Newspaper Association of America Foundation. Two hundred and eighty newspapers circulated a supplement promoting family literacy called "Reading Knows No Limits" to 50 million readers in 1998. The eighth annual literacy supplement, "Discover the World with Reading" was issued in observance of International Literacy Day in September 1999.

The Foundation has also sponsored a popular advertising campaign featuring role models, such as basketball player Grant Hill, who encourage kids to read the newspaper. According to the Foundation, imaginative serials of high interest to children, such as *Hank the Cowdog*, are boosting the numbers of school-children who read the newspaper.

Contact:
> Jim Abbott
> Manager, Education Programs
> Newspaper Association of America Foundation
> 1921 Gallows Road, Suite 600
> Vienna, VA 22182
> (703) 902-1730
> www.naa.org/foundation/index.html

USA TODAY Education

Every day in more than 25,000 classrooms, educators and students read the daily news in *USA TODAY*. The *USA TODAY* Education Experience has developed a comprehensive program that involves moral reasoning, critical thinking, problem solving, and judgment.

USA TODAY Education includes Experience TODAY, a guide to people, places, and events that shape the world. This four-page, daily lesson guide is available online and is also delivered daily to schools with their newspapers. The guide stimulates lively discussions in the classroom. Monthly themes include Careers, Diversity, Technology, Environment, Self-Esteem, Family, Problem Solving, Responsibility, Teamwork, Nutrition/Health/Fitness, Leadership, and Conflict Resolution.

In collaboration with the U.S. Department of Education, *USA TODAY* sponsors a Web site to engage parents, citizens, and educators in promising ways to improve learning and strengthen schools through the Partnership for Family Involvement in Education.

In addition, educator training is offered at no cost by *USA TODAY* National Faculty. *USA TODAY*'s online interactive connection helps educators see what other teachers across the country are doing, and helps students interact with *USA TODAY* reporters online. Students may submit book reviews they've written for publication on the *USA TODAY* Web site.

Contact:
> USA TODAY Education
> 1000 Wilson Boulevard
> Arlington, VA 22229
> (800) 757-TEACH, ext. 675
> www.usatoday.com/educate/home.htm

CHAPTER 18

The Nonprofits:
A Pro-Literacy Tradition

Hundreds of nonprofit organizations are working throughout the United States to help children read well. Nonprofit organizations are providing tutors for children, organizing book drives, and assisting teachers to instill the love of reading in children. Here is a sample of these efforts.

THE ARTS EDUCATION PARTNERSHIP

The Arts Education Partnership, representing more than 100 national organizations, researched the role of the arts in early childhood. The study sought to identify the best kinds of experiences for babies, toddlers, preschoolers, and young elementary school students to build cognitive, motor, language, and social-emotional development.

Under the philosophy that play is the business of young children, the partnership study found that the arts engage children in learning, stimulate memory, and facilitate understanding. Role-playing games, poems, songs, rhyming, dramatic storytelling, and other creative arts play can develop language skills and a love of learning.

The partnership's report, *Young Children in the Arts*, includes developmental benchmarks and appropriate arts activities for children from birth to age 8. Parents and adult caregivers are encouraged to use character voices and dramatic gestures when reading or telling stories and to make sock puppets to increase the enjoyment of the tale. Show-and-tell stories can be created with photographs, and young children can pantomime their favorite book characters before a mirror. Older children can write poems and improvise stories with simple costumes.

More arts resources, research, and programs are available through the database of the Wolf Trap Institute for Early Learning Through the Arts at www.wolftrap.org/.

Contact:
Arts Education Partnership
c/o Council of Chief State School Officers
One Massachusetts Avenue, NW
Suite 700
Washington, DC 20001-1431
(202) 236-8693
Fax: 202-408-8076
aep@ccsso.org
aep-arts.org

ASSOCIATION FOR LIBRARY SERVICE TO CHILDREN

The Association for Library Service to Children (ALSC), a division of the American Library Association, serves children from birth to age 14 and their families and caregivers.

ALSC is a major partner with the U.S. Department of Education's America Reads Challenge in promoting summer reading. ALSC helped create the new Read*Write*Now! Activity Poster for kids and Tip Sheet for adults to start a community reading program.

Virtually all of America's 16,000 public libraries have summer reading programs. Over the past 20 years, preschoolers have been added to summer reading efforts through "Read to Me" programs, where children receive recognition for books read to them by parents, older siblings, and caregivers.

Story hours for preschoolers and school-age children flourish in almost every local library. Librarians also offer staff development and training to teachers and childcare workers. ALSC encourages librarians to form partnerships with schools, museums, Head Start centers, health care providers, churches and synagogues, and other community groups. Librarians and community health centers are reaching out to new and expectant parents on the importance of reading daily to their child through national programs like Born to Read.

ALSC is also a partner with many public television programs that promote reading and literacy.

Contact:
Susan Roman
Executive Director
American Library Association
Association for Library Service to Children

50 East Huron Street
Chicago, IL 60611-2795
(800) 545-2433, ext. 2162
Born to Read
(800) 545-2433, ext. 1398
www.ala.org/alsc

CARTOONISTS FOR LITERACY

Cartoonists Across America & The World uses its members' artistic talents to promote literacy among children. Artists have painted murals on reading in 49 states and many different countries, often painting in shopping malls, on walls and billboards, buses, trucks and vans, bookmobiles, and a 53-foot truck trailer in front of the Library of Congress. The Library's Center for the Book was a sponsor of the 1999–2000 campaign, "Building a World of Readers, Artists and Dreamers."

Artists also write and illustrate books and comic books to encourage reading. The aim is to entice children away from television and into the world of art, books, and music.

Contact:
Phil Yeh
Cartoonists Across America
P.O. Box 670
Lompoc, CA 93438
(805) 735-5134
Fax: (805) 735-7542
philyeh@gte.net
www.wingedtiger.com

CENTER FOR THE STUDY OF BOOKS IN SPANISH

The San Marcos campus of California State University hosts the Center for the Study of Books in Spanish for Children and Adolescents. The center aims to help more children develop an early love of reading and to become lifelong readers. The center offers workshops and publications, and boasts an 80,000-volume lending library of children's books in Spanish, believed to be the world's largest collection of its kind. The library also includes books in English on Latino culture.

The center offers a free searchable database of 5,000 recommended books in Spanish from publishers around the world. To assist Spanish-speaking parents and others, information on each book is provided in Spanish as well as in English, including subject headings, grade-level, bibliography, and brief descriptions.

Contact:
Dr. Isabel Schon
Center for the Study of Books in Spanish for Children and Adolescents
California State University San Marcos
San Marcos, California 92096-0001
(760) 750-4070
Fax: (760) 750-4073
ischon@mailhost1.csusm.edu
www.csusm.edu/campus_centers/csb

CHILD CARE READS

Child Care READS is a new national campaign that introduces literacy development to nurturing childcare programs for young children. Childcare providers are trained to develop appropriate language and literacy skills. The caregivers then use a wide variety of books to read to children during the day and encourage parents to build skills at home.

Child Care READS also promotes after-school and summer reading programs for school-aged children. While the campaign focuses its efforts on the childcare setting, it also engages libraries, organizations, businesses, and the community to help all children become competent readers.

Contact:
Laurie Miller
Child Care READS
330 7th Avenue, 14th Floor
New York, NY 10001
(212) 239-0138

EVERYBODY WINS!

Arthur Tannenbaum, a retired New York executive, had a simple idea—why couldn't adults take time to read with children one-on-one during their lunch hours? Through Everybody Wins!, the foundation he started in 1989, office workers, police officers, executives, and Members of Congress are now doing just that.

Adult volunteers spend one hour per week reading for pleasure with an individual child. A school coordinator manages the volunteers and schedules the reading time with the child, often during what Everybody Wins! calls the "Power Lunch."

Everybody Wins! has 2,100 volunteers from 70 organizations serving 1,800 students in the New York-New Jersey-Connecticut area, and a total of 4,500 volunteers nationally, including ten United States Senators.

Contact:

> Everybody Wins!
> 350 Broadway Suite 500
> New York, NY 10013
> (212) 219-9940
> Fax: (212) 219-9917

FAMILY PLACE LIBRARY

Family Place Library is a national project operating programs in six communities. The Family Place Library in Centereach, New York recruits parents and child care providers to bring young children to the library for learning fun, beginning at birth. The Children's Services Department serves children from infancy through eighth grade, and their parents and professional caregivers. It offers abundant programming for pre-readers in early childhood. The schedule is chock-full of fun events and learning opportunities that involve singing, dancing, nursery rhymes, computers, math, science, and of course, reading.

This library also provides Storytime Kits for parents and child care providers to use in their homes. The kits include books, videos, puzzles, puppets, and activities. Educational toys, including adaptive toys for children with disabilities, are also loaned to families and caregivers.

This program offers learning opportunities based on family strengths, cultures, and interests. The Family Place Library, a joint venture between New York's Middle Country Public Library and Libraries for the Future, is funded by the Hasbro Children's Foundation.

Contact:

> Sandy Feinberg
> Middle Country Public Library
> (516) 585-9393, ext. 200
> Feinberg@mcpl.lib.ny.us
> www.mcpl.lib.ny.us

Libraries for the Future 121 W. 27th St., Ste. 1102
New York, NY 10001
800-542-1918
(212) 352-2300

FIRST BOOK

First Book's primary objective is to distribute books to children participating in community-based tutoring, mentoring, child development, and family literacy settings. First Book works through its network of volunteer-led Local Advisory Boards, which are responsible for navigating First Book activities at the community level. First Book also works with national literacy partners such as America Reads to provide new books to children most in need.

Since the organization's beginning in 1992, First Book has provided more than 4.5 million new books to hundreds of thousands of children nationwide. In 1998 alone, First Book distributed more than 2.4 million books. First Book is active in more than 215 communities throughout the 50 states and the District of Columbia.

In 1999, First Book launched Reba's First Book Club, with spokeswoman and entertainer Reba McIntyre. Joining the Club helps others to read, too. When one of McIntyre's recommended books is purchased at any Barnes & Noble store, B. Dalton Bookseller or through the First Book Web site at barnesandnoble.com, 10 percent of the book's price is donated to First Book, to buy new books for children in need.

Contact:

Lynda Lancaster
Vice President of Community Outreach
First Book
1319 F Street NW, Suite 500
Washington, DC 20004
(202) 393-1222
Fax: (202) 628-1258
fbook@aol.org
www.firstbook.org

GIRL SCOUTS: READ TO LEAD

The Girl Scouts are inspiring girls throughout the country to "Read to Lead." Girl Scouts are encouraged to read for pleasure, to learn about prominent women, to write stories and plays, and to volunteer to help younger students with their reading skills.

Southeast Pennsylvania Girl Scout Council runs a multicultural literacy program for girls whose parents are recent Asian immigrants. Through the Girl Scouts' Border Initiative, the Texas Migrant Council is fostering bilingual family literacy in three Girl Scout Council areas. Other states to adopt this initiative are Indiana, Ohio, and Wisconsin.

San Jacinto (Texas) Girl Scout Council continues its Read*Write*Now! program, and held its first Storytelling Institute in partnership with the Benefactory, Inc. Girl Scouts continue to offer community service in partnership with other organizations, including Literacy Volunteers of America's Incredible Reading Rally. The Scouts' Web site, Just for Girls, offers monthly theme activities, authors' biographies, and a new "Girl Scouting in the School Day" kit.

Contact:
Sheila Lewis
Girl Scouts of the USA
420 Fifth Avenue
New York, NY 10018-2798
(212) 852-8076
www.girlscouts.org/girls

HAWAII EDUCATION LITERACY PROJECT (HELP)

The Hawaii Education Literacy Project (HELP) designs free software to promote literacy. Their goal is to use the instruments of technology to multiply the potential of each child to read. The software may be used by educators for one-on-one sessions as well as by independent students.

The HELP Read software supports both English and Hawaiian language and has many features for the beginning reader. For example, it highlights words or sentences while reading, looks up word definitions, allows customizing of reading speed, pitch, and volume, and links to nearly 500 classic works of literature.

Contact:
Christopher Hayden
Hawaii Education Literacy Project
P.O. Box 230
Honolulu, HI 96810-0230
(808) 531-4304
reader@pixi.com
www.pixi.com/~reader1/

HOME INSTRUCTION PROGRAM FOR PRESCHOOL YOUNGSTERS (HIPPY)

HIPPY is a home-based, early intervention program. It assists parents in laying the foundations for their children's success in school. The two- to three-year program for parents targets preschool children ages three, four, and five.

Through home visits, group meetings, role playing, and structured activities, parents are provided the tools and support they need to help their children build school readiness skills. Parents spend approximately 15-20 minutes each day, five days per week, doing HIPPY activities focused on language development, problem solving, and discrimination skills.

Contact:
HIPPY USA
220 East 23rd Street, Suite 300
New York, NY 10010
(212) 532-7730
(888) 35-HIPPY
Fax: (212) 532-7899
www.c3pg.com/hippy.htm

IMAGINATION LIBRARY

The Dollywood Foundation's Imagination Library promotes early learning by encouraging and enabling families to read together. Long committed to dropout prevention, the foundation has responded to research showing that investment in early childhood can build a strong foundation for school success.

Administered by singer and actress Dolly Parton, this innovative program provides free books to families in her home region in Tennessee. Each baby born in Sevier County receives a special locomotive bookcase and a copy of *The Little Engine That Could*. The child then receives a new book each month until he or she begins kindergarten at age 5, for a total library of 60 books. The program has distributed more than 100,000 books to 5,000 pre-kindergarten children.

The Imagination Express, a specially designed train, is driven by The Imagineer, who reads aloud and promotes reading at child care centers and community events throughout the Sevier County region.

Contact:
Madeline Rogero, Executive Director
The Dollywood Foundation
1020 Dollywood Lane
Pigeon Forge, TN 37863
(423) 428-9606
www.dollywood.com/foundation/library.html

INTERNATIONAL READING ASSOCIATION

The International Reading Association is an organization whose members include classroom teachers, administrators, parents, reading specialists, psychologists and students. The Association has more than 90,000 members in 99 countries, and the group issues more than 100 print and non-print publications. The association's professional journals include *The Reading Teacher*, *Reading Research Quarterly*, and *Reading Online*, an electronic literacy journal.

In addition to the energy that the Association puts into published research, the group works to increase the level of literacy for people across the world through enthusiastic promotion of reading.

Contact:
International Reading Association
Public Information Office
800 Barksdale Road
P.O. Box 8139
Newark, DE 19714-8139
(302) 731-1600
Fax: (302) 731-1057
pubinfo@reading.org
www.reading.org

JUMPSTART

Jumpstart recruits college students to help children who are struggling in preschool. The mentors are paired for almost two years with 3- and 4-year-olds in Head Start or other programs for children living in poverty. The Jumpstart mentors work one-on-one with children to teach and reinforce basic academic and social skills.

Jumpstart forms partnerships with early childhood caregivers and involves families in their preschooler's development. The summer program provides an intensive preschool experience for young children during the two months before kindergarten.

Jumpstart serves children in Boston; New Haven, Connecticut; New York City; Washington, DC; Los Angeles; and San Francisco. The program aims to engage 1,000 college students as mentors to reach more than 12,000 children by the year 2000. Mentors may receive stipends or wages through AmeriCorps or the Federal Work-Study program.

Contact:
> Jumpstart
> 93 Summer Street, 2nd Floor
> Boston, MA 02110
> (617) 542-JUMP
> Fax: (617) 542-2557
> www.jstart.org

THE NATIONAL CENTER FOR HEARING ASSESSMENT AND MANAGEMENT

Hearing loss is a significant risk factor for reading difficulties. The National Center for Hearing Assessment and Management (NCHAM) was established in 1995 at Utah State University to promote the earliest possible detection of hearing loss and the best possible techniques for assisting people with hearing loss.

With funding from federal, state, and private sources, the center conducts research, develops training materials, provides training and technical assistance, and disseminates information about early identification and management of hearing loss.

Only 1 in 5 newborns today is screened for hearing impairment. More than 500 hospitals offer these screenings, and five states operate universal hearing screening programs. NCHAM works to build momentum toward universal newborn hearing screening.

Contact:
> Karl White
> NCHAM
> Utah State University
> 2880 Old Main Hall
> Logan, UT 84322

(435) 797-3584
Fax: (435) 797-1448
nchamhelp@coe.usu.edu
www.usu.edu

PARENTS AS TEACHERS

Parents as Teachers (PAT) is an international family education program for parents of children from birth through age 5. Parents learn to become their children's best teachers. Evaluations have shown that PAT children at age 3 have significantly enhanced language, problem-solving, and social development skills. PAT parents read more often to their children and stay involved in their children's education.

The program has four main components: 1) home visits by trained parent educators; 2) group meetings for parents to share successes, concerns, and strategies; 3) developmental screenings to determine early if a child needs assistance; and 4) families' connections with community resources, including lending libraries, diagnostic services, and help for children with special needs.

Contact:
Parents As Teachers National Center
10176 Corporate Square Drive, Suite 230
St. Louis, MO 63132
(314) 432-4330
Fax: (314) 432-8963
www.patnc.org

PHI THETA KAPPA

Phi Theta Kappa, the International Honor Society of the Two-Year College, chose the America Reads Challenge as its service project for 1998-2000. Phi Theta Kappa has thousands of chapters whose members are working in their communities to help all children learn to read. Phi Theta Kappa members serve as tutors, organize book drives, and raise funds for literacy organizations.

For example, Phi Theta Kappans at Tulsa Community College in Oklahoma created the Readers and Leaders series at a local elementary school. Tulsa's mayor, local celebrities, and athletes read children's stories to emphasize the role that reading had played in their successes. The speakers also donated the books to the school library.

Contact:
Jennifer Westbrook
Director of Chapter Programs
Phi Theta Kappa Center for Excellence
1625 Eastover Drive
Jackson, MS 39211
(800) 946-9995, ext. 532
www.ptk.org/sprogram/amreads/amreads_into.htm

PRINCIPALS IN BLUE RIBBON SCHOOLS

Innovative principals across the nation are striving to raise reading achievement for all students in their schools. Some take a school-wide approach by engaging non-teaching staff and teachers from other disciplines. Others are pairing children from different grades to read together. Many are reaching out to parents and the community to support young readers through extended learning time after school and in the home. Creative events and book challenges inspire students and motivate them to read more often. Here are some examples from award-winning Blue Ribbon Schools, compiled by the National Association of Elementary School Principals.

School-Wide Focus

At an elementary school in Cape Coral, Florida, teachers, staff, parents, and peers all serve as reading "teachers." As a supplement to classroom instruction, school-wide activities build reading and writing skills in social studies, science, health, and mathematics. A principal in Washington, Pennsylvania, rescheduled a dozen Title I teachers to reduce class sizes for longer language arts sessions. Many schools are instituting school-wide computer programs and other technology to aid, motivate, and monitor young readers.

Parents

At an elementary school in Boca Raton, Florida, parents support students in friendly competitions between teams to read the most books. Parents are coached to ask comprehension questions about each book before validating its completion, and the local newspaper publishes the pictures of top readers. School murals monitor team progress for all to see. Some schools hold Family Reading Nights each year, with vocabulary word bingo, musical chairs with phonics, computer reading games, and treasure maps for reading comprehension.

Peers

Many schools, such as one in Shreveport, Louisiana, use a "book buddy" system, which pairs an older student with a younger child for extended reading time. This approach can build skills of both learners as it boosts their motivation to read.

Another school in Talladega, Alabama, encourages older students to be "roving readers" by reading aloud before lower grade-level classes to earn certificates of accomplishment. These students build fluency and confidence as they model successful reading for younger pupils.

Community

Schools such as one in Springfield, Illinois, bring tutors into the school for supplemental reading and writing activities. Tutors may be trained through AmeriCorps, senior citizens groups, or colleges in the America Reads work-study program, among others. This approach connects the community at large with young learners who benefit from one-on-one attention to their reading progress. It also provides positive role models for pupils. Some schools, like one in Irmo, South Carolina, partner with the local library to engage elementary students in summer reading with the U.S. Department of Education's free Read*Write*Now! kits.

Fun with Books

A school in Grove City, Pennsylvania, holds an annual event at Halloween, which motivates students to dress up as characters from favorite books and tour senior centers and nursing homes. Teachers also don costumes for this Literacy Parade, which is preceded by oral book reports that develop skills in comprehension and analysis. A Houston, Texas, school uses Scrabble games to build vocabulary. A Coventry, Rhode Island, school sponsors "Reading Month," with a PTA book fair, picnic, presentations of children's original books, and a challenge to choose books over TV. Other principals promise fun rewards for the whole school for exceeding book goals, such as a hot air balloon demonstration, ice cream parties, or seeing the principal eat lunch on the roof.

Contact:

National Association of Elementary School Principals
Best Ideas For Reading from America's Blue Ribbon Schools
Corwin Press
2455 Teller Road
Thousand Oaks, CA 91320

(805) 499-9774
Fax: (800) 4-1-SCHOOL
www.corwinpress.com

REACH OUT AND READ

Developed at Boston City Hospital by Dr. Barry Zuckerman, Reach Out and Read is a national pediatric literacy program that trains pediatricians and volunteers to read aloud to children as part of their well-baby check-ups. The doctors also "prescribe" reading as essential to raising a healthy child from infancy through age 5.

At each check-up, the child is sent home with age-appropriate books, and parents are encouraged to develop the habit of reading with their children. This trailblazing program, with over 350 sites in 45 states, relies on funding from businesses and private foundations, in addition to book donations from publishing companies.

Contact:
Reach Out and Read
Boston Medical Center
One Boston Medical Center Place
South Block High Rise, 5th Floor
Boston, MA 02118
(617) 414-5701
www.reachoutandread.org

READ ACROSS AMERICA DAY

The National Education Association unites millions of Americans through Read Across America Day on March 2, the birthday of beloved children's author Dr. Seuss. On this annual celebration of reading, all citizens are asked to read with a child.

On March 2, 1998, one million teachers, parents, and community leaders put on their *Cat in the Hat* hats and shared favorite stories with ten million children, sending a crystal clear message that reading is important. 1999's celebration sounded an even louder rallying cry: all children will become good readers by the end of third grade. More than 20 million people participated, from sailors on the Navy's U.S.S. Saipan to the Tennessee principal who ate worms after his students read 10,000 books. Celebrities including Kirk Douglas, Shaquille O'Neal, Carly Simon, and Jamie Lee Curtis also donated time for reading to children.

Contact:
National Education Association
Read Across America Day
1201 16th Street, NW
Washington, DC 20036
(202) 822-SEUS
www.nea.org/readacross

READING IS FUNDAMENTAL (RIF)

Reading Is Fundamental (RIF) is the nation's largest nonprofit children's literacy organization, serving 3.5 million children annually at 17,000 locations. In
recent years, RIF's volunteer corps has grown nearly 10 percent, to 240,000.
RIF involves children in reading-related activities, encourages families to participate in their children's education, and enables children to select free books.

RIF partnered with Scholastic Inc. to donate 250,000 books to District of
Columbia schoolchildren for summer 1999 reading. By 2000, RIF was to have
placed 200 million books in the hands and homes of America's children.

Among its many innovative programs, RIF has a partnership with the Mississippi State Department of Health called Healthy Start/Smart Start. Rather
than using candy or tote bags as incentives for immunizations of small children,
state health clinics are distributing books. Every child who is immunized
receives a free book, and any accompanying siblings are also offered a book.
Volunteers read with patients and coach parents on the importance of reading.
Up to 60,000 poor children could be reached annually.

Contact:
Margaret Monsour
RIF Inc.
600 Maryland SW, Suite 600
Washington, DC 20024
(877) RIF-READ
www.rif.org

READING SUCCESS NETWORK

The Reading Success Network is a national network of schools actively pursuing schoolwide change to propel the reading achievement of every student.
Schools join the network and identify a coach, who receives ongoing support,
training, and materials, and participates in a Leadership Forum.

Coaches work with classroom teachers to provide powerful instruction in reading that allows all children to succeed, including those at risk of reading failure. Publications, a Web site, and a listserv support teachers, administrators, and parents at local Reading Success schools.

The Reading Success Network is operated by the U.S. Department of Education's Comprehensive Assistance Centers, a network of 15 regional centers designed to improve teaching and learning for all.

Based in California, the network is aligned with *Every Child a Reader*, the report of the California Reading Task Force, and *Teaching Reading*, the program advisory.

The network promotes:

- A comprehensive and balanced reading approach
- Continuous student monitoring and modification of instruction
- A proven and rigorous early intervention program
- Clear grade-level standards for student progress
- High-quality print and electronic instructional materials
- Reading as a priority of the school and community
- Continuous and ongoing staff development

Contact:

Janie Gates
9300 Imperial Highway, Suite 299
Downey, CA 90242
(562) 922-6482
Henry Mothner
(562) 922-6343
http://www.scac.lacoe.edu

ROLLING READERS

After noting the profound effects of reading aloud to his own son, the late Rolling Readers founder Robert Condon volunteered to read to children in a homeless shelter. Condon recognized how rewarding it was both for him and the children. A letter to "Dear Abby" on this experience exponentially increased the number of Rolling Readers throughout the country. Rolling Readers volunteers now read weekly to thousands of children and distribute books to the children at least three times per year. In 1997-98, 40,000 Rolling Readers served 250,000 children nationwide.

The Read Aloud program allows for collaboration between schools, local businesses and community agencies. Volunteer Readers donate an hour each week to read to a classroom of children. Twice a year, each child in the program is given a complimentary, personalized copy of a quality children's book. In 1998, more than 300,000 books were distributed to disadvantaged children nationwide.

The Tutor USA Program recruits tutors, professionally trains them, and matches tutors with students. It strives to establish, develop, and practice effective one-on-one reading strategies. In partnership with school and community-based site coordinators, tutors form a focal team to enhance child's learning capacity and comprehension of reading.

Contact:
Rolling Readers USA Headquarters
P.O. Box 4827
San Diego, CA 92164-4827
(800) 390-READ
(619) 296-4095
Fax: (619) 296-4099
www.rollingreaders.org

SCREEN ACTORS GUILD BOOKPALS

This organization tapped into its talent bank to bring the joy of reading to children in schools. The Screen Actors Guild Foundation's BookPALS (Performing Artists for Literacy in Schools) utilizes the talents of professional actors who volunteer to read aloud one day a week to children in public elementary schools.

Founded in Los Angeles in 1993 by former *Mission Impossible* television star Barbara Bain, BookPALS is reaching more than 35,000 children each week in more than 825 school classrooms in New York City; Los Angeles; San Francisco; Chicago; San Diego; Phoenix; Seattle; Minneapolis/St. Paul; Denver; Baltimore; Boston; Las Vegas; and Washington, DC.

Contact:
Marcia Smith, Executive Director
Ellen Nathan, National Director
Screen Actors Guild Foundation BookPALS
5757 Wilshire Boulevard
Los Angeles, CA 90036-3600
(323) 549-6709
www.tc.umn.edu/~mcdo0300/

APPENDIX A

How to Start an After-School, Weekend, or Summer Literacy Program

WHAT IS THE AMERICA READS CHALLENGE?

President Clinton proposed the America Reads Challenge in August 1996 to involve every American in helping our children to read well and independently by the end of third grade.

By developing and expanding current community literacy efforts, the America Reads Challenge can help many more children increase their language and reading skills and achievement. Teachers, principals, librarians, literacy organizations, businesses, national service programs, and nonprofits can all play a key role in strengthening learning through after-school, summer, and weekend reading programs. Families can serve as their child's first teacher, and community members can serve as tutors, mentors, and reading partners.

WHAT IS READ*WRITE*NOW!?

READ*WRITE*NOW! is a research-based community reading initiative that encourages students to read and write at least 30 minutes a day for 5 days a week. At least one of those days a week, children read with a learning partner or tutor. Children also learn one new vocabulary word a day and get a library card. This initiative was developed by researchers and practitioners, and is supported by over 75 national education, literacy, community, and religious organizations.

READ*WRITE*NOW! materials for families and caregivers of children from birth through grade 6, as well as free tutoring materials, are available through the Department of Education home page (http://www.ed.gov) and its toll-free 1-800-USA-LEARN number as long as supplies last.

1. Bring together family, school, library, college, and community organizations that have a stake in helping all children read well and independently by the end of third grade.

   Parents, teachers, representatives of existing literacy programs, the local library, nearby colleges and universities, local businesses, area youth service organizations, civic associations, museums, arts and cultural organizations, retired teachers, bookstores, local newspapers, and religious groups can all help.

2. Ask them to join you in starting a local America Reads Challenge: READ*WRITE*NOW! Community Reading Program.

3. Begin planning.

   ■ Ask your local school principal/s to help you identify the number of children who need extra help in reading and writing. Estimate the number of tutors needed for a program. Include children with special needs. Consider tutoring family members who cannot read or have low-level literacy skills. Contact the Corporation for National Service for a list of community service resources dedicated to supporting volunteers and tutoring activities.

   ■ Identify the resources, training, and coordination that will be needed to conduct a program and who can provide those resources. Try to provide for resources that children with special needs require.

   ■ Develop a plan for the project with time lines for starting, implementing, and evaluating it.

4. Launch your America Reads Challenge: READ*WRITE*NOW! Community Reading Project.

   ■ Set up a central point of contact in the community. Identify who will receive calls from the public and get the word out about the project. This could be a 1-800 number at the school, college, or library, serviced by volunteers from the community.

   ■ Identify a community coordinator. The coordinator can be from a school, library, college, or the community. This person should make sure that the work of the project gets done by building partnerships and calling upon the partners to conduct aspects of the program.

   ■ Find safe sites for tutoring that are convenient and inviting to students (including those with special needs) and families, and easily accessible to tutors.

- Ask principals and Title I, Head Start, and reading teachers, as well as parents at PTA and other parent meetings, to identify students that need help.

- Invite teachers and other school staff to provide special support for children with severe difficulties in reading.

- Recruit tutors. Ask parents, principals, teachers, librarians, and local media to help recruit tutors from the community. Use middle and high school students and college work-study students as tutors as well as retirees for young children. Contact your local senior center or Retired and Senior Volunteer Program office to help identify available volunteers in your community. Identify tutors who would be willing to work with children with special needs.

- Screen tutors. Follow local and state procedures for screening and using volunteers.

- Train tutors. Tutors are most effective and successful when they are trained and well coordinated. Work with your local reading teachers, local literacy groups, librarians, neighboring colleges of education, and reading supervisors in your district and state to provide training for tutors. Request assistance from your school district's special education office to provide training for volunteers working with students who have learning difficulties.

- Link students who need help with tutors. Make sure students and tutors know what is expected of them and are supported as needed. Check calendars each week to see what days and time of day tutors and students are meeting and contact them if there are any changes, especially if a back-up tutor is needed for a session. Provide follow-up with students and tutors to see if there are any questions.

- Resolve transportation and other issues that can affect students and tutors.

- Anticipate liability issues. Make sure your host site's liability insurance adequately covers the activities of this project.

- Work with local reading teachers, librarians, and literacy groups to find suitable materials. There are a number of commercial tutoring materials available for this purpose as well as free America Reads Challenge: READ*WRITE*NOW! materials. Master copies of these materials for families, teachers, librarians, and caregivers can be obtained from the U.S. Department of Education's Web site http://www.ed.gov or through the Department's toll-free number 1-800-USA-LEARN, as long as supplies last.

APPENDIX B

Reading Resources

Preventing Reading Difficulties in Young Children

This landmark 1998 report of the National Research Council synthesizes the wealth of research on early reading development. It provides an integrated picture of how reading develops and how reading instruction should proceed. The book includes recommendations for practice, as well as recommendations for further research.

Cost: $35.95
To order: The National Academy Press (800) 624-6242
               www.nas.edu

Starting Out Right: A Guide to Promoting Children's Reading Success

This guide, developed by the National Research Council, explains how children learn to read and how adults can help them. Based on the 1998 National Research Council report *Preventing Reading Difficulties in Young Children*, it provides ideas that parents, educators, policymakers, and others can use to prevent reading difficulties in early childhood and the primary grades.

Cost: $14.95
To order: The National Academy Press (800) 624-6242
               www.nas.edu

The Compact for Reading Guide and School-Home Links Kit

The Guide explains how to develop an effective compact for reading. A compact is a written agreement among families, teachers, principals, and students from kindergarten through third grade. It describes how all partners can help improve the reading skills of all children—including those with disabilities and with limited English proficiency. Tutors and other community members can also be partners in a compact for reading.

The School-Home Links Kit helps implement local reading compacts. Developed by a team of teachers in collaboration with the U.S. Department of Education, this kit includes 100 one-page reading activities for each grade from kindergarten through third. Three to four times every week, teachers can provide these easy-to-use activities to families, which encourages involvement in reading activities and support of school learning.

Cost:	Free
To order:	U.S. Dept. of Education (877) 4ED-PUBS
	www.ed.gov/pubs/CompactforReading/

Read*Write*Now! Poster, Tip Sheet, and Basic Kit

The Read*Write*Now! Activity Poster has a colorful illustration on the front and fun activities for children in kindergarten through grade six on the back. Students may write book reviews for publication on America Reads' Web site. Available in English and Spanish.

Cost:	Free
To order:	U.S. Dept. of Education (877) 4ED-PUBS

The Read*Write*Now! Tip Sheet for Developing a Community Reading Program—for librarians, teachers, camp counselors, and community leaders—offers straightforward suggestions for developing summer or after-school reading programs. Available in English and Spanish.

Cost:	Free
To order:	U.S. Dept. of Education (877) 4ED-PUBS

The Read*Write*Now! Basic Kit, created by reading experts to develop and build language and literacy skills from birth through grade 6, includes fun reading and writing activities, a vocabulary log, and a certificate.

Cost:	Free
To download:	U.S. Dept. of Education
	www.ed.gov/Family/RWN/Activ97/

NAEP 1998 Reading Report Card for the Nation

This report presents the results of the 1998 NAEP national reading assessment of fourth-, eighth-, and twelfth-grade students. Performance is indicated in terms of average scores on a 0-to-500 scale, and percentages of students attaining three achievement levels: *Basic, Proficient,* and *Advanced.* The 1998 results are compared with those in 1994 and 1992. Data for participating states is included.

Cost:	Free
To order:	(877) 4ED-PUBS
	`http://nces.ed.gov/nationsreportcard/`
	`reading/reading.asp`

Checkpoints for Progress in Reading and Writing: For Families and Communities, and For Teachers and Learning Partners

These two booklets provide developmental milestones for children from birth through grade 12 and explain what most children are able to read and write within these periods. Written for parents and community members, and teachers and tutors, the booklets outline necessary skills, suggest books for each age group to read, and offer strategies and resources to assist children.

Cost:	Free
To order:	U.S. Dept. of Education (877) 4ED-PUBS
	`www.ed.gov/americareads/`

Ready*Set*Read Early Childhood Learning Kit

This kit offers families and caregivers ideas on age-appropriate activities that help children learn about language. It includes a growth chart. Available in English and Spanish.

Cost:	Free
To download:	U.S. Dept. of Education
	`www.ed.gov/americareads/RSRkit.html`

Young Children in the Arts: Making Creative Connections

This booklet includes developmental benchmarks and appropriate arts activities for children from birth to age 8.

Cost:	$1.50
To order:	Arts Education Partnership (202) 236-8693
	`aep@ccsso.org`
	`http://aep-arts.org/tfadvoc/taskforces/ecreport.html`

Every Child a Reader

This innovative series of six-page pamphlets, written for teachers and teacher educators, presents summaries of research-based knowledge from a wide variety of sources, including the National Research Council's *Preventing Reading Difficulties in Young Children*. Effective, research-based strategies to implement in any classroom are presented in clear, concise language.

Cost: $10 per set
To order: Center for the Improvement of Early Reading
                  Achievement (CIERA) (734) 647-6940
                  ciera@umich.edu
                  www.ciera.org

Raising a Reader, Raising a Writer

This brochure for parents lays out simple ways to nurture a child into becoming a successful reader. The piece includes the characteristics of good childcare and classroom settings, and what to ask your child's teacher.

Cost: 50 cents each; 100 copies for $10
To order: National Association for the Education of
                  Young Children (800) 424-2640
                  resource_sales@naeyc.org
                  www.naeyc.org

Read With Me: A Guide for Student Volunteers Starting Early Childhood Literacy Programs

This booklet provides guidelines for placing undergraduates as literacy volunteers to work with young children and is based on the Harvard Emerging Literacy Project. The booklet discusses the role of families and communities and includes a summary of brain research, a checklist, and resources.

Cost: Free
To order: (877) 4ED-PUBS
                  www.ed.gov/pubs/ReadWithMe

Helping Your Child Become a Reader

Based on the latest research, this guide for families with children from infancy through age 6 explains how and why to use language skills—talking, listening, reading, and writing—to help children grow into readers. It offers ideas for everyday activities to encourage a child's love of reading.

Cost: Free
To order: U.S. Dept. of Education (202) 219-1556
                  velma_allen@ed.gov

READ*WRITE*NOW! Tutoring Manual

This manual provides the reading tutor with tools and strategies for one-on-one tutoring of school-age in children grades 1 to 6.

196

Cost: Free
To order: Hadassah (212) 303-8042
                `curtis@hadassah.org`
                `www.ed.gov/americareads`

Beginning to Read

This article gives an overview of the critical role that phonological awareness and word recognition play in teaching beginning reading to children with diverse learning needs. It includes tips for teachers.

Cost: Free
To download: `www.ldonline.org/ld_indepth/reading/ericE565.html`

Learning to Read, Reading to Learn Information Kit

The kit provides information for parents and teachers to help children with learning disabilities succeed. It includes a resource guide, a list of principles for learning to read, an article from *American Educator*, and a bibliography.

Cost: Free
To order: U.S. Dept. of Education (877) 4ED-PUBS
                `www.ed.gov/americareads`

On the Road to Reading: A Guide for Community Partners

The guide advises community partners on how to become involved in the America Reads Challenge. It presents a step-by-step process and describes how most children learn to read, how tutors can help young readers, and how community partnerships support the progress of literacy.

Cost: Free
To order: U.S. Dept. of Education (877) 4ED-PUBS
                `www.ed.gov/pubs/RoadtoRead/`

Reading Helpers: A Guide for Training Tutors

This manual outlines 36 hours of preservice and inservice training for tutors working with children from preschool through third grade. Lesson plans, handouts, and an extensive resource list are included. This manual is used with *On the Road to Reading*.

Cost: Free
To order: National Service Resource Center
                `www.etr-associates.org/NSRC/`

Where to Find Inexpensive or Free Children's Books

This brochure lists organizations and publishers to contact about free books and ideas for holding a community book drive.

Cost: Free
To download: LEARNS
                www.nwrel.org/learns/resources/startup/
                inexpensive.html

Even Start: Facilitating Transitions to Kindergarten

This report presents promising strategies for transition to school used by Even Start projects. Even Start is a federal family literacy program for low-income children and adults that focuses on early childhood educational opportunities.

Cost: Free
To order: U.S. Dept. of Education (800) 4ED-PUBS

Guidelines for Tutoring English Language Learners

This brochure lists simple guidelines for tutoring students whose home language is not English. It includes tips for the tutor and links to relevant resources.

Cost: Free
To download: LEARNS
                www.nwrel.org/learns/resources/ell/index.html

Including Your Child

This booklet for parents with special-needs children covers the first eight years of life. It includes helpful suggestions for parents to help them relate to their special-needs children and to find support services for their children and themselves.

Cost: First copy free; $10 each additional
To order: National Library of Education
            (800) 424-1616 (single copies only)
            (202) 512-1800 (multiple copies)

Museums and Learning: A Guide for Family Visits

This guide for parents and teachers of children between the ages of 4 and 12 shows how museums can inspire, inform, and build skills for both classroom and lifelong learning. It is full of helpful suggestions for parents and teachers on how they can make the most of their museum visits for their children.

Cost: Free
To order: U.S. Dept. of Education (877) 4ED-PUBS

Federal Resources for Educational Excellence (FREE)

This on-line directory offers hundreds of educational resources supported by agencies across the U.S. federal government. Topics include language arts, educational technology, math, science, and arts. FREE includes extensive links to Web sites for children's learning.

Cost: Free
To use: U.S. Dept. of Education
              www.ed.gov/free

International Reading Association

The International Reading Association provides a variety of resources for teachers, reading specialists, tutors, researchers, parents, and others concerned about literacy. Topics include balanced reading instruction, tutoring, assessment, classroom discussion strategies, integrated instruction, motivation for reading, and teaching English as a Second Language.

Cost: Varies by product
To order: International Reading Association (302) 731-1600
              www.reading.org/publications

Learning Disabilities Online (LD Online)

This Web site offers easy-to-understand information and resources on learning disabilities, including dyslexia. It is a service of The Learning Project at WETA-TV, in cooperation with the Coordinated Campaign on Learning Disabilities.

Cost: Free
To use: LD Online
              www.ldonline.org

U.S. Department of Education Publications

The U.S. Department of Education publishes a wealth of information for teachers, administrators, policymakers, researchers, parents, students, and others on reading and other educational topics.

Cost: Free
To order: U.S. Dept. of Education
              (800) USA-LEARN for guidance
              (877) 4ED-PUBS to order
              www.ed.gov/pubs

Federal Work-Study Directory

This is a listing of more than 1,100 institutions of higher education that pay literacy tutors and mentors through the Federal Work-Study program. In 2000, every college or university receiving work-study funds will offer a reading tutor program.

Cost:	Free
For contact information:	Corporation for National Service
	(202) 606-5000, ext. 280
	jgale@cns.gov
For summaries	
of some programs:	Federal Work-Study On-line Directory
	www.ed.gov/americareads

Additional Information about America Reads

The toll-free number for comments or questions:
(800) USA-LEARN or (800) 437-0833 (TTY)

The toll-free number for ordering publications:
(877) 4ED-PUBS or (877) 576-7743 (TTY)

America Reads staff may be reached at (202) 401-8888. The fax number is (202) 401-0596.

The America Reads Web site: www.ed.gov/americareads

The America Reads Listserv is a forum for interested parties to ask questions and discuss best practices regarding children and reading. To subscribe, send an e-mail to majordomo@etr-associates.org.

APPENDIX C

Literacy Assistance Resources

America Reads Challenge: READ*WRITE*NOW! Materials

The READ*WRITE*NOW! Basic Kit: A basic literacy kit to get children preschool through grade six and reading partners started. The kit includes an activities book, a vocabulary log, a bookmark, and two certificates. Every public library in the country will have kits.

The Early Childhood Kits READY*SET*READ: Two basic literacy kits—one for parents and one for caregivers to enhance the language skills of young children from birth to age five. Each kit includes an activities book, a growth chart, and a calendar of activities for children.

The READ*WRITE*NOW! Learning Partners Guide: A guide to help tutors and learning partners work with children to develop their reading and writing skills.

The READ*WRITE*NOW! Just Add Kids! Resource Directory: A list of national organizations that can be useful in starting and supporting community reading projects.

Learning to Read, Reading to Learn: A kit for teachers and learning partners to help children with learning disabilities learn to read and become better readers. Each kit includes information about how children learn to read, tips for parents and teachers, a bibliography of early reading instruction, and a resource guide.

Checkpoints for Progress: Developmental milestones that describe the reading and writing skills children should attain by developmental period to show reading readiness or reading on level. Reading examples by grade level are also provided within each developmental period. The checkpoints are divided into two documents—one for families and communities and one for teachers and learning partners.

All of these publications are available on the Internet at `http://www.ed.gov`. For more information on the America Reads Challenge: READ*WRITE* NOW!, call 1-800-USA-LEARN.

Federal Sources of Assistance for Children Birth Through Grade Six

Title I and Even Start

U.S. Department of Education
Compensatory Education Programs
Office of Elementary and Secondary Education
400 Maryland Avenue, SW
Washington, DC 20202-6132

U.S. Department of Education
Office of Educational Research and Improvement
555 New Jersey Avenue, NW
Washington, DC 20208

Head Start

U.S. Department of Health and Human Services
Administration for Children and Families
Office of Public Affairs
370 L'Enfant Promenade, SW
Washington, DC 20202

Child Care Bureau

U.S. Department of Health and Human Services
Administration for Children and Families
Office of Public Affairs
370 L'Enfant Promenade, SW
Washington, DC 20202

Parent Training and Information Systems Program

Office of Special Education Programs
U.S. Department of Education
400 Maryland Avenue, SW
Washington, DC 20202

Additional Sources of Assistance If Your Child Has a Reading or Learning Disability

Office of Special Education Programs

U.S. Department of Education
400 Maryland Avenue, SW
Washington, DC 20202

Learning Disabilities Association of America

4156 Library Road
Pittsburgh, PA 15254
http://www.ldanatl.org

NICHCY

P.O. Box 1492
Washington, DC 20013-1492
http://www.nichcy.org

The National Library Service for the Blind and Physically Handicapped

Library of Congress
1291 Taylor Street, NW
Washington, DC 20542

ERIC Clearinghouse on Disabilities and Gifted Education

The Council for Exceptional Children
1920 Association Drive
Reston, VA 22091

National Association of Developmental Disabilities Councils (NADDC)

1234 Massachusetts Avenue, NW
Suite 103
Washington, DC 20005

National Center for Learning Disabilities
381 Park Avenue South
Suite 1420
New York, NY 10016

Additional Literacy Resources

Corporation for National Service
1201 New York Avenue, NW
Washington, DC 20525
http://www.cns.gov

National Institute for Literacy (NIFL)
800 Connecticut Avenue, NW
Suite 200
Washington, DC 71309-1230
http://www.nifl.gov

Reading Is Fundamental, Inc. (RIF)
Publications Department
Smithsonian Institution
400 Maryland Avenue, SW
Washington, DC 20024
http://www.si.edu/rif

American Library Association (ALA)
50 East Huron Street
Chicago, IL 60611
http://www.ala.org/alsc

International Reading Association
800 Barksdale Road
P.O. Box 8139
Newark, DE 19714-8139

National Center for Family Literacy
Waterfront Plaza
Suite 200
325 West Main Street
Louisville, KY 40202-4251

Summaries of Recent State Laws on Reading for Children in Grade 3 and Younger

1996–June 1999

These are some examples of legislative action being taken by states with regard to reading for children in grade 3 and younger. These examples were compiled primarily through the U.S. Department of Education's Office of Intergovernmental and Interagency Affairs, the Education Commission of the States, and various state education agencies. Readers should keep in mind that in reviewing any particular legal questions, they should consult the underlying state legislation, and that nothing in the following summaries of that legislation reflects the position of the U.S. Department of Education as to the meaning or effect of any state legislation or legal requirement.

Arizona

HB 2130; enacted 5/98
Required that beginning in the 2000-2001 school year, school districts that provide education for kindergarten through third grade shall implement research-based, balanced, comprehensive, language arts instruction, which includes instruction in listening, speaking, reading, and writing. The measure allows parents to select the method of language arts instruction for their child. The bill also changes teacher certification requirements and appropriates $1 million for teacher training, including $25,000 toward the development of a statewide reading curriculum.

HB 2293; enacted 5/98
Makes technical changes to existing requirements regarding pupils who do not meet the literacy and reading comprehension standards set by the Board of Education by providing intensive reading instruction, without instruction in any other subject matter, until the pupil can meet set standards. Requires

intensive reading instruction for pupils who cannot pass an "Arizona Instrument to Measure Standards" test, created by the Board of Education.

SB 1006; enacted 4/99
Appropriated an additional $6,533,500 in FY 2000 and $7,067,300 in FY 2001 to enhance reading programs for students enrolled in grades kindergarten through third grade.

California

AB 1086; The Reading Instruction Development Program; enacted 1997
Extends the multi-faceted California Reading Initiative by establishing two grant programs for inservice training in reading instruction, as follows: 1) grants for inservice training for certificated employees teaching kindergarten and grades 1 through 3, inclusive, and site administrators, and 2) grants for inservice training for certificated employees teaching grades 4 through 8, inclusive, and site administrators. Separate applications are required for kindergarten through third grade and grades 4 through 8.

AB 1178; enacted 9/96
Requires the Commission on Teacher Credentialing to develop, adopt, and administer a reading instruction competence assessment to measure an individual's knowledge, skill, and ability relative to effective reading instruction. Applies to kindergarten through third-grade reading teachers.

AB 3482; Teacher Reading Instruction Development Program; enacted 7/96
Enacts the Teacher Reading Instruction Development Program, which would effectuate legislative intent, expressed in the bill, that each certified teacher of pupils enrolled in kindergarten and grades 1 through 3, inclusive, possess the knowledge and skills to effectively teach pupils to read. Enacts The Comprehensive Reading Leadership Program, which would encourage members of governing boards of school districts and teachers to implement comprehensive reading programs for kindergarten through third grade.

AB 2x; enacted 3/99
Establishes and provides funding, in the amount of $94 million, for six of Governor Davis' initiatives in kindergarten through third grade reading instruction and teacher and principal preparation.

Elementary School Intensive Reading Program. Authorizes local school districts to provide multiple, intensive reading opportunities to students in grades kindergarten through fourth grade. Instruction is to be offered four hours per day for six continuous weeks during the summer or when school is not regularly in session (although instruction may also be offered at other times, including before school, after school, on Saturdays, and during inter-sessions.) Appropriates $75 million for allocation by the Superintendent of Public Instruction to local school districts.

Governor's Reading Award Program. Establishes awards of up to $5,000 per school site, to be distributed by the Secretary of Education based on the number of books read per student. Appropriates $2 million to the Superintendent of Public Instruction for this program.

Public Involvement Reading Campaign. Establishes a reading campaign to promote the message that reading is a key to success in life and the responsibility of all Californians. Appropriates $4 million to the Secretary of Education for this campaign.

Governor's Teacher Scholars Program. Requests that the University of California establish a rigorous teacher preparation program for talented students at the UC-Los Angeles and UC-Berkeley campuses. When fully operational, the program is expected to serve 400 students—200 at each campus. Participants will receive scholarships equivalent to tuition and campus-based resident fees, be required to teach for at least four years in a low-income school, and be required to repay their scholarship assistance if they teach for less than four years. Appropriates $500,000 to the University of California to develop this program (scholarships are to be funded through private donations.)

Governor's Principal Leadership Institute. Requests that the University of California establish a rigorous, two-year administrator preparation program for talented students at the UC-Los Angeles and UC-Berkeley campuses. When fully operational, the program is expected to serve 400 students—200 at each campus. Participants will receive scholarships equivalent to tuition and campus-based resident fees, be required to serve for at least four years in a public school, and be required to repay their scholarship assistance if they serve for less than four years. Appropriates $500,000 to the University of California to develop this program (scholarships are to be funded through private donations.)

California Reading Professional Development Institutes. Requests that the University of California, California State University, and independent colleges and universities provide intensive reading instruction training to kindergarten through third-grade teachers—or those who supervise beginning reading teachers. The program began in 1999 for up to 6,000 participants. Each participant receives a $1,000 stipend. Appropriates $6 million to the University of California to administer this program and $6 million to the Superintendent of Public Instruction to fund the stipends.

Colorado

HB 1139; Colorado Basic Literacy Act; enacted 5/96

A kindergarten reading readiness level is established by State Board. State Board will identify and approve instruments for assessing kindergarten reading readiness and the literacy and reading comprehension level of each pupil in first, second, or third grade. No later than the 1998-99 school year, each district must assess on an annual basis the reading readiness or literacy and reading comprehension level of each pupil enrolled in kindergarten or first, second, or third grade using the state assessment. The bill also outlines an individual literacy plan for each student if literacy falls below the level established by the state. The General Assembly declares that reading is the most important skill to learn in school.

HB 1296; enacted 1998

Creates the Early Education and School Readiness Program to provide funding for programs that advance coordination of early education and school readiness programs at the local level, to help achieve school readiness goals for at-risk children. Grants under the program may be used for the following activities: age-appropriate reading readiness tutoring, which may include parental education programs to further family involvement in reading activities; the purchase of age-appropriate reading readiness materials to serve early childhood programs; grants for nonprofit and for-profit early childhood and education care centers, and family child care homes to become accredited; and grants for early childhood teacher or caregiver professional development.

Connecticut

HB 5657; enacted 5/98

Requires each local or regional board of education to develop and implement a three-year plan to improve the reading skills of students in kindergarten through third grade. The plan must be designed to allow all students to attain the standard of reading competency developed by the Connecticut State Board of Education. Requires the Department of Education to provide technical assistance to local boards.

Idaho

HB 176aa; enacted 3/99

Identifies the Idaho Comprehensive Literacy Plan, adopted in January 1999, as the standard for student achievement in reading for grades kindergarten through third grade. Requires a kindergarten through third-grade reading assessment at least twice annually, with follow-up intervention for students with special needs. Charges the State Department of Education with publicizing the results of the assessments by school and district. States the Legislature's intent that textbooks align with the Idaho Comprehensive Literacy Plan.

HB 177aa; enacted 3/99
Establishes an extended-year reading intervention program for students in kindergarten through third grade who are below grade-level in reading. Provides that the costs of the program, including a transportation allowance, will be reimbursed to the district by the state (subject to an appropriation.)

HB 178aa; enacted 3/99
Establishes a performance-based exam, consistent with the Idaho Comprehensive Literacy Plan, which new teachers must pass to be certified to teach in the state. Requires that kindergarten through eighth grade, special education, and Title I teachers and administrators must complete three credits, or the equivalent, in state-approved reading instruction to be recertified every five years. Creates opportunities for exemptions and "testing out" of the instruction.

Illinois

HB 2887; Reading Improvement Block Grant Program; enacted 2/98
Amends the School Code on the Reading Improvement Block Grant Program (105 ILCS 5/2-3.51). Permits school districts participating in the Reading Improvement Block Program to use assessment methods other than the reading portion of the IGAP tests to measure student reading skills; provides that districts not demonstrating performance progress using an approved assessment method shall not be eligible for subsequent funding until such progress is established.

Indiana

SB 006; Budget Bill; enacted 5/97
Among other provisions, this bill appropriates money for early intervention programs for reading in kindergarten through third grade. Also provides for improving school libraries' printed material for kindergarten through eighth grade. Part of a two-year budget that extended through FY 1998-99.

Iowa

HB 743; enacted 4/99
Provides school districts with resources for kindergarten through third grade early intervention efforts in basic skills instruction, especially reading. Earmarks funding for school districts to reduce class size in kindergarten through third grade to 17 students for every one teacher in basic skills instruction. Allows school districts the flexibility to use the funding to support reading

programs. Requires school districts to notify parents at least twice each school year of the reading progress of individual students. Parents will also be notified of steps taken to improve students' reading ability. Appropriates $100 million over four years for the initiative ($10 million in FY 2000.)

Kentucky

SB 186; enacted 4/98
Establishes the Early Literacy Incentive Fund; provides grants to schools to implement reading models, including phonics instruction; requires the State Board to establish an application process and the criteria for funding grants; requires applicants to allocate matching funds; creates The Collaborative Center for Literacy Development of the University of Kentucky to promote literacy development, including training educators.

Louisiana

HB 2444; Implementation of Reading Programs; enacted 6/97
Requires implementation of reading programs at each public elementary school to teach students to read at grade-level by the end of the first grade and provides for certain reports.

Mississippi

SB 2944; Reading Sufficiency Program; enacted 1998
Directs the State Board of Education to develop and implement a comprehensive Reading Sufficiency Program of Instruction—specifically designed to enable each student to reach the appropriate grade level of reading skills. Likewise, local school districts will be instructed to devise reading plans, including the following elements: additional in-school instruction time; readiness intervention programs; utilization of research-based training methodologies; and professional development for teachers and administrators.

New Hampshire

HB 229; Reading Recovery Training Program; enacted 4/97
Establishes a Reading Recovery Training Program in the Department of Education to provide training to all eligible first-grade teachers.

Ohio

SB 055; Fourth-Grade Guarantee; enacted 8/97
Establishes what has become known as the Fourth-Grade Guarantee to ensure students are reading at least at grade-level before going on to the more

demanding rigors of middle school and then high school. Among other requirements, the Fourth-Grade Guarantee includes: assessing each student at the end of first, second, and third grade to identify those reading below their grade-level; and providing intervention services following third grade, including intensive summer reading programs, to those students who need them.

HB 1; enacted 3/99

Involves recruiting, training, and organizing 20,000 tutors to work one-on-one with students to enhance their reading and comprehension skills. Creates an 11-member OhioReads Council, whose duties include awarding OhioReads grants, evaluating the progress of the initiative, and developing a strategic plan to recruit and train volunteers. Five members are appointed by the governor, one of whom must be a reading specialist and one of whom must represent an Ohio college of education. H.B. 1 abolishes the Council on July 1, 2004.

Establishes the OhioReads Classroom Reading Grants Program and the Ohio-Reads Community Reading Grants Program. Establishes the OhioReads Office, within the State Department of Education, as the fiscal agent for the classroom and community reading grants. Permits recipients of OhioReads grants to request criminal record checks (including fingerprinting) on individuals applying to provide services directly to children. Requires the OhioReads Council, in collaboration with the State Department of Education and the Ohio Board of Regents, to review each university and college approved by the State Board to train teachers. Appropriates $25 million for the initiative.

Oklahoma

HB 2017; Common Education-Literacy Act; enacted 6/97

Beginning with the 1998-99 school year, schools were required to assess all students enrolled in the first and second grades by multiple ongoing assessments for the acquisition of reading skills at that grade-level. Any student who is found not reading at grade-level will be given a reading assessment plan designed to enable the student to acquire the appropriate reading skill. Students who are on an individual education plan, have limited English proficiency, or for whom English is a second language are exempted.

HB 2878; The Reading Sufficiency Act; enacted 6/98

Requires each district to adopt and annually update a district reading plan that outlines how each site will comply with the Reading Sufficiency Act. Its modifications clarify that after-school tutoring does not count toward the 180-school-day-per-year requirement, specify the elements of reading instruction to be included in assessment plans, and call for a Reading Report Card for each elementary site.

South Carolina

HB 3696; enacted 6/99
Appropriates $3 million in initial funding for the Governor's Institute of Reading, which will focus on the reading skills of students in kindergarten through third grade. The Institute will aim to strengthen reading programs statewide by providing expertise in research and techniques, grants to local schools, and professional development for teachers.

HB 3620; enacted 6/99
Provides $20 million for the Governor's First Steps initiative for improving early childhood development. First Steps would prepare children up to age five for kindergarten by providing subsidies to make childcare better and more affordable. It would also provide grants to involve parents in their children's education.

Texas

HB 001; General Appropriations Act; enacted 1997
The budget includes $32 million ($7 million in 1998 and $25 million in 1999) for reading academies—"schools-within-schools" that focus on reading. Also created was the Read to Succeed program for early diagnosis of reading problems in kindergarten through second grade. Read to Succeed will be funded through the sale of special automobile license plates.

HB 107; enacted 6/97
Establishes Texas Education Code 28.006 for reading diagnosis. Among other requirements, the commissioner shall develop recommendations for school districts for administering reading instruments to diagnose student reading proficiency; for training educators in administering the reading instruments; and for applying the results of the instruments to the instructional program. Also, the commissioner is required to adopt a list of diagnostic student reading instruments for which schools may use state funds. Each school district shall administer, at the kindergarten through second grade levels, one of these reading instruments.

Utah

HB 067: Student Assessments of Reading Proficiency; enacted 3/97
Provides for an assessment of emerging and early reading skills of children entering kindergarten and the first grade; provides that school districts make available material to parents to assist in helping their children to master emerging reading skills and early reading skills.

HB 8; enacted 3/99

Appropriates $250,000 to community-based literacy efforts, $150,000 to volunteer training, and $100,000 to the Read to Me education campaign. Governor Leavitt had proposed $10 million for his literacy initiative, including a plan for mandatory extra classroom time for children not reading up to grade-level. Lawmakers passed a revised package.

HB 312; enacted 3/99

Commits $5.2 million to local school districts to develop personalized instruction plans for readers in first through third grades.

Vermont

HB 527; enacted 6/97

Requires the State Board of Education, in collaboration with the Agency of Human Services, to develop a plan for services for early education to ensure that all children will read by the end of third grade and directs public schools to offer early reading instruction as well as intervention when necessary.

Virginia

HB 4001; Appropriations for Virginia Reading Recovery Program; enacted 1998

Appropriates $141,581 to the Virginia Reading Recovery Program. The Virginia Reading Recovery Program was enacted in 1994 for those students identified at risk for reading failure in elementary schools. The purpose is to develop strategies that promote reading and independent learning skills, and better equip teachers to provide reading instruction. The funding is for the 1998-2000 biennium.

HB 1859; Remedial Instructional Programs; enacted 4/97

Requires students who do not pass the literacy tests to obtain the Literacy Passport to participate in summer school or after-school remediation programs; requires School Boards to establish remediation program standards committees, consisting of administrators, teachers, parents, and the community at large.

SB 558; Reading Incentive Grants; enacted 3/98

Establishes the Reading Incentive Grants Program and Fund, to be administered by the Board of Education; incentive grants would be awarded on a competitive basis to public schools demonstrating low pupil academic performance and be used to support successful reading programs, including but not limited to, the Virginia Reading Recovery Program.

HB 426; enacted 5/98
Allows school boards to employ reading specialists for each elementary school; provides that funding for such programs will be apportioned as given in the appropriation act.

Washington

HB 2909; Effective Reading Programs for Elementary Students; enacted 3/96
Directs the Center for the Improvement of Student Learning, or its designee, to develop and implement a process for identifying programs that have been proven to be effective using scientifically valid research in teaching elementary students to read.

SB 2849; enacted in 1998
Focuses on raising reading scores by requiring school boards to set three-year improvement goals for kindergarten through third grade reading. Plans were mandated by 12/15/98, with frequent reports to parents and the media.

SB 6509; Reading Instruction Training Act; enacted in 1998
Provides funds for additional reading instruction opportunities that use tutors in the summer, during breaks, and during school hours. Provides funds for professional development and instructional material for beginning (kindergarten through second-grade) reading programs. Allows schools to apply for staff development, instructional material, and tutoring funds, with priority given to schools with low-scoring students.

SB 5180; enacted 5/99
Appropriated $8,000,000 in FY 2000 and $8,000,000 in FY 2001 for the existing Washington Reading Corps, a volunteer tutoring program.

West Virginia

HB 4306; WV Reads; enacted in 1998
Based on the recommendations of the State Commission on Educational Quality and Equity, establishes a new reading grant program: WV READS (Reading Excellence Accelerates Deserving Students). WV READS specifically targets kindergarten through fourth-grade students who do not perform at a grade-level by prioritizing schools with low test scores. County boards, or a community partner with the county board, are responsible for submitting the grant application, which will be used to fund both summer schools and intensive reading instruction during the regular school year.

CITATIONS

Alexander, K. & Entwisle, D. (1996). *Early Schooling and Inequality: Socio-economic Disparities in Children's Learning.* In Falmer sociology series, ed. J.S. Coleman, 63–79. London: Falmer Press.

Andrews, J. & Mason, J.M. (1986). *How Do Deaf Children Learn about Reading?* American Annals of the Deaf., 131:210–217.

Archibold, R.C. (1998). *Getting Tough on Teachers.* The New York Times, November 1.

Arnold, C. (1997). *Read with Me: A Guide for Student Volunteers Starting Early Childhood Literacy Programs.* Washington, D.C.: U.S. Department of Education, National Institute on Early Childhood Development and Education. ECI 97–9017.

Azer, S. & Eldred, D. (1998). *Training Requirements in Child Care Licensing Regulations,* June. Boston: The Center for Career Development in Early Care and Education, Wheelock College.

Azer, S. & Caprano, K. (1997). *Data on Child Care Licensing.* Boston: The Center for Career Development in Early Care and Education, Wheelock College.

Baker, C., Serpell, R., & Sonnenschen, S. (1995). *Opportunities for Literacy Learning in the Homes of Urban Preschoolers.* In Family Literacy: Connections in Schools and Communities, ed. C.M. Morrow, Newark, Del.: International Reading Association.

Baker, L., Scher, D., & Mackler, K. (1997). *Home and Family Influences on Motivations for Reading.* Educational Psychologist, 32(2):69–82.

BeautyTech. (1999). *State Board Reciprocity.* BeautyTech Online, March 12.

Blakes-Greenway, D. (1994). *Increasing Parental Involvement in the Preschool Program by Offering Alternative Communication Strategies Between Parents and School Staff.* Unpublished practicum, Nova Southern University, Ft. Lauderdale, Fla.

Blank, R., Manise, J., Braithwaite, B., & Langesen, D. (1999). *State Education Indicators with a Focus on Title I, 1998.* Washington, D.C.: Council of Chief State School Officers. February.

Booth, C.L. (1999). *National Institute of Child Health and Human Development Study of Early Child Care*. Paper presented at the symposium of the American Association for the Advancement of Science, Anaheim, Calif.

The Boston Globe. (1998). *Toward Better Teachers*. Editorial, June 23.

Boyer, E.L. (1991). *Ready to Learn: A Mandate for the Nation*. Princeton, N.J.: Carnegie Foundation for the Advancement of Teaching. Lawrenceville, N.J.: Princeton University Press.

Bryant, J. (1999). *Evaluation of PBS Ready to Learn Service*, an unpublished survey analysis. Institute for Communications Research, University of Alabama.

Cervantes, H.T., Baca, L.M., & Torres, D.S. (1979). *Community Involvement in Bilingual Education: The Bilingual Educator as Parent Trainer*. National Association for Bilingual Education Journal, 3(2):73–82.

Cohen, P.A., Kulik, J.A., and Kulik, C.L.C. (1982). *Educational Outcomes of Tutoring: A Meta-analysis of Findings*. American Educational Research Journal, 19:237–248.

Commission of Education of the Deaf. (1988). *Report to Congress and the President*. Washington, D.C.

Cost, Quality and Child Outcomes Study Team. (1995). *Cost, Quality and Child Outcomes in Child Care Centers*. Department of Economics, University of Colorado. Denver: Author.

Council of Chief State School Officers. (1998). *Young Children and the Arts: Making Creative Connections*. A Report of the Task Force on Children's Learning and the Arts, Birth to Age Eight. Goals 2000 Arts Education Partnership, June. Washington, D.C.

Council for Exceptional Children. (1997). *Reading Difficulties vs. Learning Disabilities*, CEC Today, 4(5), November/December.

Cummins, J. (1979). *Linguistic Interdependence and the Educational Development of Bilingual Children*. Review of Educational Research, 49: 222–251.

Cummins, J. (1989). *Empowering Minority Students*. Sacramento: CABE.

D'Agostino, J.,Wong, K., Hedges, L., & Borman, G. (1998). *The Effectiveness of Title I Parent Programs: A Multilevel Analysis of Prospects Data*. Paper presented at the annual meeting of the American Educational Research Association, San Diego, April.

Darling-Hammond, L. (1996). *The Quiet Revolution: Rethinking Teacher Development*. Educational Leadership, 53(6):4–10.

De La Rosa, D. & Maw, C. E. (1990). *Hispanic Education: A Statistical Portrait 1990*. Washington, D.C.: National Council of La Raza.

Dickinson, D.K., ed. (1991). *Bridges to Literacy: Children, Families, and Schools*. Blackwell Press.

Dodge, D.T. & Colker, L.J. (1996). *The Creative Curriculum for Early Childhood*. 3rd edition. Washington, D.C.: Teaching Strategies, Inc.

Dwyer, Piontek, Seager, DiMartino & Graham. (1998). *The Massachusetts Literacy Study: Report of Phase 1 Findings*. Providence, R.I.: Northeast and Islands Regional Educational Laboratory at Brown University.

Ebener, R., Lara-Alecio, R., & Irby, B. (1997). *Supportive Practices among Low-Income Parents of Academically Successful Elementary Students in Even Start Programs*. ERIC Clearinghouse on Reading, English, and Communication. ED40511, Indiana University. Educational Testing Service. (1995). *The Pennsylvania State Literacy Survey*. Adult Literacy in Pennsylvania: Author.

Education Commission of the States. (1997). *Compulsory School Age Requirements*. Education Commission of the States Clearinghouse. Denver: Author.

———. (1997). *Early Childhood Education Programs*. Education Commission of the States Clearinghouse. Denver: Author.

———. (1997) *State Characteristics: Kindergarten*. Education Commission of the States Clearinghouse. Denver: Author.

Education Trust Inc. (1998). *Dispelling the Myth: High Poverty Schools Exceed Expectations*. Draft. In collaboration with the Council of Chief State School Officers.

Elley, R. (1992). *How in the World Do Students Read?* Hamburg: The Hague International Association for the Evaluation of Educational Achievement.

Espinosa, L.M. (1995). *Hispanic Parent Involvement in Early Childhood Programs*. ERIC Digest. Clearinghouse on Elementary and Early Childhood Education. EDO-PS-95-3, May.

Espinosa, L. & Lesar, S. (1994). *Increasing Language—Minority Family and Child Competencies for School Success*. Paper presented at the annual meeting of the American Educational Research Association, New Orleans, April 4.

Families and Work Institute. (1994). *The Study of Children in Family Child Care and Relative Care*. New York: Author.

Federal Interagency Forum on Child and Family Statistics. (1997). *America's Children: Key National Indicators of Well-Being*. Washington, D.C.: U.S. Government Printing Office.

Ferreiro, E. & Teberosky, A. (1982). *Literacy Before Schooling*. Portsmouth, N.J.: Heinemann.

Fingeret, H.A., (1990). *Let Us Gather Blossoms Under Fire...* Paper presented at a conference on literacy for a global economy: A Multicultural Perspective. El Paso, Texas, February 21.

Fleischman, H.L. & Hopstock, P.J. (1993). *Descriptive Study of Services to Limited English Proficient Students*. Arlington, Va.: Development Associates, Inc.

Fletcher, J.M. & Lyon, G.R. (1998). *Reading: A Research-Based Approach*. In What's Gone Wrong in America's Classrooms, ed. W.M. Evers, 49–90. Stanford, Calif.: Hoover Institution Press.

Foorman, B. et al. (1998). *The Role of Instruction in Learning to Read: Preventing Reading Failure in At-risk Children*. Journal of Educational Psychology, 90: 37–55.

Fuller, B. & Liang, X. (1995). *Can Poor Families Find Child Care?* Cambridge, Mass.: Harvard University.

Fuller, B., Eggers-Pierola, C., Holloway, S.D., Liang, X., & Rambaud, M. (1994). *Rich Culture, Poor Markets: Why Do Latino Parents Choose to Forego Preschooling?* Washington, D.C.: American Educational Research Association and National Science Foundation.

Galinsky, E., Howes, C., & Kontos, S. (1995). *The Family Training Care Study: Highlights of Findings*. New York: Families and Work Institute.

Gambrell, L.B. & Coulso, D. (1998). *Reading Is Fundamental: 1998 Delaware Running Start Initiative*. University of Maryland Research Report.

General Accounting Office. (1998). *Child Care: Use of Standards to Ensure High Quality Care*. (GAO.HEHS-98-223R). Washington, D.C.: Author.

Graves, M. F. & Slater, W. H. (1987). *Development of Reading Vocabularies in Rural Disadvantaged Students, Intercity Disadvantaged Students and Middle Class Suburban Students*. Paper presented at the American Education Research Association conference. Washington, D.C.

Gomby, D., Larner, M., Terman, D., Krantzler, N., Stevenson, C., & Behrman, R. (1996). *Financing Child Care: Analysis and Recommendations*. The Future of Children: Financing Child Care, 6(2):5–25.

Goodlad, J. (1997). *Producing Teachers Who Understand, Believe and Care*. Education Week, 16(48):36–37.

Hanson, R., Siegel, D., & Broach, D. (1987). *The Effects on High School Seniors of Learning to Read in Kindergarten*. Paper presented at the annual meeting of the American Educational Research Association. Washington, D.C.

Hart B. & Risley, T.R. (1995). *Meaningful Differences in the Everyday Experiences of Young American Children*. Baltimore: Paul H. Brookes Publishing Co.

Hart, P.D. (1994). Graph for survey in *Learning to Read, Reading to Learn: The First Chapter in Education*. The American Federation of Teachers and Chrysler Corporation survey, p.1.

Haselkorn, D. & Harris, L. (1998). *The Essential Profession*. Belmont, Mass.: Recruiting New Teachers, Inc.

Hayes, D. P. & Grether, J. (1969). *The School Year and Vacations: When Do Students Learn?* Revision of a paper presented to the Eastern Sociological Association Convention, New York.

Hayes, D.P. & Ahrens, M.G. (1988). *Vocabulary Simplification for Children: A Special Case of 'Motherese'?* Journal of Child Language, 15(2):395–410.

Hess, R.D. & Holloway, S. (1984). *Family and School as Educational Institutions*. In Review of Child Development Research, ed. R.D. Parke, 179–222. Chicago: University of Chicago Press.

Heyns, B. (1987). *Schooling and Cognitive Development: Is There a Season for Learning?* Child Development, 58:1,151-1,160.

Hiebert, E.H., Pearson, D., Taylor, B., Richardson, V., and Paris, S.G. (1997). *Every Child a Reader*. A series of pamphlets prepared for the Center for the Improvement of Early Reading Instruction. Ann Arbor, Mich.

Hofferth, S. C. (1998). *Healthy Environments, Healthy Children: Children in Families*. Ann Arbor, Mich.: University of Michigan Institute for Social Research.

Interagency Commission on Learning Disabilities. (1987). *Learning Disabilities: A Report to the U.S. Congress*. Washington, D.C.

International Reading Association/The National Association for the Education of Young Children. (1998). *Learning to Read and Write: Developmentally Appropriate Practices for Young Children: A Joint Position Statement.* Washington, D.C., and Newark, Del.: Authors.

Juel, C. (1988). *Learning to Read and Write: A Longitudinal Study of Fifty-Four Children from First through Fourth Grade.* Journal of Educational Psychology, 80:437–447.

Kagan, S.L. & Cohen, N.E. (1997). *Not by Chance: Creating an Early Care and Education System for America's Children.* New Haven, Conn.: Yale University, The Bush Center for Child Development and Social Policy.

Kagan, S.L. (1995). *Normalizing Preschool Education: The Illusive Imperative.* In Changing Populations/Changing Schools: Ninety-fourth Yearbook of the National Society for the Study of Education, eds. E. Flaxman & A.H. Passow, 840-101. Chicago: National Society for the Study of Education.

Karoly, L.A., et al. (1998). *Investing in Our Children.* Santa Monica, Calif.: RAND.

Karweit, N., Ricciuti, A., & Thompson, B. (1994). *Summer Learning Revisited: Achievement Profiles of Prospects' First Grade Cohort.* Draft document. Cambridge, Mass.: Abt Associates.

Kisker, E.E., Hofferth, S.L., & Phillips, D.A. (1991). *Profile of Child Care Settings Study: Early Education and Care in 1990,* submitted to the U.S. Department of Education, Office of Planning, Budget and Evaluation (Princeton, N.J.: Mathematica Policy Research Inc., 1991) and unpublished tabulations, 1992.

Klass, P., MD. (1998). *Sense and Dispensability: My Patients Want More Than a Medical Diagnosis—And So Do I.* The Washington Post, November 29.

———. (1998). *Children and Books at a Crossroads.* Speech delivered to the National Symposium of the National Children's Book and Literacy Alliance, Boston, October 9.

Kontos, S., Howes, C., Shinn, M., & Galinsky, E. (1994). *Quality in Family Child Care and Relative Care.* New York: Teachers College Press.

Lally, R.J. (1997). *Brain Research, Infant Learning, and Child Care Curriculum.* Unpublished paper prepared for the Child Care Information Exchange.

Landerholm, E., Rubenstein, D., & Losch, M. (1994). *Involving Parents of Young Children in Science, Math and Literacy Activities.* Unpublished manuscript, Northeastern Illinois University, Chicago.

Leibowitz, A., Waite, L., & Witsberger, C. (1988). *Child Care for Preschoolers: Differences by Child's Age.* Demography, 27:112–133.

Lewis, M.C. (1993). *Beyond Barriers: Involving Hispanic Families in the Education Process.* Washington, D.C.: National Committee for Citizens in Education.

Liberman, I.Y. & Shankweiler, D. (1991). *Phonology and Beginning to Read: A Tutorial.* In Learning to Read: Basic Research and Its Implications, eds. L. Rieben and C.A. Perfetti. Hillsdale, N.J.: Lawrence Erlbaum Associates Inc.

Liontos, L.B. (1992). *At-Risk Families & Schools: Becoming Partners.* Eugene, Ore.: ERIC Clearinghouse on Educational Management. ED 342 055.

Love, J. & Kisker, E. (1996). *What Choices Do They Have? The Supply of Center-based Child Care in Low-income Neighborhoods.* Princeton, N.J.: Mathematica Policy Research Inc.

Lyon, G.R. (1998). *Overview of Reading and Literacy Initiatives.* Prepared statement to the Committee on Labor and Human Resources, U.S. Senate, April 28.

———. (1997). *Report on Learning Disabilities Research.* Prepared statement to the Committee on Education and the Workforce, U.S. House of Representatives, July 10.

———. (1996). *Learning Disabilities.* In The Future of Children: Special Education for Students with Disabilities, 6:54–76.

Lyon, G.R., Vaassen, M., & Toomey, F. (1989). *Teachers' Perceptions of Their Undergraduate and Graduate Preparation.* Teacher Education and Special Education, 12: 164–169.

Macias, R.F. (1998). *How Many School-Aged Limited-English-Proficient Students Are There in the U.S.? How Many in Each State?* NCBE No. 1. Washington, D.C.: National Clearinghouse for Bilingual Education.

McCormick, S. (1999). *Instructing Students Who Have Literacy Problems.* 3rd edition. Columbus, Ohio: Prentice-Hall.

McCutchen, D., Harry, D., Cunningham, A., Cox, S., & Covill, A. (1998). *Subject-Matter Knowledge of Teachers of Beginning Reading.* Paper presented at the annual meeting of the American Educational Research Association, San Francisco, Calif., April.

McInerney, M., Riley, K., & Osher, D. (1998). *Technology to Support Literacy Strategies for Students Who Are Deaf.* Chesapeake Institute of the American Institutes for Research.

The McKenzie Group Inc. (1999). *Student Achievement and Accountability Systems in Urban Districts*. Draft. Washington, D.C.: The McKenzie Group.

Miller, M.L. & Shontz, M.L. (1997). *Small Change: Expenditures for Resources in School Library Media Centers, FY 95–96*. School Library Journal, October.

Moats, L.C. (1995). *The Missing Foundation in Teacher Education*. American Educator. American Federation of Teachers, summer.

Moats, L.C. & Lyon, G.R. (1996). *Wanted: Teachers with Knowledge of Language*. Topics on Language Disorders, 16(2):73–86.

Moss, M. & Puma, M. (1995). *Prospects: The Congressionally Mandated Study of Educational Growth and Opportunity. First Year Report on Language Minority and Limited-English-Proficient Students*. Cambridge, Mass.: Abt Associates.

Murnane, R. (1975). *The Impact of School Resources on the Learning of Inner City Children*. Cambridge, Mass.: Ballinger.

NAEP 1998 Reading Report Card: See U.S. Department of Education, Office of Educational Research and Improvement, National Center for Education Statistics, 1999. *The NAEP 1998 Reading Report Card for the Nation*.

NAEP 1996 Trends Report: See U.S. Department of Education, Office of Educational Research and Improvement, National Center for Education Statistics, 1997. *NAEP 1996 Trends in Academic Progress*.

Nathenson-Mejia, S. (1994). *Bridges between Home and School: Literacy Building Activities for Non-native English Speaking Homes*. The Journal of Educational Issues of Language Minority Students, 14 (winter):149–164.

National Association of Elementary School Principals. (1998). *Best Ideas for Reading from America's Blue Ribbon Schools: What Award-Winning Elementary and Middle School Principals Do*. Thousand Oaks, Calif.: Corwin Press.

National Center for Early Childhood Development and Learning. (1998). *NCDEL Kindergarten Transitions*, July.

National Center for the Early Childhood Workforce. (1989). Executive summary for *The National Child Care Staffing Study*. Washington, D.C.: Author.

National Center for Family Literacy. (1996). *The Power of Family Literacy*, 2nd edition. Louisville, Ken.:National Center for Family Literacy.

National Education Association. (1998). *Promoting Quality in Early Care and Education: Issues for Schools*. Washington, D.C.: Author.

National Education Goals Panel. (1997). *Special Early Childhood Report.* Washington, D.C.: Author.

————. (1995). *Data Volume for the National Education Goals Report.* Volume 1: National Data. Washington, D.C.: U.S. Government Printing Office.

National Governors Association. (1996). *Improving Services for Children in Working Families,* a report prepared for the Center for Best Practices. Washington, D.C.: Author.

————.(1998). *Early Childhood Activities in the States, 1996–1998.* Results of a survey by the National Governors Association. Washington, D.C.: Center for Best Practices.

National Household Education Survey, 1996: See U.S. Department of Education, Office of Educational Research and Improvement, National Center for Education Statistics, 1995.

National Institute for Child Health and Human Development. (1997a). *Mother-Child Interaction and Cognitive Outcomes Associated with Early Child Care.* Early Child Care Research Network: Author.

————.(1997b) *NICHD Study of Early Child Care: The Relationship of Child Care to Cognitive and Language Development.* Presented at the Society for Research in Child Development meeting, April 3–6, 1997. Washington, D.C.

National Institute for Literacy. (1998). *Fast Facts on Literacy & Fact Sheet on Correctional Education.* Washington, D.C.: National Institute for Literacy.

National Research Center on English Learning & Achievement. (1998). *Effective Early Literacy Instruction: Complex and Dynamic.* English Update: 1(8), spring.

National Research Council. (1998). *Preventing Reading Difficulties in Young Children.* Washington, D.C.: National Academy Press.

Needlman, R., Fried, L., Morley, D., Taylor, S., & Zuckerman, B. (1991). *Clinic-based Intervention to Promote Literacy.* American Journal of Diseases of Children, 145:881–884, August.

Neuman, S.B. (in press). *Books Make a Difference: A Study of Access to Literacy.* Reading Research Quarterly. July/August/September 1999.

New York Times. (1997). *Teaching Johnny to Read.* January 25.

Nicolau, S. & Ramos, C. L. (1990). *Together Is Better: Building Strong Relationships between Schools and Hispanic Parents.* New York City: Hispanic Policy Development Project.

Nicolau, S., Ramos, C., & Palombo, B. (1990). *Dear Parents: In the United States…It's Our School Too.* New York City: Hispanic Policy Development Project. (English version: ED-325–541; Spanish version: ED-325–542.)

Office of Technology Assessment, U.S. Congress. (1993). *Adult Literacy and New Technologies: Tools for a Lifetime.* OTA-SET-550. Washington, D.C.: U.S. Government Printing Office.

Olsen, C.R. (1979). *The Effects of Enrichment Tutoring upon Self-concept, Educational Achievement, and Measured Intelligence of Male Under-achievers in an Inner-city Elementary School.* Palo Alto, Calif.: Unpublished paper.

Orton Dyslexia Society. (1997). *Informed Instruction for Reading Success: Foundations for Teacher Preparation.* Baltimore: Orton Dyslexia Society.

Padden, C. & Hanson V. (1999). *Transitions in Skilled Reading in Signing Deaf Children.* In The Signs of Language Revisited: An Anthology in Honor of Ursula Bellugi and Edward Klima, eds. K. Emmorey, and H. Mahwah-Lane, N.J.: Lawrence Erlbaum & Associates.

Padden, C. & Ramse, K. (1998). *Reading Ability in Signing Deaf Children.* Topics in Language Disorders, 18:30–46.

Pelavin, S. & David, J. (1977). *Evaluating Long-term Achievement: An Analysis of Longitudinal Data from Compensatory Education Programs.* Menlo Park, Calif.: Stanford Research Institute.

Pianta, R.C., & Cox, M.J. (in press). *The Transition to Kindergarten: Research, Policy, Training, and Practice.* Baltimore: Paul Brookes.

Rack, J.P., Snowling, M.J., & Olson, R.K. (1992). *The Non-word Reading Deficit in Developmental Dyslexia: A Review.* Reading Research Quarterly, 27:29–53.

Recruiting New Teachers Inc. (1998). *The Essential Profession: A National Survey of Public Attitudes Toward Teaching, Educational Opportunities and School Reform.* Belmont, Mass.: November 17.

Reisner, E., Petry, C., & Armitage, M. (1990). *A Review of Programs Involving College Students as Tutors or Mentors in Grades K–12.* Washington, D.C.: Policy Studies Associates.

Riley, J. (1996). *The Teaching of Reading.* London: Paul Chapman.

Risko, V.J., Peter, J.A., & McAllister, D. (1996). *Conceptual Changes: Preservice Teachers' Pathways to Providing Literacy Instruction.* In Growing Literacy, eds. E.G. Sturtevant and W.M. Linek, 104–119. Commerce, Texas: College Reading Association.

Risko, V.J. & Kinzer, C.K. (1997). *Videodisc, Case-based Reading Instruction in Pre-service Reading Education.* New York: McGraw-Hill.

Rock, D. (1993). *A Preliminary Look at the "Summer Learning Deficit" of First-Graders.* Unpublished manuscript.

Sauerwein, K. (1999). *State Weeds Out Old, Inaccurate Books at Schools.* Los Angeles Times, May 30.

Scarborough, H.S. (1998). *Early Identification of Children At-risk for Reading Disabilities: Phonological Awareness and Some Other Promising Predictors.* In Specific Reading Disability: A View of the Spectrum, eds. B.K. Shapiro, P.J. Accardo, and A.J. Capute, 77–121. Timonium, Md.: York Press.

Schwartz, W. (1996). *Hispanic Preschool Education: An Important Overview.* ERIC Clearinghouse on Urban Education. EDO-UD-96-2. Number 113, July.

Shaywitz, S.E., Shaywitz, B.A., Fletcher, J.M., & Escobar, M.D. (1990). *Prevalence of Reading Disability in Boys and Girls: Results of the Connecticut Longitudinal Study.* Journal of the American Medical Association, 264:998–1002.

Shaywitz, S.E., Escobar, M.D., Shaywitz, B.A., Fletcher, J.M., & Makuch, R. (1992). *Evidence that Dyslexia May Represent the Lower Tail of a Normal Distribution of Reading Ability.* New England Journal of Medicine, 326:145–150.

Shaywitz, S.E., Fletcher, J.M., & Shaywitz, B.A. (1996). *A Conceptual Model and Definition of Dyslexia: Findings from the Connecticut Longitudinal Study.* In Language, Learning and Behaviour Disorders, eds. J. H. Beichtman, N. Cohen, M.M. Konstantareas, and R. Tannock, 199–223. New York: Cambridge University Press.

Shaywitz, B.A., et al. (1997). *The Yale Center for the Study of Learning and Attention: Longitudinal and Neurobiological Studies.* Learning Disabilities: A Multidisciplinary Journal, 8:21–30.

Shore, R. (1997). *Rethinking the Brain: New Insights into Early Development.* New York City: Families and Work Institute.

Siegel, G. & Loman, A. (1991). *Child Care and AFDC Recipients in Illinois: Patterns, Problems, and Needs.* St. Louis, Mo.: Institute of Applied Research.

Slavin, R.E., Karweit, N.L., & Madden, N.A. (1989). *Effective Programs for Students At Risk.* Boston: Allyn and Bacon.

Smart Start Evaluation Team. (1999). *North Carolina's Smart Start Initiative: 1998 Annual Evalution Report.* Chapel Hill, N.C.: Frank Porter Graham Child Development Center at University of North Carolina, Chapel Hill.

Snow, C. & Tabors, P. (1996). *Intergenerational Transfer of Literacy in Family Literacy: Directions in Research and Implications for Practice,* eds. L.A. Benjamin and J. Lords. Washington, D.C.: Office of Educational Research and Improvement, U.S. Department of Education.

Snow, C. E. & Ninio, A. (1986). *The Contracts of Literacy: What Children Learn from Learning to Read Books.* In Emergent Literacy: Writing and Reading. Norwood, N.J.: Ablex.

Torgeson, J., Wagner, R., & Rashotte, C. (1997). *The Prevention and Remediation of Severe Reading Disabilities: Keeping the End in Mind.* Scientific Studies in Reading, 1:217–234.

U.S. Department of Education, Office of Educational Research and Improvement, National Center for Education Statistics. (1999). *Teacher Quality: A Report on the Preparation and Qualifications of Public School Teachers,* NCES 1999-080, by Lewis, L., Parsad, B., Carey, N., Bartfai, N., Farris, E., Smerdon, B., and Greene, B., project officer. Washington, D.C.

———. (1999). *The NAEP 1998 Reading Report Card for the Nation.* NCES 1999-459, by Donahue, O.L., Voelkl, K.E., Campbell, J.R., and Mazzeo. J., Washington, D.C.

———.(1997). *NAEP 1996 Trends in Academic Progress.* Washington, D.C.: National Center for Educational Statistics. By Campbell, J.R., Voekl, K.E., and Donahue, P.L.

———. (1996). *Child Care and Early Education Program Participation of Infants, Toddlers, and Preschoolers.* Statistics in Brief. NCES 95-824. Washington, D.C.: Author.

———. (1996). *Reading Proficiency and Home Support for Literacy.* NAEP facts 2(1). NCES 96-814R. Washington, D.C.: Author.

———. (1996). *Reading Literacy in the United States: Findings from the IEA Reading Literacy Study.* Washington, D.C.: Author.

———. (1996). *National Household Education Survey, 1995.* Washington, D.C.: Author.

———. (1994). *National Household Education Survey, 1991 and 1993. Family-Child Engagement in Literacy Activities: Changes in Participation between 1991 and 1993.* Statistics in Brief. NCES, December 1994.

————. (1993). *Dropout Rates in the United States: 1993.* NES 940669, by McMillen, M., Kaufman, P., & Whitener, S. Washington, D.C.

U.S. Department of Education. (1999). *Promising Results, Continuing Challenges: The Final Report of the National Assessment of Title I.* Washington, D.C.: U.S. Department of Education.

————. (1998). *Baby Boom Echo Report III. A Back to School Special Report on the Baby Boom Echo: September 8, 1998.* Washington, D.C.: Author.

————. (1998). *Longitudinal Evaluation of School Change and Performance: Some Preliminary Findings from First Two Years.* Draft. Washington, D.C.: U.S. Department of Education.

————. (1998). Office of Bilingual Education and Minority Languages Affairs. OBEMLA *Data from Special Issues Analysis Center:* Author.

————. (1997). *Prospects: Student Outcomes Final Report.* Washington, D.C.: U.S. Department of Education.

————. (1996). *Reading: The First Chapter in Education.* Office of Special Education and Rehabilitative Services and National Center to Improve the Tools of Educators. Washington, D.C.: Author.

————. (1992). Office of Special Education Programs. *Deaf Policy Guidance.* Washington, D.C.: 57 Fed. Reg. 49274, October 30.

U.S. Department of Health and Human Services. (1997). *Child Care Bureau Frequently Asked Questions.* Washington, D.C.: Administration for Children and Families.

U.S. Department of Labor, Bureau of Labor Statistics. (1999a). *Occupational Employment Projections to 2006.* Silvestri, G.T., Monthly Labor Review, November 1997, Table 3, 77.

————.(1999b). *Usual Weekly Earnings of Wage and Salary Workers, First Quarter 1999.* Washington, D.C.: Government Printing Office.

————. (1998). *Occupational Employment Statistics: 1997 National Occupational Employment and Wage Estimates.* Washington, D.C.: Government Printing Office.

U.S. General Accounting Office. (1998). *Child Care: Use of Standards to Ensure High Quality Care.* A report prepared for the Hon. Sander Levin, the Hon. Fortney "Pete" Stark, the Hon. Matthew Martinez, and the Hon. George Miller, U.S. House of Representatives. GAO HEHS-98-223R.

University of Colorado, Boulder. (1999). *Overview: Marion Downs National Center for Infant Hearing.* Boulder, Colo.: Marion Downs.

Utah State University. (1999). *Fact Sheet: Universal Newborn Hearing Screening.* Logan, Utah: National Center for Hearing Assessment and Management.

Vellutino, F.R., Scanlon, D.M., Sipay, H., & Denckla M. (1996). *Cognitive Profiles of Difficult–to-remediate and Readily Remediated Poor Readers: Early Intervention as a Vehicle for Distinguishing between Cognitive and Experiential Deficits as Basic Causes of Specific Reading Disability.* Journal of Educational Psychology, 88:601–636.

Wells, C.G. (1985). *Preschool Literacy-Related Activities and Success in School.* Literacy, Language, and Learning. London: Cambridge University Press.

West, J., Wright, D., & Hausken. (1995). *Child Care and Early Education Program Participation of Infants, Toddlers and Preschoolers.* Washington, D.C.: National Center for Education Statistics, U.S. Department of Education.

Whitebook, M., Howes, C., & Phillips, D. (1990). *The National Child Care Staffing Study.* Oakland, Calif.: National Center for Early Childhood Workforce.

Withrow, F. (1989). *Literacy and the Hearing Impaired: Living, Moving, Dynamic Text.* Washington, D.C., ED-353–734.

Young, K.T., Davis, K., & Schoen, C. (1996). *The Commonwealth Fund Survey of Parents with Young Children.* New York: The Commonwealth Fund.